THE DUTY TO RESCUE

THE DUTY TO RESCUE
THE JURISPRUDENCE OF AID

Edited by

MICHAEL A. MENLOWE
Lecturer in Philosophy, University of Edinburgh

and

ALEXANDER McCALL SMITH
Reader in Law, University of Edinburgh

With contributions from:

Alberto Cadoppi
Daniel W. Shuman
Stephen C. Neff

Dartmouth
Aldershot • Brookfield USA • Hong Kong • Singapore • Sydney

Published by
Dartmouth Publishing Company Limited
Gower House
Croft Road
Aldershot
Hants GU11 3HR
England

Dartmouth Publishing Company
Old Post Road
Brookfield
Vermont 05036
USA

British Library Cataloguing in Publication Data
Duty to Rescue: Jurisprudence of Aid. –
(Dartmouth Series in Applied Legal
Philosophy)
  I. Menlowe, Michael   II. Smith, R. A.
  McCall   III. Series
  340.1

Library of Congress Cataloging-in-Publication Data
The Duty to rescue / edited by Michael A. Menlowe, and Alexander
  McCall Smith ; with contributions from Alberto Cadoppi, Daniel W.
  Shuman, and Stephen C. Neff.
      p.   cm.
  Includes index.
  ISBN 1-85521-396-6 : $69.95 (approx.)
    1. Assistance in emergencies.   I. Menlowe, Michael A., 1943–   .
  II. McCall Smith, Alexander, 1948–   .   III. Cadoppi, Alberto.
  IV. Shuman, Daniel W.
  KF830.Z9D88   1993
  344.73'0320425–dc20
  [347.304320425]   93–22672
                                                                      CIP

ISBN 1 85521 396 6

Printed in Great Britain at the University Press, Cambridge

Contents

Notes on the Authors

Alberto Cadoppi is Professor of Criminal Law at the University of Trento. He has written extensively on criminal law, including a study of liability for omissions, *Il reato omissivo proprio* (1988), and an analysis of the crime of failure to rescue, *Il reato di omissione di soccorso* (1992).

Michael A. Menlowe is Lecturer in Philosophy at the University of Edinburgh. He is author of a number of articles on the philosophy of law and co-editor (with Eric Matthews) of *Philosophy and Health Care* (1992).

Stephen C. Neff is Senior Lecturer in Public International Law at the University of Edinburgh. He is the author of *Friends But No Allies: Economic Liberalism and the Law of Nations* (1990) and is currently writing a general history of the law of neutrality.

Daniel W. Shuman is Professor of Law at Southern Methodist School of Law in Dallas, Texas and an adjunct Professor of Psychiatry at the University of Texas, Southwestern Medical School. His publications include *Psychiatric and Psychological Evidence* (1986) (winner of the 1988 American Psychiatric Association Manfred S. Guttmacher Award), *Law and Mental Health Professionals* (1990) and *The Psychotherapist Patient Privilege: A Critical Examination* (with Weiner, 1987).

Alexander McCall Smith is Reader in Law at the University of Edinburgh. He has written several works on law and medicine, including *Law and Medical Ethics* (3rd edition 1991) and *Butterworth's Medico-Legal Encyclopedia* (both with J.K. Mason) (1987). In the area of criminal law, he is author of *The Criminal Law of Botswana* (1992) and *Scots Criminal Law* (1992).

Series Preface

The objective of the Dartmouth Series in Applied Legal Philosophy is to publish work which adopts a theoretical approach to the study of particular areas or aspects of law or deals with general theories of law in a way which focuses on issues of practical moral and political concern in specific legal contexts.

In recent years there has been an encouraging tendency for legal philosophers to utilize detailed knowledge of the substance and practicalities of law and a noteworthy development in the theoretical sophistication of much legal research. The series seeks to encourage these trends and to make available studies in law which are both genuinely philosophical in approach and at the same time based on appropriate legal knowledge and directed towards issues in the criticism and reform of actual laws and legal systems.

The series will include studies of all the main areas of law, presented in a manner which relates to the concerns of specialist legal academics and practitioners. Each book makes an original contribution to an area of legal study while being comprehensible to those engaged in a wide variety of disciplines. Their legal content is principally Anglo-American, but a wide-ranging comparative approach is encouraged and authors are drawn from a variety of jurisdictions.

TOM D. CAMPBELL
Series Editor
The Faculty of Law
The Australian National University

Introduction

This book unites five different perspectives into a comprehensive jurisprudential analysis of our duty to rescue. Our first reactions to the rescue of those in distress are deceptively simple. We praise heroes; we sympathise with those who find heroism beyond them; we condemn those too callous to care. However, the slightest reflection on these reactions provokes puzzlement. What *is* required of the vast majority of us who are neither heroes nor callous bystanders? Do we have any duty to act? If so, at how great a risk or inconvenience to ourselves? If we have some moral duty to act, is it a duty that is, or ought to be, recognised by law? If the duty is recognised by law, is it only an individual duty or is it a collective duty of the state? In this volume we set out to establish the grounds on which a duty to rescue may be said to exist, and we examine the extent to which this duty is, or may be, recognised by the law.

It is widely accepted by philosophers that there is a moral requirement to rescue, although the basis on which this requirement is founded is controversial. A prominent problem which arises for two of the most influential philosophical theories is that of deciding whether rescue is always required, no matter what the cost to the rescuer, or whether there are limits to be placed on any obligation of this nature. In the opening chapter, Michael Menlowe discusses the difficulties inherent in the tension between an easily shouldered obligation (a duty to effect easy rescues of those most immediate to us) and an extensive duty to attempt the rescue of a wide range of people. He is primarily concerned with the adequacy of a variety of consequentialist arguments in favour of the duty. A moderate position, which admits a relatively narrowly defined duty, is essentially unstable. Hence the recognition of any duty at all rapidly projects one into an acknowledgement of extensive and burdensome duties, and thus requires a radical change in the way in which most of us think about what we are morally required to do.

The implication of Menlowe's argument in Chapter 1 is that, in recognising any duty to rescue, a legal system will need to resolve the conflict between the practical necessity of limiting a legal obligation to rescue and the theoretical requirement that the obligation must be extensive. In Chapters 2 and 3, we examine two different resolutions of that conflict. It is a truism of comparative law that there is a marked difference in the area of criminal liability for failure to rescue between the common law systems of the English-speaking world and the civilian systems of European continental provenance. There is no criminal offence of failure to rescue in the common law world, whereas in the civil law world those who do not attempt to rescue when they could easily do so may be prosecuted. So runs the common belief, and it is, to an extent, quite true. Yet the position of the common law systems is not one of utter hostility to rescue, as Alexander McCall Smith shows in Chapter 2. The common law is unhappy about liability for omissions to act, but still imposes criminal liability in many such cases. It recognises, too, that there may be liability in certain specific cases – as where there is a relationship between the parties – and certainly it allows for civil liability in a number of cases where the non-rescuer is under a duty of care to act. The basic conceptual background for a legal duty to rescue therefore exists in the common law world, and its recognition by legislation would not represent a sharp break with recent developments in the law.

In Chapter 3, Alberto Cadoppi examines the experience of continental legal systems in recognising a more extensive legal duty to rescue. The distinction in the civilian legal tradition between pure crimes of omission and crimes of commission by omission facilitates the creation of criminal statutes imposing a duty to rescue. Most European and Latin American countries now have such statutes. These statutes illustrate a legal solution to the problem of rescue in striking contrast to that of the common law, as explained in Chapter 2. They are not the exact, limited provisions which, according to the common law lawyer, a predictable system of criminal justice requires. They are, in fact, loosely drafted and appear to impose a wide-ranging liability for non-rescue. In many ways they are the kind of legal requirement which the philosophical arguments of Chapter 1 would lead one to expect. For those persuaded of the essential correctness of the common law's approach in attempting to limit the duty to rescue, the fact that the scope of the law has in some cases been extended by the continental courts applying the legislation in question is a further cause for concern. Cadoppi suggests that the explanation of the difference between the common law and civilian legal systems has more to do with historical development than with philosophy. Codification makes duty to rescue statutes easy to create, and their creation satisfies the desire of the codifiers to appear progressive.

Rescues often require collective action. For the reasons given in Chapter 1, the state's duty to rescue is continuous with that of the individual. The final two chapters examine the state's duty to rescue.

It is widely assumed that the state has some duty to rescue certain vulnerable citizens. Daniel Shuman examines that assumption in Chapter 4. His perspective is that of therapeutic jurisprudence. The therapeutic approach focuses on the role of law in facilitating reconciliation and healing, outcomes which a mechanistic application of legal rules may fail to produce. In his analysis of state intervention in child abuse cases in the United States, Shuman argues that the state should come to the rescue of vulnerable children only when the intervention will be therapeutic. Since it is often not, it would be inappropriate to impose a duty on the state to rescue. Such an analysis is very different from the more doctrinaire approach frequently adopted in the literature, and sounds a cautionary note in the face of the enthusiastic endorsement of a duty to rescue.

In Chapter 5, Stephen Neff examines the problem of rescue in international law. This is an area not previously given adequate attention in discussions of rescue and the law, and yet it is in the international arena that the most dramatic rescue issues of our time are being played out. Is a state required to rescue a victim state from aggression, or to rescue refugees, or to provide economic assistance to poor states? In his examination of these and other questions, Neff detects a common theme. The early law, based on natural law, took a sympathetic view of the duty to rescue, but this attitude gave way to the principle of non-intervention in the affairs of autonomous states. The moral concerns of the early Christian writers with such concepts as the just war are replaced by national interests. There are many obvious parallels in this chapter with the discussion of non-interference in Chapter 1. For example, the idea that states can be neutral in the face of aggression has similarities with the view that a bystander has no duty to rescue. Neff's discussion of the international law relating to refugees provides a vivid illustration of the difficulty, elaborated in Chapters 1 and 2, of defending a duty to rescue without that duty becoming too extensive. Neff concludes his chapter with a discussion of a vigorously debated and topical matter in international law – the right to intervene for humanitarian purposes.

What emerges from our discussion is that there are no conclusive objections to a legal duty to rescue (although there may be reservations about whether the duty is appropriate in particular cases). The duty to rescue, at least insofar as such a duty is imposed on the individual, is one which is both philosophically defensible and legally enforceable. It falls, however, into that category of duties which are wider in their moral than in their legal dimension. We have presented the case both for and against the expansion of the legal duty. Collective duties pose questions of even greater complexity. There are those who are inclined to deny the existence of these duties altogether. Yet recent developments may suggest that it is becoming less acceptable for states, just as it may be for individuals, to decline to alleviate the suffering of others.

1 The Philosophical Foundations of a Duty to Rescue*

MICHAEL A. MENLOWE

1 Introduction

There is no shortage of philosophical theories defending a moral requirement to rescue. Post-medieval natural law theory advocated the ideal of Christian brotherhood and invoked the Biblical notion of being my brother's keeper. Kant argued for a moral obligation to help those in distress. He thought that the obligation could be seen as a requirement of the supreme principle of morality. Contemporary philosophers such as Gewirth, Nagel, O'Neill and Rawls have all argued at length that a duty to rescue is part of a certain view of moral philosophy that places rationality at its centre.[1] Within the consequentialist tradition, the major utilitarian philosophers, Bentham, Mill and Sidgwick, all held that there is a duty to rescue, at least in those cases where rescue promotes the greatest happiness of the greatest number. Jurisprudentialists writing on the law of torts are contributing additional philosophical ideas. For example, it has recently been argued that a feminist theory of torts and a jurisprudence of compassion would make caring for others the central value of the law of torts.[2]

There is, then, wide philosophical support for the view that there is a moral requirement to rescue. It is therefore interesting that in the law in English-speaking common law countries there is no general duty to rescue in either the criminal or the civil law. The common law recognises specific limited exceptions to that bad samaritan rule based, it is usually claimed, on certain legally significant relationships. By contrast, most European legal systems do have a duty to rescue. Part of my task is to explore that contrast. The relation between law and morality is complex, but there are at least two possible explanations for this remarkable difference. Simply stated, the first explanation is that, for reasons perhaps similar to Kant's, there cannot be a legal obligation to rescue. The nature of the moral duty to rescue is such that it is a duty of virtue and one that cannot be externally compelled. On this view, the common law jurisdictions have got it right, and the continental systems have got it wrong. The second explanation shares much with legal positivism. It says that moral requirements can always in principle be made into legal ones if there is good reason to do so. If there are convincing arguments for a moral obligation to rescue, there is some reason to consider whether there ought to be a legal obligation.

In this chapter I shall explore primarily the second explanation since it relates more closely to issues discussed in this book. The most important questions are these. Are there convincing arguments for a moral requirement to rescue? Supposing that moral obligations can be turned into legal ones, does the best philosophical justification of the moral requirement to rescue lead to the common law position that there is no duty to rescue or to the position that there ought to be one?

The view I shall defend is that consequentialist theories have difficulties in finding grounds for a moral or a legal obligation to rescue. Solving these difficulties requires major changes in our view of what we are morally required to do. I am inclined to think that part of the explanation for the common law's dedication to the principle that there is no duty to rescue is the recognition of these philosophical difficulties. In Chapter 2, Alexander McCall Smith illustrates the connection between those philosophical difficulties and recent developments in the law of torts in English-speaking countries. Our view is that tort law concerning rescues has failed to develop (or, more properly, has developed only very slowly in limited areas) because of a familiar philosophical problem about consequentialism, namely the difficulty in setting limits to the duty to act.

I begin by trying to uncover the main philosophical issues. I shall explain why I think it is difficult to defend the view that there is no moral requirement to make at least an easy rescue. I shall then move on to my main concern, the difficulties facing consequentialist theories in defending a moral requirement to rescue.

2   Describing the Problem

Imagine an easy rescue. A child is drowning in a pond and Jones is walking past the pond. All he has to do to rescue the child is to reach down and pull the child out of the water. Suppose that Jones decides not to rescue the child. I want to say that Jones ought to have rescued the child because it is wrong to fail to make an easy rescue and that Jones therefore ought to be blamed or punished for failing to rescue. I imagine an opponent would say that Jones ought to have rescued, meaning it would be good if Jones had rescued; however, the opponent says that Jones is to be neither blamed nor punished for his failure. Underlying the opponent's view is a familiar categorisation of actions: those which are morally required and one can be blamed or punished if one fails to do them; those actions which are not morally required but one can be praised for doing them.

There are several views one might hold about rescues: (a) rescues are never morally required; (b) rescues are sometimes morally required; for example, only when the rescue is very easy; (c) the requirement to rescue is extensive: it is a requirement to rescue everyone one can. My view is that (a) is to be rejected, and that (b) cannot be defended because it collapses into (c). In Section 3, I take seriously the moral minimalism implied by (a), but I argue that there are no persuasive grounds to adopt it. In Sections 6 and 7, I argue that (b) is an unstable position. It is not possible to argue on consequentialist grounds that *only* easy rescues are required. If we are required to rescue, we are also required to promote the good of others more extensively.

The preceding paragraphs offer only a very rough formulation of the problem. There are complex conceptual issues involved which will determine how we describe the problem. I take it that a fundamental philosophical question to be asked in this context is: *ought* one to make a rescue, at least when the rescue is easy? Such agreement as there is among writers who hold that one ought to make an easy rescue is deeply misleading. Writers who agree that one ought to make an easy rescue frequently disagree about why one ought and what is to be said about the person who fails to do what she ought to do. Some writers say that one ought because one has a duty; others say that one ought because one has an obligation; yet others say that one ought even if one has neither an obligation nor a duty. Some writers say that someone who fails to do what she ought is doing wrong; while others say that it would be appropriate to blame or punish such a person even if she does not do wrong. The disagreements are not only substantive disagreements about the duty to rescue. They are also differences about fundamental conceptual issues. Because there is a lack of agreement about fundamental conceptual issues, the philosophical literature on the duty to rescue is confusing.

This is not the place to go into these conceptual issues.[3] I shall therefore state what I take to be the crucial question: does one who fails to rescue, particularly when the rescue is easy, do wrong; or does that person merely fail to do good? If the former, blame or punishment may be appropriate; if the latter, it is probably not. If blame or punishment is appropriate, then there is a reason for a legal obligation to rescue. The view I shall defend is that one who fails to make an easy rescue does what is wrong and is therefore liable to blame or punishment. Further, I think that one does wrong in failing to rescue even if one does not have an obligation or duty to rescue, at least according to some accounts of those concepts. I shall use the word 'requirement' to include both obligations and duties. Anyone who fails to do what is morally required does what is wrong, and is liable to blame or punishment. The crucial issue could be put thus: is one morally required to make an easy rescue; or does one merely fail to do good in making an easy rescue? The view I shall consider is that one is morally required to rescue, particularly when the rescue is easy, because one is morally required to promote some good.

What I take to be the crucial issue is obscured by agreement that Jones ought to rescue. I can now put my intuition about Jones more clearly. I think Jones ought to have rescued because there is a moral requirement to make an easy rescue. It is wrong to fail to make an easy rescue, and he therefore ought to be blamed or punished for failing to rescue. I imagine an opponent would say that Jones ought to have rescued, but meaning that it would be good if Jones had rescued; however, Jones has not done wrong and is to be neither blamed nor punished for his failure because there is no moral requirement to promote the good.

3   Liberty and Another's Good

Those who hold that rescues are never morally required, as well as some of those who hold that rescues are sometimes morally required, may think that one of the central issues is the extent to which it is permissible to limit the liberty of the potential rescuer for the sake of promoting the good of another. It is difficult to find elaborated arguments for the view that there is no moral requirement to rescue. There are at least two different kinds of arguments that might be made. First, there is an argument based on the claim that some principle of liberty is fundamental. Second, there is the argument that we have certain rights to do as we like which exclude certain demands on us.

Let us first consider the view that some principle of liberty is a fundamental value. If there were such a principle, then it might be argued that the right to refuse to rescue is derived from that principle alone. The problem is to explain what principle is invoked by the claim that liberty is fundamental. One plausible principle is this: everyone is entitled to the most extensive liberty compatible with like

liberty for all. Suppose that one were to interpret liberty as the presence of options and the absence of coercion. Then liberty is increased
whenever some individual has more uncoerced options, and the most
extensive system of liberty would be that which provides such options for most people. On this view, one could argue that there is no
duty to rescue because the system in which there is no such duty
provides the most extensive liberty. In other words, the absence of
such a duty increases options for most people.

I follow Will Kymlicka in thinking that there are two things wrong
with this argument.[4] First, it is strongly counter-intuitive. If the most
extensive liberty is the largest number of uncoerced options, then, for
example, a society without traffic lights and without freedom of religion will have more liberty than a system with traffic lights and
freedom of religion. [5] This view is counter-intuitive because our
intuitions are against a purely quantitative assessment of liberty. But
notice that it is this counter-intuitive view that is being appealed to
when the argument is made to support the absence of a duty to
rescue. To justify the absence of the duty to rescue on this view, we
have to claim that the most extensive system of liberty is that in
which there is no such duty. That entails that the potential rescuer's
option of not reaching out to save the drowning child is more valuable than the liberty of the child. If this is plausible at all, it is only
plausible on the basis of a purely quantitative comparison of liberty.
The person who defends the duty to rescue on this ground has to
maintain that a society with no traffic lights is freer than a society
with traffic lights and more substantial freedoms (such as freedom of
religion) as well. However, it may be doubted whether such quantitative comparisons are possible to make. We lack a principled way of
individuating acts; and so we lack a principled way of summing the
quantity of liberty produced by these acts.[6]

It would be possible to interpret the principle of the most extensive
liberty as requiring not a quantitative assessment but some qualita-
tive assessment. For example, one might measure liberties relative to
purposes. But Kymlicka argues that this is not an improvement, since
the principle of the most extensive liberty is doing no work. Consider
this claim: the liberty provided by the freedom to worship is more
extensive than the liberty provided by the absence of traffic lights –
because the former promotes more important interests or purposes.
The more important liberty is simply being redescribed as the most
extensive. So the most extensive liberty principle, on this interpretation of it, is a disguised assertion of the importance of liberty.[7]

There are reasons to think that no form of the most extensive liberty principle is tenable[8] and reasons to think that the theory that
liberty is a fundamental value is confused.

Our commitment to certain liberties does not derive from any general right to liberty, but from their role in the best theory of equality (or mutual advantage). The question is which specific liberties are most valuable to people, given their essential interests, and which distribution of those liberties is legitimate, given the demands of equality or mutual advantage? The idea of freedom as such, and lesser or greater amounts of it, does no work in political argument.[9]

Let us therefore consider the second kind of argument mentioned above, the argument that we have certain rights to do as we like which exclude certain demands upon us. Such an argument is associated with John Locke, but Locke was equivocal about some of the implications of his view.[10] He held, for example, that, although everyone had a right to use his possessions as he liked, there was also a duty of charity; but what he meant by this is unclear.[11] Locke influenced the foremost modern exponent of the view we are now considering, Robert Nozick,[12] but, as we shall see, the same equivocation occurs in Nozick's view.

3.1   Nozick's Water-hole

Nozick's basic idea is that people have rights, and no one can interfere with those rights. In Nozick's terms we might say that rights, specifically the right to use one's energies and possessions as one likes, are side-constraints on goals. Compelling someone to benefit another, for example by redistributing some portion of that person's wealth by taxation, violates that person's rights. Ultimately we are separate persons and rights as side-constraints preserve our separateness.

Nozick's basic right is the right of self-ownership; that is, the right over oneself. He treats this as an interpretation of the Kantian principle of treating persons only as ends in themselves and never as means.[13] The idea of treating people as ends in themselves prohibits using persons as resources for others.[14] The notion that people are distinct ends in themselves is implemented by means of a strong right of self-ownership, which limits the demands that one person can make of another. The right of self-ownership, by means of an argument from Locke, can be extended so that goods can become one's private possessions. Provided that some good was either previously unowned or legitimately owned, ownership can be transferred by means of recognised procedures. For example, since I have a right of self-ownership, I can make a piece of unowned land my own by working on it.

A critical discussion of the right of self-ownership is beyond the scope of this chapter. However, two criticisms may be mentioned.

The claim that the right of self-ownership entails absolute property rights is central to Nozick's project. But this claim seems doubtful. Kymlicka argues that the Lockean proviso (see below) fails to provide an adequate account of the initial acquisition of property, without which Nozick's claim – that self-ownership entails absolute property rights – fails.[15] Secondly, as an interpretation of the principle that we are to treat people only as ends in themselves, the notion of a strong right of self-ownership which permits us to ignore the needs of others seems curious. As Kant recognised, a duty to help those in distress does not violate the prohibition against treating people (such as potential rescuers) as means. It is odd, to say the least, to interpret the principle so that it is compatible with the great inequalities that arise from absolute property rights.[16]

It is reasonably clear how the right of self-ownership might be used to argue that there is no duty to rescue: in virtue of my right of self-ownership, your needs cannot become demands to which I am required to respond. But Nozick's position is more complicated than this. Because of the account he gives of how we can legitimately come to own private property, Nozick cannot use the right of self-ownership to attempt to justify *complete* indifference to the needs of others. On the contrary, Nozick recognises a limitation on rights that amounts to a limited duty to rescue. As I shall argue, it is not possible to use Nozick's self-ownership argument to bolster the claim that there is no moral obligation to rescue.

Suppose that Bob is drowning and that the only safe way to rescue him is by throwing him a rope. There is only one available rope and now, by a process recognised as giving her a right of ownership, Alice makes it her rope and refuses the use of it to save the drowning Bob.

Nozick argues that Alice cannot come to own the rope in such circumstances. This is because of the Lockean proviso. According to the Lockean proviso, one can acquire previously unowned things only if the acquisition does not worsen anyone's overall condition. Thus: 'A process normally giving rise to a permanent bequeathable property right in a previously unowned thing will not do so if the position of others no longer at liberty is thereby worsened.'[17] For example, one could not acquire the only water-hole in a desert. The Lockean proviso applies also to pre-existing ownership. If I own a water-hole and all the other water-holes in the area dry up, I cannot charge what I like for my water. Notice that I cannot even charge a fair price for it if those who need it cannot afford to pay. My ownership is limited by the circumstances. The notion that scarcity can affect ownership rights is an old one. Hugo Grotius argued that a shortage of necessities resurrected a primitive *property* right of all persons to own all things. Thus the destitute had a property right to whatever they needed. Grotius's view was criticised by Pufendorf, who argued that the destitute had only a personal right to the charity of the affluent. This controversy is discussed by Stephen Neff in Chapter 5, Section 3.

So we can conclude that Nozick's position is that certain needs of others limit individual liberty in respect of the acquisition and the use of property. Thus he is committed to some kind of duty to rescue. I cannot deny thirsty people my water, nor a drowning man the use of my rope. But the duty he is committed to extends only to the use of one's property, and is therefore negative. The obligation is not to refuse the use of one's property in certain circumstances. Nothing positive is required. However, insisting on drawing the line there seems rather arbitrary.

Suppose I own the only water-hole in the desert. The thirsty person needs a rope and a bucket to extract the water from my well. By the argument just considered, I cannot refuse him the use of those things if I have them handy. But, apparently, I have no obligation to obtain them if I do not. Suppose that the bucket and rope are some distance away, too far for the weak, thirsty person, but only a few minutes' walk for me. Or suppose that the thirsty person is too weak to draw the water with a bucket and rope, but if I help him pull on the rope the two of us can manage easily. Nozick may want to say that I do not owe the thirsty person anything other than non-intervention. His needs limit my property rights; they do not create obligations. However, the motivation for the argument is now obscure. Why is it that some person's needs justify a limitation on my property rights but do not impose an obligation to provide the minimum necessary to enable that person to satisfy her needs?

A rescuer is, of course, a monopoly supplier of a service. To adapt another of Nozick's examples, I have no right to refuse the drowning person space on my boat. But apparently I can refuse to throw her a rope so that she can climb aboard. As Stephen Neff points out, this is in fact the position in international law with regard to refugees.[18]

Nozick's theory of property requires certain limitations on property rights. That commits him to what is in effect a limited duty to rescue. However, it is obscure why that duty should be limited as it is. It leaves obscure why the owner's rights are limited but he has no obligations to ensure the means to satisfy the very needs that caused his rights to be limited.

It is, of course, possible to argue that liberty is a fundamental value and therefore there *is* a moral requirement to rescue just because it greatly increases the liberty of the person rescued. Such an argument has been made, for example, by J.S. Mill in his essay *On Liberty*.[19] This thought underlies much consequentialist justification for a duty to rescue. Kant also makes a similar argument.

4 Kant's View of a Duty to Rescue

I mentioned at the beginning of this chapter that both consequentialists and non-consequentialists have held that there is a moral requirement to rescue. The tradition on which I concentrate in this chapter is the consequentialist one. However, Kant's view on the duty to rescue has been very influential. For example, the preceding discussion on liberty is one to which Kant had a great deal to contribute. Non-consequentialist theories often appeal to the intuition that there is something irrational about not accepting that there is a moral requirement to help others in distress. The theory in which Kant develops this intuition is not without difficulties.

In the *Groundwork of the Metaphysic of Morals*, Kant distinguishes perfect and imperfect obligations.[20] A maxim creates a perfect obligation if its converse could not be conceived: 'The very attempt to think of the maxim as universally adopted breaks down owing to some incoherence in the way the world would have to be if it were universally acted on. '[21] A maxim creates an imperfect obligation if its converse cannot be willed as a universal law: 'A contradiction in the will is not a contradiction in thinking, but a contradiction between the thought experiment of universalising a maxim and the background conditions of the lives of specifically *finite* rational agents.'[22] Kant claims that we have an imperfect duty to aid others in distress.[23] That is, although a rational being could will not to aid another in distress, no rational being could aim for the state of affairs in which he would not be aided were he in distress.

> Self-sufficiency is an incoherent goal for finite rational beings; at most they can coherently aim to minimise their dependence on others. They cannot universalise maxims either of refusing to accept any help or of refusing to offer help, since help may be needed for the survival of their agency. The thought experiment of willing a world of principled nonbeneficence is not one that finite beings can make consistent with an awareness of the limitations of their own agency, on which all their plans for action ... are premised. A duty of beneficence grounded in this way is only an imperfect duty: It demands only the rejection of a maxim of refusing (to give or receive) any help, and not the adoption of a maxim of providing or accepting all help (which would in any case be impossible). Which particular forms of help should be offered or accepted by finite rational beings must vary.[24]

There may be problems about how best to describe the distinction. One immediate worry is this: to what do imperfect duties commit one? If I must reject the maxim of refusing to aid others in distress, then I must aid some who are in distress; but whom or when and to what extent and at what cost? Apparently, Kant does not think that the maxim can settle such questions. As Mary Gregor says, 'it should be recalled that, according to the non-rigoristic view of Kant's theory on imperfect duty, the law enjoining beneficence also leaves room, between our maxim and our action, for arbitrary, subjective factors determining whom we shall help, to what extent and by what means'.[25] In considering whether we ought to aid someone in distress, we need to consider our own resources, the relationship between ourselves and the person in need, and that person's own conception of happiness.[26] We can be selective about imperfect duties.[27] So asking to whom and when we owe imperfect duties reveals an important point, not only about the nature of imperfect duties, but about Kantian deliberation in general. 'Kantian reasoning does not even aim to provide an algorithm for action ...'[28] In order to assess the adequacy of Kant's theory, it would be necessary to consider Kant's theory of moral reasoning, and that cannot be undertaken here. However, this aspect of Kantian deliberation may seem very unsatisfactory to some. If we consider the imperfect duty of beneficence, it could be argued that a crucial moral question is how much of a sacrifice one can be required to make for others.

Given the concerns of this chapter, there is a different reason why Kant's imperfect duty of beneficence is problematic as a possible foundation for a duty to rescue. Kant thought that all imperfect duties were duties of virtue and not duties that could be externally compelled. Hence, on Kant's view there could not be a legal obligation to rescue. An explanation of that point requires a brief consideration of Kant's theory of right.[29]

Kant conceives of man as both noumenon and as phenomenon. As noumenon, man is a potentially rational agent motivated by duty. That is, his will is determined by the categorical imperative. Noumenal man is the subject of ethics, that is, those actions done from the motive of duty alone. Kant deals with ethics in both the *Groundwork of the Metaphysic of Morals* and in the *Metaphysics of Morals* (*Metaphysik der Sitten*).[30] Man as phenomenon is a partially rational being living in the empirical world. Man as phenomenon is thus motivated by inclinations and desires. Kant's philosophy of right deals with phenomenal man. The object of the philosophy of right is to outline those conditions essential for external freedom (hereafter 'liberty', as distinguished from the freedom of the autonomous individual). The theory of right concerns those maxims of ethics which are capable of being made into external laws, which in turn provide the conditions of liberty. However, not all the maxims of ethics figure in Kant's theory of right. That is because Kant's conception of liberty is that of non-interference with the liberty of others. The theory of right sets out the conditions for liberty irrespective of an agent's individual purposes. Thus, unlike Hegel, Kant sees law as regulating the conflicting wills of individuals. Coercion is justified in order to permit each to pursue his own goals to the same extent as any other.

Thus there is no straightforward connection between ethics and the theory of right. Ethics concerns those maxims which the autonomous rational individual legislates for herself. Freedom consists in this self-legislation and in obedience to duty from the motive of duty alone. The theory of right concerns individuals who are only partially rational. The question for the theory of right is *not* what would partially rational individuals will? The question is, rather, what conditions are required for partially rational individuals to carry out their purposes, whatever those purposes are?

Kant thought that the theory of justice was concerned with perfect duties. Thus only perfect duties could be externally enforced by law. Imperfect duties are not part of the theory of right, but the theory of virtue. The imperfect duty to aid others, which Kant establishes in the *Groundwork*, would not figure in his theory of right. If that is so, it is because the duty to aid others is not required for liberty (conceived of as non-interference). Thus, considering only the imperfect duty of beneficence, Kant would have opposed a legal duty to aid others in distress. Rather, the imperfect duty to aid others in distress would figure only in Kant's doctrine of virtue.[31]

There is, however, a way of reading Kant that would produce a different conclusion. Instead of treating the duty to rescue as a Kantian imperfect duty, we should consider whether it could be a perfect obligation. So far I have been assuming that for Kant any duty to rescue could be derived *only* from the imperfect duty to aid others in distress, that rescue is for Kant a matter of beneficence rather than justice. That means that we can be selective in whom we aid, when and to what extent. This selectivity may be regarded as a merit of Kant's account of the imperfect duty of beneficence. Selectivity is essential in order to avoid an overload of obligations. Thus I have a duty to give to some beggars, but not to all beggars. Of course, it still needs to be asked whether the duty to aid others is an imperfect duty in Kant's sense. Perhaps extensive obligations are indeed morally required. That claim will be considered in Section 7. Here I wish to consider a more restricted problem. Selectivity clearly has two aspects. On the one hand, it means that our imperfect obligations, such as beneficence, can be limited. On the other, it may mean that they can be so limited as to be morally unacceptable. I take it that it would be unacceptable if our only duty to aid the poor of the Third World were our imperfect duty to aid and if that duty could be satisfied by giving one penny a year to a charity. It would be ludicrous to argue that one did not have to rescue a drowning child from a shallow pond because one had performed a rescue two weeks ago. The idea behind imperfect obligations seems to be that there must be some limit to what an individual can be required to do. But it would be unacceptable if the individual were able to set the burden as low as he could. The point is well explained by Onora O'Neill.[32] She argues that the selectivity of imperfect obligations is ethically acceptable only because the duties of justice are prior.

O'Neill explains that one part of Kant's perfect duty of justice is the duty to avoid coercion. It is often the case that those in need are coerced by their needs or by the circumstances which create their needs. O'Neill is thinking of the poor of the Third World. Many political and economic institutions coerce the poor of the world since the poor have no real option but to accept the terms offered by the rich. The perfect duty of justice requires us to change the existing political and economic institutions. Therefore the perfect duty to avoid coercion aids those in need. Our perfect duty to create just institutions is prior to our imperfect duty of beneficence. What we must do first is to create the conditions of justice. Since the greatest *needs* of others will be satisfied when we satisfy our perfect duty of justice, the demands for beneficence will be less urgent, and it is therefore more ethically acceptable that we cannot be equally beneficent to all: 'In a just society, with few failures to meet needs, imperfect duty might seldom have to focus on unmet needs, and could turn to making good lesser impediments to action'.[33] The selectivity of imperfect duties is acceptable because the imperfect duty to aid those in distress supplements rather than replaces the duty of justice.[34]

O'Neill's reading of Kant points in the direction of several conclusions relevant to the concerns of this chapter. Her argument is that we have a perfect duty of justice to avoid coercion, and that duty makes it incumbent upon us to aid the poor of the Third World. The point seems capable of generalisation. Insofar as a duty to rescue can be represented as a duty to avoid coercion, the duty is perfect and the rescue is required. O'Neill further argues that we are morally required to seek collective institutional solutions at the national and international level. Presumably, we may also be required to create and support political solutions to national poverty, such as redistributive taxation, as well as other rescue services. Solving the problems closer to home may result in extensive legal duties on individuals to rescue.

But our perfect duty to avoid coercion cannot be only the duty to participate in collective remedies. When we consider what else our duty to avoid coercion might require, O'Neill's argument seems to have the implication that there is an extensive individual duty to rescue. That is partly because she seems to interpret the duty to avoid coercion as including the duty to change coercive circumstances (for example, coercive political and economic institutions) as well as to prevent coercion.[35] If her argument is that the duty to avoid coercion is a duty which includes preventing coercion, then many rescues are perfect duties and not imperfect ones. Furthermore, if there is no reason to think that the duty is only to assist in providing collective solutions, then it seems to be that the individual has an extensive perfect duty to aid those in distress whenever the distress can be regarded as coercive. O'Neill understands that the problem of rescuing those in urgent need cannot be left as a matter of imperfect obligation only. She makes it a matter of justice, a matter of perfect obligation. The problem of selectivity is neatly solved, but the problem of requiring a great deal of individuals seems to remain.

I shall not pursue Kant's view further. Although it is attractive as a justification for a duty to rescue, there are a number of problems. There is a problem about what an imperfect duty to rescue would entail. No imperfect duty could be the basis of a legal duty to rescue. However, it might be possible to argue that there is a perfect duty to rescue. But to interpret Kant in this way invites the same objection that is often made to consequentialist theories, namely, that it is not possible to have a duty to rescue without it turning into an extensive and onerous duty to aid others. This is a point to which I will return in Section 6.

5   Other Objections to a Duty to Rescue

In *Harm to Others*,[36] Joel Feinberg discusses a number of common objections to the view that there ought to be a legal duty to rescue. Feinberg's chapter provides a very useful overview of these objections and some convincing rejoinders. However, I think he frequently undervalues the objections and thus fails to make a strong case for a duty to rescue.

Causation.   One objection to a duty to rescue is that people are required only not to cause harm; they are not required to prevent harm. Thus I am required not to push someone into a dangerous river; I am not required to warn them about the danger or to rescue them once they are in danger. This is one important objection I shall not touch upon in this chapter. I recommend Feinberg's reply to the reader.[37] Feinberg notes that the objection has two forms. The first form is that there is a morally significant difference between causing harm and failing to prevent it. That difference justifies restricting liability to blame or punishment to cases of causing harm. Feinberg denies that there is a morally significant difference, at least in the rescue context, between positive and negative duties. The second form of the objection is to deny that omissions can be causes of harm. Feinberg's reply is that there is no reason to doubt that omissions can be *a* cause.

Whether an omission is *the* cause will depend on our reasons for wanting to determine the cause. If what is in question is blame, then omissions can be *the* cause.[38]

Undue interference with liberty; Macaulay's line-drawing.   There are three other objections, but I am much less persuaded by Feinberg's treatment of these. All three will be dealt with in the course of this chapter. There is the objection that a legal duty to rescue is an undue interference with liberty. Feinberg's reply, that the interference is outweighed by the good produced, is rather superficial. I have already discussed this objection in Section 3, and I shall return to it again in Section 7. The third objection Feinberg considers is the famous objection from Lord Macaulay.[39] Macaulay thought that there could only be a legal obligation to assist those with whom one had a special relationship. Macaulay thought that if you did not draw the line there, then no non-arbitrary line could be drawn and one would have to recognise an extensive legal obligation of beneficence. In the latter case, one would have to recognise that a surgeon might have a legal duty to suffer the enormous inconvenience of travelling vast distances in great discomfort if he were the only person who might save a dying patient.[40] Feinberg's conclusion is that Macaulay's fear was exaggerated. But Feinberg does not address the more interesting problem that Macaulay's objection is an even better objection to the claim that there is a *moral* requirement to rescue. It is that issue that I discuss in Section 7.

No duty to confer a benefit.   The fourth objection that Feinberg considers is the objection that rescues are benefits; and since there is no duty to confer a benefit, there can be no duty to rescue. Feinberg argues that this view is based on a confused account of what counts as a benefit. Preventing harm and making a gratuitous present may both be benefits, but it is a confusion to argue that, since there is no duty to do the latter, there is no duty to do the former. But, once again, Feinberg seems unwilling to give the objection its full force. What the objection may ineptly express is the worry that, if one allows that there is a moral requirement to promote some good of others, there may not be any limit to what one can be required to do for the sake of others. I think that both Macaulay's objection and this objection are bottomed on the same anxiety: that once one grants a duty to rescue one must grant an extensive duty of beneficence. That is the important issue that Feinberg does not confront and which I will address shortly.

5.1   *Feinberg's Argument for a Duty to Rescue*

Before leaving Feinberg, one should note his own solution to the duty to rescue problem, a solution which many might find attractive in its simplicity. He suggests that there is a right to be rescued.[41] This looks like a more significant position than I think it is. Feinberg takes as opponents some of those who deny that there is a right to be rescued. The opponents' view is pictured as depending on a certain account of imperfect duties. For example, Mill apparently distinguished perfect and imperfect obligations or duties on the basis that the former, but not the latter, give rise to correlative rights.[42] Thus Mill was able to distinguish those benefits that someone could claim as a right (such as the right to what was promised) and those benefits which ought to be given but no one has a right to claim (such as charity). The distinction is ambidextrous. On the one hand, one could use it to argue: since the duty to rescue is a perfect duty, then allowing a duty to rescue does not entail a *general* duty of charity, and the problem of an unlimited duty of beneficence does not arise. Feinberg is here confronting the alternative argument: since the duty to rescue is an imperfect duty, no one's rights are violated by a failure to rescue. The failure is at most a lack of beneficence but not an injustice. Since we are not required to be beneficent, someone who fails to rescue does not do what is wrong.

Feinberg's reply is to argue that Mill's distinction between perfect and imperfect duties is based on whether the person to whom the duty is owed is determinate or indeterminate. A duty is indeterminate 'when there are more persons to be assisted than there are personal resources effectively to aid them'.[43] If determinate, then the duty is perfect and gives rise to a correlative right. If imperfect, the duty is indeterminate and does not give rise to a right.[44] Feinberg then claims that the duty to rescue can be perfect whenever the person who needs to be rescued is determinate. Hence there is a right to be rescued.

There are a number of points in this argument that are unclear to me. For example, suppose that there are more people who need to be rescued than can be rescued by the only available rescuer. In such a case, Feinberg says the rescuer has an imperfect duty and that each person in need of rescue has a right that the rescuer save as many as he can. [45] That account of the matter is apparently inconsistent, since imperfect duties are those that give rise to no rights. Moreover, if that account were correct, it would be possible to argue that the starving of the Third World have a right that I feed as many of them as I can. Yet, as I shall explain, Feinberg denies that they have that right. I leave aside such difficulties because I wish to pursue a more general point. This argument works if the only issue is the correct interpretation of the distinction between perfect and imperfect duties. That is, Feinberg's opponents have to agree that there is a duty to rescue but, because imperfect, it confers no right. The more interesting question is whether Feinberg could demonstrate that there is a right to be rescued without first assuming that there is a duty to rescue.

Feinberg's account of the nature of rights is given in two earlier articles.[46] The essence of his view is that rights are valid claims. A claim is valid if it is justified within a system of rules or principles.[47] This seems to be a necessary and sufficient condition for a *legal* right.[48] Thus one could say that a slaveowner has a legal right to beat his slave provided that there is a system of rules within which such a claim is justified. However, moral rights require something more. Moral rights are valid claims based on certain interests.[49] Not all interests will ground moral rights but welfare interests (for example, the interest in living) indisputably do.[50]

I think Feinberg has a problem in trying to extract a right to be rescued from this account of rights. Consider this question: do all welfare interests give rise to rights? I think that Feinberg wants to deny that they do. In several places he argues that the starving have a claim to be fed but no right to be fed.[51] The reason for this is not clear, but the options appear to be these: (a) According to his earlier articles, Feinberg held that a moral right is a claim, based on certain interests (welfare interests, for example) within a valid system of rules. The starving have no right to be fed because there is no moral rule that those with more than they need have a duty to feed the starving. (b) Those with more than they need have an imperfect duty to feed the starving; but the starving have no right because they are indeterminate.

Option (b) appears to contradict option (a). If there is an imperfect duty to feed the starving, then there is a relevant moral rule and, according to his earlier accounts, Feinberg should hold that there is a moral right. If his view is option (a), then he has yet to address what I think is the most significant question. If it is plausible to deny that the starving have a right to be fed because there is no relevant moral principle, it also must be plausible to deny that there is a right to be rescued because there is no relevant moral principle. At least, one cannot conclude that there is the right to be rescued without first assuming that there is a duty to rescue.

It appears that Feinberg needs to assume at least the imperfect duty to rescue (which can become perfect) in order to refute the view that the person in distress has no right to be rescued. But there is an inconsistency between this assumption and his earlier accounts of rights. Furthermore, even if his argument succeeded, it would not refute those who hold that there is no right to be rescued because there is no duty to rescue; rescues are acts of supererogation which are morally praiseworthy but not morally required. Nothing in Feinberg's discussion of this objection refutes that view.[52] Feinberg's appeal to rights does not advance what I think is the main argument. What is in dispute is whether there is a moral principle that a by-stander ought to rescue someone in distress and does wrong if he fails to rescue, at least if the rescue is easy. If we agree that there is such a principle, I see little to be gained by then concluding that the person in danger has a right to be rescued correlative to the duty of the bystander.

6 Consequentialism

I suggested earlier (Section 2) that one had to consider three positions about the moral requirement to rescue. I have so far dealt with the first, namely, the view that there is no moral requirement to rescue. Many consequentialists who have felt the pull of the argument that individuals ought not to be compelled to act for the good of another have been tempted by the second position, the position that there is some moral requirement to rescue. They have sought a balance be-tween promoting another's good and compelling an individual against her desires to promote it. I will argue that this balance is illusory. The second position is unstable and so a consequentialist is committed to the third position, that the moral requirement to aid is extensive.

It seems evident that a utilitarian theory will treat some rescues (for example, easy ones) as morally required. Both Bentham and Mill supported a requirement to rescue. In the *Introduction to the Principles of Morals and Legislation*, Bentham argued that, although benevolent acts were in general not the concern of the legislator,

> The limits of the law on this head seem, however, to be capable of being extended a good deal farther than they seem ever to have been extended hitherto. In particular, in cases where the person is in danger, why should it not be the duty of every man to save another from mischief, when it can be done without prejudicing himself, as well as to abstain from bringing it on him?[53]

It is interesting that, in *Specimen of a Penal Code*, Bentham made the obligation much wider: 'Every man is bound to assist those who have need of assistance, if he can do it without exposing himself to sensible inconvenience.'[54]

This general approach to the problem is vulnerable to two related objections, which I shall bear in mind in what follows. The first objection is that discussed in Section 3, namely that one ought not to require a person to restrict his liberty for the sake of the needs of another, except by voluntary agreement (the bad samaritan principle). The second objection, which has been mentioned several times already, is that a requirement to rescue requires too much. This is an aspect of the familiar objection that utilitarianism creates an obligation to be beneficent that is far too extensive (the overload of obligations objection). I think it is the most serious difficulty for a utilitarian justification of a duty to rescue.

The writers with whom I shall first be concerned (in Sections 6.1 and 6.3) emphasise the first of these quotations from Bentham, and give it a certain interpretation. They suppose that a duty to rescue arises only *in certain circumstances* and the problem lies in determining the circumstances. In Bentham's view, the duty arises only in situations of danger and when the rescue can be effected without prejudice to the rescuer. In adopting this approach to the problem of a duty to rescue these writers have tried to formulate theories that are sensitive to the importance of individual liberty. I shall argue that they have not been successful. I shall then discuss whether the second quotation from Bentham indicates the way in which a utilitarian theory must develop.

6.1   Sidgwick's View

Henry Sidgwick's approach to the morality of rescue clearly exemplifies that form of utilitarianism just described.[55] His utilitarianism seeks to maximise individual liberty by insisting on the importance of voluntary agreements, while subjecting those agreements to certain overriding limitations. Thus the duty to rescue becomes a justified exception to the principle that voluntary agreements generally maximise utility.[56]

The first important premise in Sidgwick's argument is his claim that Bentham's requirement that everyone is to count for one in the utilitarian calculus does *not* mean that happiness has to be distributed equally.

> Bentham's dictum must be understood merely as making the conception of the ultimate end precise – laying down that one person's happiness is to be counted for as much as another's (supposed equal in degree) as an element of the general happiness – not as directly prescribing the rules of conduct by which this end will best be attained.[57]

In other words, Bentham's dictum prescribes only the end that equal amounts of happiness should count equally in calculating the greatest happiness of the greatest number. The means by which the greatest happiness of the greatest number is achieved is left open. So Sidgwick is free to claim that the greatest happiness of the greatest number is in fact produced by an unequal distribution of happiness. He argues that *in general* the means of producing the greatest happiness of the greatest number is to allow individuals to contract freely to exchange goods.

> As political economists have explained, the means of happiness are immensely increased by that complex system of cooperation which has been gradually organised among civilised men: and while it is thought that under such a system it will be generally best on the whole to let each individual exchange such services as he is disposed to render for such return as he can get for them by free contract, still there are many large exceptions to this general principle.[58]

There are two main kinds of exceptions: the duties arising from special affection, such as the familial duties; the duties arising from 'special needs'. The duties which arise from special needs include the duty to alleviate poverty in an emergency, and the duty to rescue in an emergency.[59] Sidgwick's claim is that these exceptions to the general principle are justified on utilitarian grounds. We can see why if we examine the duty to rescue. Sidgwick maintains that there is a duty to rescue when the following conditions are satisfied:[60]

1 a person finds himself in a situation where he cannot ward off an evil without assistance that he cannot purchase 'on the ordinary commercial terms';[61] and
2 because of the exceptional nature of that situation – an emergency – rendering assistance does not have the undesirable effect of weakening the self-reliance of the person assisted; and
3 the assistance is not burdensome to the giver.

Sidgwick believes that the conditions will be satisfied in the case in which 'I could save a man from drowning merely by holding out my hand.'[62] In such a case, I presume that Sidgwick would conclude that it is wrong to fail to rescue. Futhermore, although he is describing the *moral* duty, he is at least prepared to consider that there ought to be a *legal* obligation to assist when these conditions are satisfied.[63]

The strategy of Sidgwick's argument is clear. It is evident, he thinks, that the greatest happiness of the greatest number is produced by imposing a duty to rescue in certain circumstances. So an exception is required to the general principle that the greatest happiness of the greatest number is produced by allowing individuals freely to contract their services. But the exception is itself justified on utilitarian grounds because it maximises happiness without undesirable side-effects. The undesirable side-effects are ruled out by the three conditions listed above.

6.2   Criticism of Sidgwick

My contention is that this account of when it is wrong to fail to rescue is seriously incomplete. Either it offers us no account of when the duty to rescue arises because condition (3) fails to answer the question as to when, on utilitarian grounds, one is required to make a rescue; or it begs the question in favour of a certain answer.

Let us consider the matter with regard to Sidgwick's claim that there is a duty to alleviate poverty. He denies that it is a duty for a rich man to give away all of his surplus wealth. That is not a duty, he says, because it weakens the self-reliance of the poor. However, in an emergency, it *is* a duty to alleviate poverty because the indirect evil of weakening self-reliance does not arise. This argument works only because Sidgwick assumes that condition (3) is satisfied, that is, that it is not burdensome to the rich man. He is, of course, not entitled to assume that. Indeed, the problem with the argument is that, if Sidgwick did not assume that condition (3) is satisfied, it would not be clear what would follow from the three conditions.

So let us begin again. Sidgwick's view ought to be that giving aid to the poor is a duty whenever conditions (1)–(3) are satisfied. I am not certain that I understand what the first of Sidgwick's conditions means. It appears to require in effect that ordinary contractual relations are impossible in the circumstances. So the first condition is not so much an exception to the general principle but a requirement that the general principle cannot apply. Condition (2) is arguably always satisfied in the case of the poor. It could be read in two ways: either as (2a) limiting the duty to emergencies, or as (2b) limiting the duty to those cases in which self-reliance is not weakened. If (2a), Sidgwick owes us an explanation of what counts as an emergency, and some justification for that restriction. So I shall read (2) as (2b) and, according to that way of reading it, emergencies are just an example of situations in which aid does not weaken self-reliance. Read as (2b), the condition does not impose any significant limitation on the duty to aid the poor. To make only the most obvious point, the truly destitute do not have self-reliance as an option. [64] Giving them aid does not weaken their self-reliance because they cannot rely on themselves. Either we aid them, or they die. Aiding may induce reliance but, if we give them the right kind of aid, that will be temporary.[65] Similarly, condition (2) will usually be satisfied in the case of rescues. Persons in need of rescue from serious harm do not have their self-reliance weakened if they are rescued.

So even if conditions (1) and (2) are satisfied, Sidgwick is committed to an extensive duty of beneficence – the duty to aid the truly destitute – and perhaps an extensive duty to rescue. This duty could clearly be very burdensome and, if Sidgwick intends to avoid that conclusion, then condition (3) must do all the work. But condition (3) could be taken in several ways, and Sidgwick does not guide us. The first possibility is that the condition is meant to reflect the outcome of a utilitarian calculation performed, perhaps, by some impartial spectator. Thus some act is not burdensome to the giver whenever some impartial spectator would judge that the act produces more utility overall. But that is clearly too strong a claim for Sidgwick. It might entail that the rich man, and some not-so-rich men, have to give away much of their money to the truly destitute. The second possibility is that what is burdensome is a matter for the giver to decide. If this is correct, objections could be made: (a) we are left with no clear guidance about when the duty to aid does arise; (b) if the duty can arise only when condition (3) is satisfied, and if that judgement is left up to the individual giver to make, then the duty to aid arises only when the potential giver wants it to arise. Giving aid is thus part of a voluntarist theory of obligation; it is not an exception to it.

At best, the discussion of the duty to rescue and the duty to aid is incomplete. Conditions (1) and (2) might be satisfied, and yet there would be an extensive duty to aid or to rescue. So the argument depends crucially on condition (3). On one account of condition (3), there might still be an extensive duty. On a different account of condition (3), the discussion is irrelevant or unhelpful. I discuss later, in Section 7, other reasons for thinking that condition (3) is the crucial condition in any consequentialist argument. It is, in effect, what Shelly Kagan calls the appeal to costs argument.[66]

It can now be seen why I emphasised that Sidgwick assumed that the rich man would not be burdened by giving to the poor in an emergency. His argument only works when it seems clear that the action is not burdensome; hence his other example that there is a duty to rescue when I need only stretch out my hand to someone who is drowning. Sidgwick's discussion appears question-begging. The discussion inclines to the conclusion that a duty to rescue arises only when the duty is *clearly* not burdensome. In other words, the duty arises only when there is no significant interference with individual liberty. Thus it is not surprising that Sidgwick believed he had accomplished the reconciliation of a duty to rescue or a duty to aid with his view that voluntary obligations generally maximise utility. The non-voluntary obligations are either really voluntary or so minimally inconvenient that no one could object to her liberty being restricted.

It may of course be true that the only duty to rescue that can be defended on utilitarian grounds is a very limited one. However, Sidgwick has not demonstrated that. It is interesting to look at another theory very similar to Sidgwick's. What makes E.J. Weinrib's theory particularly interesting in this connection is that his theory is explicitly fashioned so as to minimise the infringement on individual liberty.

6.3   Weinrib's View

Weinrib's article, 'The Case for a Duty to Rescue',[67] is an interesting and influential attempt to defend (with reservations) a legal duty to rescue on utilitarian grounds. Weinrib has adopted much of Sidgwick's argument and developed it into a defence of a legal duty in tort to rescue. Like Sidgwick, he argues that the duty to rescue is an exception to the principle that *in general* the greatest happiness of the greatest number is produced by allowing people to distribute goods and resources by contract. Weinrib believes that he can demonstrate a duty in tort to rescue which is consistent with principles of the common law, which respects individual liberty and which is consistent with utilitarianism. He claims to be able to deal with two objections to a duty to rescue I mentioned earlier: that it is an infringement of individual liberty and that the duty is indistinguishable from a wider duty of beneficence.

In the first part of his argument, Weinrib claims that a tort duty to rescue would be a simple extension of a principle of the common law. He takes it that the common law regards the law of contract as prior to the law of torts. The law of contract is connected in a fundamental way with individual liberty. The priority of the law of contract is an expression of the political value that individuals should have the maximum liberty to organise their own affairs. So the common law is very reluctant to interfere with the liberty to contract by imposing obligations that override it.

But, of course, the law of torts does impose obligations that override the liberty to contract. Weinrib's view is that the general principle of the common law is that tort liability is created only when there is no 'social value in the liberty to contract'.[68] He illustrates this with the Canadian Supreme Court case of *O'Rourke* v. *Schacht*.[69] In that case a policeman was held negligent in tort because he failed to erect a warning sign on the highway. Tort liability could be imposed in such a case because there is no social value in allowing a policeman to contract with individual motorists. The policeman is not a market agent. Similar explanations can be offered for the obligations on members of families. Moreover, in the circumstances of a rescue, contracts have been held void because of duress.[70]

It must be questioned whether *O'Rourke* v. *Schacht* offers very persuasive support for Weinrib's theory of the common law. There are interesting cases with considerable authority that are apparently irreconcilable with it. For example, in *Hill* v. *Chief Constable of West Yorkshire*,[71] the House of Lords held that the police were not liable in tort for the inefficient investigation of a number of rapes.[72] More recently, in *Ancell and Another* v. *Chief Constable of Bedfordshire and Others* the English Court of Appeal decided that the police were not liable for damages in respect of a failure to warn the public of danger.[73] The facts in that case were very similar to those in *O'Rourke* v. *Schacht*. The police spotted a spillage of oil on the roadway but took no steps to warn the public. The plaintiff's wife and daughter were in a car which skidded on the oil and hit an oncoming lorry, killing the wife. In his decision, Lord Justice Beldam said: 'It is exceptional to find in the law a duty to control another's actions to prevent harm to strangers. Such a duty of care would impose upon a police force potential liability of almost unlimited scope.' As I shall explain, I believe that Lord Justice Beldam has identified the crucial issue.

I leave aside these doubts about Weinrib's use of *O'Rourke* v. *Schacht* and return to his argument that there is a principle of the common law that tort liability can be imposed only when there is no social value in upholding the liberty to contract. A tort duty to rescue would not be inconsistent with this principle and thus a tort duty would not interfere with individual liberty. Weinrib clearly regards this principle of the common law as a gloss on the first of Sidgwick's conditions.

I emphasise that Weinrib is claiming that, for a duty to rescue to arise, there can be no social value in upholding the liberty to contract. In order to defend that claim he has to draw the following distinction:

> In the rescue context, the resource to be expended (time and effort directed at aiding the victim) cannot be traded on the market. ... In the charity context, by contrast, the resource to be expended (money) can be traded on the market.[74]

Weinrib has to draw this distinction because in any situation involving a market commodity there will be *some* social value in upholding the liberty to contract.

Thus far the argument is that a tort duty to rescue (as defined) is not inconsistent with the principles of the common law. The tort duty does not interfere with the individual's liberty to contract because the duty arises only when that liberty is valueless. Moreover, the tort duty can be limited by adding two conditions which Weinrib thinks can be justified on utilitarian grounds. There is the condition that the duty arises only in an emergency. Weinrib provides a gloss on 'emergency'. He thinks that this condition captures the utilitarian worry that aid is justified only when it does not 'induce reliance' on the giver.[75] Emergencies do not induce reliance because 'an emergency is not only a desperate situation; it is also a situation that deviates from society's usual pattern'.[76] Therefore, poverty and homelessness are not emergencies.[77] There is also the condition that the rescue is not burdensome to the rescuer. This condition is justified because of the disincentive effect of setting too high a standard:

> Accordingly, a utilitarian will be restrained and circumspect in the elaboration of legal duties. In particular, he will not pitch a standard of behaviour at too high a level: the higher the standard, the more oner-ous it will be to the person subjected to it, the greater the pleasure he must forgo in adhering to it, and the greater his resistance to its de-mands. A high standard entails both more severe punishment and a more elaborate apparatus of detection and enforcement. Applied to the rescue situation, this reasoning implies that some convenience restric-tion should be adopted as part of the duty.[78]

When set out, Weinrib's argument is very similar to Sidgwick's. A tort duty to rescue arises whenever:

1   There is in the situation no social value in upholding the liberty to contract; and
2   the situation is an emergency; hence the aid does not 'induce reliance' on the giver; and
3   the rescue is not burdensome to the rescuer.

Like Sidgwick, he argues that the duty in tort to rescue is an excep-tion to the priority of voluntary obligations, an exception which is justified on utilitarian grounds.

6.4   Criticism of Weinrib

I think Weinrib has inventively elaborated Sidgwick's argument, but I do not find his argument convincing. My main objection is to Weinrib's first condition, *viz.*, that a necessary condition for a legal duty to rescue is that there is no social value in upholding the liberty to contract. It is not entirely clear what Weinrib means. He seems to mean that the rescuer is not a market agent in the sense that what is required of him for the rescue is not something that he could sell on the market. Hence Weinrib's point that rescues are defined as requir-ing only time and effort.

I find this point just baffling. Clearly rescuers of human life can market their services: for example, doctors, private emergency para-medical services, owners of helicopters in search and rescue opera-tions. It is precisely because there is a market in rescues that there is a market for insurance against the costs of rescue. Moreover, the at-tempt to distinguish rescues from charity in this way fails. Anything which uses a market commodity cannot be a rescue, according to this account. But a doctor or paramedic will need expensive technology; a lifesaver may need a boat, or a buoy or a rope. By this definition, a rescue involving a rope becomes an act of charity and is not a suitable case for a tort duty to rescue. Not only is this conceptually unattractive for the reasons given earlier, in Section 3, it defeats what I take to be the object of the argument, which is to create liability in tort for someone who does not throw a rope to a drowning person.

I might make two further criticisms of the view that rescues cannot involve market goods. First, it seems to me that a rescuer might be justified in using *someone else's property*, as when he takes a boat or trespasses on land. Second, it is in recognition of the fact that rescues require marketable commodities that rescuers can obtain compensation under the principles of *negotiorum gestio*. I think that Weinrib has got himself into a predicament with his first condition because he recognises that he needs to distinguish rescues from charity in order to limit the duty to rescue,[79] but has not found a way to do it.

The alternative interpretation of Weinrib's first condition is that he is claiming that the rescuer *ought not* to be allowed to act as a market agent. This interpretation would explain Weinrib's reference to *Post v. Jones* and the duress rule.[80] In that case, the United States Supreme Court held unenforceable a contract to save whalers marooned in the Arctic. The Court seems to have recognised that the rescuers had something to sell, but would not permit them to sell it. But why not? Presumably because the defendant's liberty to contract was of less social value than the marooned whalers' lives. But allowing this kind of balance is not enough for Weinrib's argument, since it clearly opens up the possibility of wider duties of beneficence.

I appreciate that Weinrib's first condition is an attempt to keep the duty to rescue within bounds that a libertarian might accept. Crudely, the condition attempts to limit the duty to rescue to those cases in which the liberty to refuse to rescue has no social value. However, my view is that Weinrib's first condition is wrong. Perhaps it is only overrestrictive. It could be argued that tort liability is very influenced by policy considerations, and the social value of allowing individuals to govern their duties to each other is *one* such policy consideration. On my view, it can be outweighed by even more pressing considerations.

Given the earlier comments about Sidgwick (Section 6.2), there is no need to discuss Weinrib's second and third conditions in detail. I think that they are both question-begging. For example, Weinrib's definition of an emergency in his second condition is that emergencies must 'deviate from society's usual pattern'. This is just another way of distinguishing rescues from charity. But the question at issue is precisely whether a utilitarian can draw that distinction in any principled way.

6.5   Summary

Thus far, I have been examining one kind of utilitarian attempt to justify a duty to rescue. It has two features:

1   The duty to rescue is thought of as a justified exception to the principle that allowing liberty to be restricted only by voluntary obligations maximises utility.
2   The duty to rescue has to be circumscribed in some way so that it does not turn into a general duty of charity or beneficence.

So far we have seen that this approach appears to work only by limiting the duty to rescue to cases in which there is no conflict or no substantial conflict with individual liberty. The duty to rescue is a very limited exception to the principle that voluntary obligations maximise utility, since it arises only when the rescuer has almost no good reason not to rescue. However, it is arguable that utilitarianism requires more than can be provided by rare exceptions to the principle that voluntary obligations maximise utility. In that case we would need to try an entirely different approach. The requirements for a different approach are that it gives up treating the duty to rescue as an exceptional duty, that it accepts that there is no relevant distinction between rescues and charity and that it gives up any attempt to reconcile the duty to rescue with individual liberty. Such an approach is adopted by Robert Goodin in his book, *Protecting the Vulnerable*.[81]

6.6   Goodin's View

Robert Goodin distinguishes two different 'theories of obligation', as he calls them.[82] The voluntarist theory claims that obligations (requirements) arise only from voluntary actions. The voluntarist takes the notion of a promissory obligation as the paradigm of all obligations (requirements). The voluntarist would probably see contractual obligations in general as the core of the notion of obligation. Insofar as the voluntarist recognises special obligations or duties, he treats them as peripheral to the core. For example, the voluntarist can hardly deny the special duties of a parent to his child, but those duties do not fit easily or at all into the voluntarist theory. A duty to rescue, as we have seen, creates difficulties for the voluntarist theory. As I have just argued, someone like Sidgwick or Weinrib who makes voluntary obligations normatively central can include a duty to rescue only by making it such a limited exception that it does not affect the voluntarist's view.

Goodin contrasts the voluntarist theory with the vulnerability theory. The central intuition of the vulnerability theory is that vulnerability gives rise to moral requirements. According to the vulnerability theory, the moral requirement that some person does something for another arises from the fact that the latter is vulnerable to the former for some harm. Thus the paradigm moral requirement according to the vulnerability theory is the requirement to assist those in special need – the destitute, the drowning, and so on. So the duty to rescue, far from being a problem for the theory, is in fact its paradigm case. The proponents of the vulnerability theory believe they can explain contractual obligations as well as, if not better than, the voluntarist.

The distinction between voluntarist and vulnerability theories of obligation (requirement) offers the tempting explanation of the difficulties in the previous arguments that it is the voluntarist theory that is the source of the difficulty. The central role assigned to voluntary obligations creates an insoluble difficulty with the duty of charity and the duty to rescue. Would we do better, then, by placing the vulnerability theory at the centre of our theory, as Goodin argues? At first sight, this seems improbable. One of the objections to the previous theories has been that the vulnerability-based requirements are unlimited. Goodin thinks that he can deal with that problem. I think that he is much less successful than he thinks. Without saying more that needs to be said about the vulnerability theory, let me turn directly to that problem.

According to the vulnerability theory, person A is morally required to do some act in respect of person B if and only if B is vulnerable to A in respect of B's interests or welfare.[83] That means that A is in a position either to harm B or to prevent harm to B. In that circumstance, A is responsible for the protection of B's interests. Goodin thinks that the vulnerability theory is well placed to deal with the problem of allocating responsibility. The theory holds that 'the strength of ... responsibility depends strictly upon the degree to which' A can affect B's interests, either by harming them or by preventing harm to them.[84]

Now we add a familiar point from Mill and Sidgwick. *As a matter of fact*, they claim, we are capable of affecting the interests of only a limited number of people. Moreover, we most affect the interests of those nearest to us because they are most vulnerable to us. Furthermore, because we have more intimate knowledge of the welfare of those nearest to us, we can more efficiently promote or prevent harm to their interests. So the vulnerability theory allows us to pay more attention to the interests of those nearest to us than to the distant starving millions. In effect, Goodin is accepting that we do have an extensive beneficent duty to others, but argues that the duty is not burdensome to individuals. More precisely, the claim is that the scope of the duty to aid is extensive but that the burden on individuals can be limited.

6.7   Criticism of Goodin

The difficulty with this argument is that the central fact it relies on seems to me arguably false. That alleged fact is: 'On balance, persons relatively near to us in space and time probably *will* be rather more vulnerable to us. Their interests are more likely to be affected more heavily by our own actions and choices than are the interests of persons more distant.'[85] Consider this example. I have £23 in my bank account that I don't need. I could give it to my wife or I could send it to Oxfam. Today £23 sent to Oxfam will keep a starving person in East Africa alive for six months. There is nothing (I am glad to say) that my wife could do with £23 that would be as worthwhile. As a matter of fact, she is not more vulnerable to me than some nameless starving East African. Far from this being an exceptional situation, I think it is a common situation. My counter-example works because the strength of my obligation varies inversely with levels of welfare.

There is an ambiguity in the vulnerability theory's claim that the strength of the requirement A must satisfy 'depends strictly upon the degree to which' A can affect B's interests. To bring out this ambiguity, I will make use of the idea of a welfare baseline.[86] B's welfare baseline is her current level of welfare. Now the vulnerability theory claims that A is morally required to do some act in respect of B whenever A can change B's welfare baseline, either up or down. But the vulnerability theory might be making either of two different claims about the *strength* of the requirement.

1   The strength of the requirement on A varies in proportion to the relative difference in baselines between A and B. The lower B's baseline relative to A, the greater the requirement. But if this is the theory, then it is not true that my stronger obligations will generally be to those most immediate to me.
2   The strength of the requirement on A is directly proportional to the degree to which A can change B's baseline, either up or down. But if this is what the theory means, the counter-example still works because of marginal utility. If I give £23 to a starving African, I will move her baseline up more increments than I could increase the baseline of anyone nearer to me.

So on either interpretation of what the vulnerability theory is claiming, there will be cases in which the requirement that I aid those distant starving millions will *in fact* be stronger than any requirement I must satisfy for those nearest to me. Goodin seems to have neglected the fact that the level of B's welfare baseline will affect the strength of the requirement on A in respect of B at least as much as the causal relations between A and B. So the alleged fact that he and some utilitarians have relied on is not true.

Goodin has replied by rejecting the counter-example.[87] He argues that my wife is vulnerable to me almost uniquely; if I don't give her £23, no one else will. However those whom Oxfam supports are equally vulnerable to everyone with spare cash, and so there is a collective obligation to support Oxfam. An individual's obligation to those whom Oxfam supports is less than my obligation to my wife because the collective obligation is divided in so many ways. Thus it is true that as individuals we have stronger obligations to those nearest us.

This reply does not seem to meet my point, which is that the strength of obligation varies with the need as well as with the numbers of those who could satisfy it. Goodin's reply suggests an odd account of the strength of an obligation. Suppose it is true that my wife is uniquely vulnerable to me because I am the only one who knows of the need and can satisfy it. I think that nothing follows about the strength of my obligation. Suppose that I am the only person who could save a drowning child. Coincidentally, I am the only person who can then take to hospital a passer-by who is suffering from a painful but not life-threatening injury. If the only fact relevant to the strength of my obligation were that I was the only person who could assist, then both obligations would be equally strong. However, I think that they are not. The strength of my obligation varies with need.

It seems that we need two concepts where Goodin uses only the concept of strength. For the sake of a rough illustration, call the amount needed to satisfy the need in question the quantum, and call his liability that portion of the quantum which any individual is required to supply. In my wife's case, my liability is high but the quantum is low. In the Oxfam case, my liability is low but the quantum is very high. Which is the stronger obligation? The question cannot be answered by reference to liability alone. (There is a rough parallel here with the common law approach to torts. In negligence cases, one must decide first whether there is a duty of care. Only if there is does one ask about the standard of care; that is, how much care was owed by the individual upon whom the duty fell. If talk about the strength of one's obligation were meaningful here, it would typically refer to the standard of care question.)

Suppose my wife's needs are relatively slight. Now imagine some group P of unfortunates who could be helped by N individuals. Goodin seems to be arguing that P divided by N will usually be a smaller quotient than my wife's needs divided by one. But that depends on so many factors (principally the needs that P has) that I see no reason to suppose that contingencies will favour those nearest to us. As investors in the Lloyd's insurance market learned, if the losses are great enough, even a collective obligation can result in an enormous burden for individuals.

A different reply to my counter-example would be to dispute the facts. My argument assumes that as an individual I can make a worthwhile improvement in the welfare of a starving person in the Third World. Goodin denies that. He argues that I can only improve the welfare of a starving person in the Third World by 'restructuring the recipient's whole community'.[88] Such a restructuring is beyond my power as an individual. So the obligation here is what Goodin calls a group obligation. Goodin believes that, as a matter of fact, the necessary restructuring is even beyond the capacity of organised charities and isolated national governments. So the obligation of a citizen in the First World is primarily to engage in political action to make certain that effective aid schemes are organised.[89] Once such a scheme is organised the individual's obligation is to cooperate in bearing 'a fair share of the costs' of discharging the obligation.

Goodin's reply is unconvincing, I think. I am inclined to believe that one individual can affect another Third World individual. But perhaps Goodin has only over-stated his case. Perhaps all that he needs to argue is that an individual will be much more effective if he acts as a member of a group than as an individual. So, as an individual, his primary duty is to create the group obligation. The group obligation limits the burden of my individual obligation, but not its scope. As an individual, I do have an obligation to the Third World, but it is primarily the obligation to bear my fair share of costs in some collaborative effort.

The modification I am suggesting may not be entirely satisfactory. For one thing, the idea of a primary obligation is misleading. Surely my duty to the Third World is to contribute what I can out of my own resources *and* to advocate a group obligation. Only when the group obligation is so effective that my additional contribution is no longer required can I cease my individual contribution. Secondly, it may well be that the individual's fair share of the group obligation is still onerous. If the obligation is to give enough to the Third World for it to be approximately equal in welfare to the First World, the obligation may well require diverting resources from those nearest to me and lowering their welfare. So I think that Goodin is committed to requiring individuals to recognise burdensome obligations. He has defended an extensive duty to aid and has failed, I think, to prevent it from being potentially very burdensome on an individual. (The problem of sharing an extensive burden of rescuing, and the failure of efforts to co-ordinate sharing the burden, are vividly illustrated by refugees – see Chapter 5, Section 4.3.)

I think that Goodin's approach is preferable to that of Sidgwick and Weinrib. Goodin accepts that in order to defend a moral requirement to stretch out my hand to save a drowning person, one has to defend an extensive moral requirement to aid. This may seem inevitable because, contrary to what Mill appears to have thought, there is no distinction between the obligations of rescue and charity that can be justified on consequentialist grounds. If Mill thought that the distinction between charity and rescue was such that the distinction itself could limit our charitable obligations, I think he was wrong.[90] The only difference between perfect and imperfect obligations is that the former are specific in the way that the latter are not.

However, Goodin's approach makes it impossible to draw a distinction between moral requirements and acts of supererogation. That is because his starting-point is that vulnerability is sufficient to give rise to an obligation for those with the relevant power. Moreover, if, as he maintains, the strength of A's obligation to B varies with B's vulnerability, then A may have a very strong *obligation* to act heroically to save B. The main issue here is whether an adequate moral theory must have space for doing more than is required. I shall discuss that issue in Section 7. For the moment let us suppose that it is an objection to Goodin's theory that he makes it impossible to distinguish moral requirements from acts of supererogation. In that case, we would prefer a consequentialist theory which (a) concludes that the requirement to promote others' good is extensive, and is thus unlike Sidgwick's; and (b) maintains that there is a distinction between moral requirements and acts of supererogation, and is thus unlike Goodin's.

Such a theory has been defended by Peter Singer.[91] His basic principle is: 'if it is in our power to prevent something bad from happening, without thereby sacrificing anything of comparable moral significance, we ought, morally, to do it'.[92] Singer uses this basic principle to justify a very extensive duty to aid the poor of the Third World. He claims that our duty is to reduce our standard of living to that level at which giving further charity to the poorest reduces the level of our utility below theirs.

For present purposes, the key phrase in Singer's principle is 'comparable moral significance'. The libertarian may well claim that his ideal of non-interference is of comparable moral significance. Therefore he will argue that, even if Singer's principle is sound, it does not entail that there is a duty to rescue.[93] So Singer's view would fail to satisfy our requirement for a theory that acknowledges an extensive requirement to promote others' good. Presumably, Singer would attempt to rebut that reply by arguing that the judgement of comparable significance has to be made from some impartial or universal point of view, and that from that point of view non-interference is simply not of comparable moral significance.[94] The libertarian could simply deny that. However, Singer's reply would invite difficulty from a different direction. It is a question whether from the impartial or universal point of view one would decide that, for example, I am required to do no more than reduce my standard of living to that of the very poorest. The impartial or universal point of view might require more. In that event, Singer's theory would be unable to satisfy the second of our requirements of sustaining a distinction between what we are required to do and what it would be good to do, even if not required.

6.8   Summary

I will now summarise the discussion in Section 6. Someone who wants to defend a duty to rescue on consequentialist grounds faces two main problems: (a) the libertarian objection discussed in Section 3 (the bad samaritan principle); and (b) the objection that a duty to rescue requires too much because it cannot be distinguished from a requirement of extensive beneficence (the overload of obligations objection). One approach, exemplified by Sidgwick and Weinrib, tries to accommodate the libertarian by claiming that voluntary obligations maximise utility. The duty to rescue is treated as a limited exception to that principle. I have argued that this strategy is unsuccessful.

Let me summarise that argument by returning to Sidgwick's account. It is far from clear what Sidgwick's first condition is but, as elaborated by Weinrib, it will not do. It seems to be an attempt to retain the priority of the value of individual liberty (or of contract values) so that blame or punishment (or tort liability) can be imposed only when the liberty to contract is useless. It is an essential feature in the strategy of accommodating the libertarian, so, if this condition goes, perhaps the accommodation goes as well. The difficulty with Sidgwick's second condition is that it appears to be too restrictive to be justified on utilitarian grounds. While it may be acceptable to insist that a condition of giving aid is that it does not weaken self-reliance, that condition is not satisfied only in what would ordinarily be called emergencies. The third condition, limiting the duty to rescue to cases where the rescue is not burdensome, probably cannot be justified either. The correct points here are that one must not create a standard so high that it is a disincentive; otherwise, aid is required unless it creates a preponderant disutility. So a duty to rescue as described by Sidgwick and Weinrib is either too limited or so extensive as to be indistinguishable from a general duty of beneficence.

I conclude that the Sidgwick–Weinrib approach is fundamentally flawed. The essence of that approach is that one starts with the principle that obligations are created by voluntary agreements and then creates good samaritan duties by making exceptions to it. The good samaritan duties are created by describing the conditions under which the imposition of a duty to aid others maximises utility. The assumption is that those conditions will be satisfied only exceptionally, since what motivates this approach is the desire to limit non-voluntary duties. Of course, I have not shown that this approach is unsuccessful but I have suggested two problems: first, that it is not easy to define the appropriate conditions; second, there is a pressure from the principles of utilitarianism for a broad duty to aid others, not a duty in only exceptional circumstances.

To put it simply, the Sidgwick–Weinrib approach is looking for what is special about duties to rescue such that they form a limited exception to the general principle that there is no duty to rescue. The approach needs to distinguish rescues from some broader duty of charity. I think that Sidgwick and Weinrib have failed to discover what is special about rescues. Mill, too, tried this strategy in Chapter V of *Utilitarianism*, where he tried to distinguish perfect and imperfect obligations, and I think that Mill, too, failed to find a feature that distinguishes charitable from other obligations.[95] My own view is that this strategy is bound to fail because there is no crucial difference between the duty to rescue and other charitable obligations.

A different approach – exemplified by Goodin – does not seek any accommodation with the libertarian, nor does it deny that there is an extensive duty to aid. It claims that moral requirements can be imposed on us by the vulnerability of others (that is, the vulnerability of others is what makes it wrong for us to fail to aid them) and tries to manage the extensive obligation as an allocation problem. Goodin argues that our obligation to others is extensive but manageable, so that no individual carries an insupportable burden. I argue that Goodin fails to show that the individual burden is not very onerous. Moreover, even if I am wrong about that, Goodin's approach faces a major problem: an implication is that there could be requirements which it would be unreasonable to blame someone for not fulfilling.

This second approach treats the duty to rescue as indistinguishable from other moral requirements, perhaps (following Goodin) a central case of a moral requirement, of something it would be wrong to fail to do. Hence one cannot work out a view on rescue *after* one has worked out one's view on other obligations in general; it must be the other way around. Moreover, because there is no distinction between rescue and charity, one cannot justify the duty to rescue without committing oneself to an extensive duty to aid. The consequentialist's dilemma might be that the central case of a moral requirement, of something it is wrong to fail to do, commits him to too much.

7   The Requirement to Promote the Good

I argued in Section 6 that the consequentialist foundation for a duty to rescue turns it into a duty of extensive beneficence. That is because the second of the two positions I listed in Section 2 – the moderate position that there is some duty to rescue – collapses into the third position – that there is an extensive duty to rescue. If it is correct that the moderate position is untenable, then an objection to utilitarianism becomes pertinent. This objection is similar to that considered in Section 3, but is more profound. In Section 3, I considered the objection that a duty to rescue was inconsistent with individual liberty. Here I consider the objection that a consequentialist-based extensive duty of beneficence is inconsistent with individuality; that is, with the agent's sense of himself or herself as a person.

Here is a sketch of the objection. The more I have to do for other people, the less I can do for myself. Utilitarianism requires that I give my projects no more than equal weight with the equally valuable (considered impartially) interests or projects of others. If I am required to promote the good, and if the needs of others are great, then, as the argument in the preceding section demonstrates, I will be required to sacrifice my interests to satisfy the interests of others. My own projects cannot be special to me just because they are my own. This point can be extended: the needs of those with whom I have a special relationship cannot receive special treatment simply in virtue of their relationship to me. A number of philosophers have argued that my interests or projects *are* special just because they are mine.[96] That is because part of what is involved in being myself is that I have certain interests. If I am prohibited from regarding those interests as special then, as Bernard Williams has put it, my integrity is threatened.[97] The more extensive the duty to rescue, the more an agent's individuality is threatened.

The most extensive and persuasive reply to this objection has been given by Shelley Kagan in *The Limits of Morality*.[98] Kagan's most general concern in that book is to defend the view that morality does require us to promote the good of others even at the expense of our own interests. Kagan distinguishes three positions which correspond roughly to the three views about the duty to rescue which I distinguished earlier, in Section 2. Here we need only be concerned with two of them. The extremist holds that morality *requires pro tanto* that we do all we can to promote the good.[99] The moderate believes that there is a reason to promote the good but that we are not *required* to promote the good. The moderate believes that morality includes both options and constraints. Options permit us not to promote the good when there are countervailing considerations that outweigh our reason to promote the good (when, for example, it is at the cost of our own interests).[100] Options allow agents to give special weight to their own interests. Constraints *inter alia* prohibit us from promoting the good when promoting the good entails some forbidden act. The moderate believes that there is some reason to promote the good even when some sacrifice is required. Thus the moderate believes that we are required to save a drowning child when the rescue is easy. So promoting the good is sometimes required but the occasions are limited.[101] Most of Kagan's argument in *The Limits of Morality* is devoted to showing that the moderate's position collapses into the extremist's because the moderate cannot defend the existence of either constraints or options. Kagan's argument supports much of the argument developed so far in this chapter. It is worth pausing for a moment to explain how.

I began by rejecting in Section 3 what Kagan calls the minimalist position, the position that there is no duty to rescue. I then argued in Section 6 that the moderate's position is unstable. Sidgwick and Weinrib cannot defend a duty to rescue without it becoming an extensive duty of beneficence. This is as much as to say that, if there is an option to give special weight to one's own interest, that option is very limited. Therefore the moderate's position collapses into the position that there is an extensive requirement to promote the good. Kagan and I thus agree that the consequentialist cannot defend a duty to make an easy rescue without committing himself to an extensive duty to promote the good. That is the crucial conclusion of Section 6.

However, a complication arose at the end of Section 6. We are faced with a choice of two consequentialist theories, both of which require extensive beneficence. One theory (Goodin's) denies a distinction between what is morally required and what is supererogatory. It is therefore an example of what Kagan calls an extremist theory, a theory which holds that morality does not include options. The other theory (of which Singer's is an example) includes options, but maintains that the option of favouring one's own interest is very limited. Strictly speaking, this second theory is a moderate position, according to Kagan's use of the term, because it allows options. To take account of this difference, I need to add to the list of possible positions mentioned in Section 2.

From the standpoint point of this chapter, a crucial distinction needs to be drawn between two positions, both of which allow for options. On the one hand, there is the position that the requirement to promote the good of others at the expense of one's own good can be limited. That is the position of Sidgwick and others, which I reject in Section 6, and is the second of the three positions I distinguish in Section 2. On the other hand, there is the position that the option of favouring one's own interest at the expense of promoting the good is limited. That is the position illustrated by Singer, and exemplifies the third of the three positions distinguished in Section 2. There is a requirement to promote the good which is extensive (but not unlimited). The difference I wish to stress between the second and the third positions is that, whereas both allow for options, the third position is that the option to give special weight to one's own interest is very limited. Theoretically, according to the third position, one can give special weight to one's own interest when and only when it is of comparable moral importance to the good of others.

In the interests of clarity, I should now add as a fourth possible position the extremist's position as defined by Kagan. The fourth position is that the requirement to promote others' good is unlimited by any options because morality contains no options. Goodin's theory is an example of the fourth position. The difference between the second, third and fourth positions is the extent to which the requirement to promote the good can be limited by an option to pursue one's own interests. It is sufficient for the purposes of this chapter to show that the only defensible form of consequentialism entails either the third or fourth position. The moderate's view (position two) is untenable; the duty to rescue cannot be restricted to, for example, only easy rescues in situations of dire and immediate peril. Consequentialism requires at least that the option of favouring one's own interests is very limited (position three). Whether consequentialism in fact requires even more (position four) is the question currently under discussion. However, the concerns of this chapter do not require that we finally settle that question here. Let us now return to Kagan's argument.

That part of Kagan's argument most pertinent here is her discussion of the moderate's view that there is no requirement (that is, no duty nor an obligation) to promote the good because morality must include options. The moderate's basic argument is to appeal to costs.[102] He argues that the cost to the agent of promoting the good is too high. Morality cannot demand that we sacrifice our interests in order to promote the good. This captures the basic intuition of some that easy rescues may be morally required but difficult, dangerous, that is, costly, rescues cannot. Let us now look at the appeal to costs argument,[103] the crux of which is that there is some truth about persons which is inconsistent with a requirement to promote the good. The most basic appeal to costs argument is this:

1   Persons have a point of view from which objects have special importance or weight. Persons care most about their wants being satisfied.
2   An acceptable system of morality *must reflect* the fact that persons

lack the motivation to promote the good (at the expense of their interests).

3   Only a moral system with options is acceptable because only such a system reflects the facts about persons.

Kagan thinks that this argument can be refuted.[104] We must distinguish systems which *fully* reflect the facts and systems which *minimally* reflect the facts. If the moderate claims that a moral system must minimally reflect the facts, the extremist agrees with (2) but denies (3). If the moderate means that system must *fully* reflect the facts, then the extremist denies (2) and (3). In other words, the extremist agrees that only a system with options fully reflects the nature of persons but denies (a) that a system without options fails minimally to reflect the nature of persons and (b) that a system which only minimally reflects the facts is flawed. The moderate defends the appeal to costs argument with negative and positive arguments.

The negative argument attempts to establish that systems without options fail even minimally to reflect the facts about persons.[105] The crucial fact which they fail to reflect is that persons are psychologically incapable of always promoting the good. Therefore, if for a reason to ground a moral requirement it must be capable of motivating the agent, there cannot be a requirement to promote the good. Kagan's reply is to distinguish pale and vivid beliefs. Vivid beliefs are those beliefs whose significance we fully comprehend. If our beliefs were vivid, we would act from the standpoint of impartial concern for the interests of all (the extremist's counter-factual). Kagan offers some evidence for the extremist's counter-factual. For example, we are familiar with the fact that it is more difficult to refuse aid to someone immediately to hand than it is to refuse aid to someone distant, even if we recognise that the plight of the latter is as serious. The explanation is that we are unable to make the plight of the latter as vivid; but, if we could, we would regard their need as equally compelling. This suggests, Kagan claims, that 'in *all* cases where there is greater objective reason overall for taking on some sacrifice, the agent is *capable* of being appropriately motivated'.[106]

The conclusion of the extremist's argument is very strong. Kagan claims to have proved that generally the promotion of the good is a reason capable of motivating agents to sacrifice their own self-interest. If this is correct, it would not be an objection to Goodin's view that it fails to leave room for supererogation. Rather, the extremist would object to the view (as, for example, held by Singer), that there are limits to what can be required of an agent in order to promote the good. The important step in the argument is the extremist's counter-factual.

The moderate would seem to be on firm ground if he insists that there is no reason to believe that we would all overcome all of the bias in favour of our own interests even if our beliefs were vivid. This debate looks destined to be inconclusive since it is difficult to know what one would do if one were so different. Kagan is persuasive in arguing that it is more difficult for the moderate to make his case than it would appear. Eventually, the moderate will want to move to his positive argument, namely that there is some source of value missing from a system that does not include options.

The positive argument is that an adequate moral system must fully reflect the facts about persons.[107] The crucial fact now is that persons have biases in favour of their own interests and it is undesirable that they should be required to act contrary to their interests any more than is absolutely necessary. Every agent has subjective reasons to promote her own interests, reasons different from, and above and beyond, the reason to promote the good. Sometimes these subjective reasons (that is, reasons which have to do with the agent's own interests) will outweigh a reason to promote the good, especially when the cost to the agent's interests of promoting the good is considerable. Thus a system of morality which fully reflects the nature of persons must recognise that subjective reasons are sources of value by including options that allow the agent to protect her own interests.

The moderate then needs to defend the claim that subjective reasons are sources of value that cannot be adequately recognised by a system that has a requirement to promote the good. Kagan considers five arguments that the moderate might offer, and rejects them all. They are worth considering briefly. The first argument is that the extremist's system produces a grey world with no fun, like collecting stamps or going to the ballet. Second, the extremist's system requires so much that it prevents the good life; that is, the sort of life worth living. Kagan's reply to both of these is the same. The extremist can recognise the value of agents' acting on subjective reasons, pursuing their own interests rather than promoting the good. However, the extremist claims that, in the world as it is, agents must sacrifice their own interests. This reply entitles Kagan to claim only that the moderate has not demonstrated that the extremist's view is inadequate.

The third argument is an influential one to the effect that the extremist's willingness to sacrifice his interests shows a lack of commitment.[108] Truly valuing an interest or a project is incompatible with a willingness to sacrifice it. I entirely agree with Kagan that this objection is question-begging. The fourth argument is that the extremist's willingness to sacrifice his interests shows that he does not value those interests *directly*, and direct attachments are things we value highly. But this argument is a *non sequitur*. The willingness to sacrifice one's own interests does not indicate that those interests are not valued directly. It merely indicates that those interests are valued less than promoting the good. The final argument is that the extremist cannot adequately value love or friendship. The claim is that loving someone requires a willingness to favour that person even at the cost of promoting the good. Kagan thinks that it is plausible to deny this account of love.

A pattern emerges from the moderate's positive argument. The moderate points to values which, it is claimed, can be recognised only from a subjective point of view; that is, from the point of view of subjective reasons, the point of view from which the agent's bias in favour of his interests is seen as valuable. The extremist replies that these values can be recognised from an objective point of view, but that they are not endorsed as dominant values, all things considered, from that point of view.[109] Thus the moderate has failed to establish that the system which has a requirement to promote the good is inadequate because it fails to include subjective sources of value.

But even if the moderate should be able to improve upon these arguments, a further problem awaits him. The moderate's argument must not show that subjective reasons are morally decisive, for the argument would then undermine his claim that a morality must include options. If subjective reasons are decisive, then agents are morally required to promote their own interests, even if a greater good might be produced by sacrificing them. However, most moderates maintain that such sacrifices are at least morally permissible.

Let me review the argument as it applies to the concerns of this chapter. A moderate holds the second of the three positions I distinguished in Section 2. He holds that rescues are sometimes morally required (for example, to save a drowning child when the rescue is easy), but denies that rescues are invariably required (for example, to donate much of one's income in order to mitigate the effects of famine). A plausible way of drawing the relevant distinction is to insist that only rescues which are not burdensome can be required (see, for example, Sidgwick's third condition in Section 6.1). This is what Kagan calls the appeal to costs argument. There are two ways of defending the appeal to costs argument. Both ways involve the claim that an appeal to costs must be allowed because a moral system that does not allow such an appeal (a system without options) fails to reflect important facts about the nature of persons. The negative argument claims that a system without options ignores the fact that people cannot be motivated by a requirement to promote the good. The positive argument attempts to demonstrate that an adequate morality must recognise subjective reasons as sources of value. Kagan argues persuasively that both the negative and positive arguments fail to demonstrate a defect in the extremist's position. They fail to demonstrate that there is something significant about the nature of persons which a moral system without options fails to include. At the very least, Kagan's arguments defend the extremist against that charge that his view is fundamentally flawed because it commits the extremist to positions that are obviously indefensible. Kagan's argument offers support to the claims in this chapter that the moderate accounts of the duty to rescue are untenable because they collapse into extremist accounts, and yet that consequentialism may provide an adequate foundation for a moral requirement to rescue.[110]

8   From Morality to Legal Obligation

Let us now suppose that there is a good case for a moral requirement to rescue. When considering whether that moral requirement should be a legal obligation, there are two problems to bear in mind: (a) to what extent should the law, especially the criminal law, be used to enforce our moral convictions?; and (b) assuming a consequentialist justification for a moral requirement to rescue, there is a problem about limiting the corresponding legal duty.

The question to what extent the law ought to enforce our moral convictions is a familiar and complex matter. On the one hand, one may argue that the function of law is to promote the common good or the greatest happiness of the greatest number. On the other, it may be argued that, when moral opinions differ, a tolerant society should use law to enforce the moral convictions of some only when absolutely necessary. As we have seen in Section 4, although the Kantian supports a moral duty to rescue, the question whether there ought also to be a legal duty depends on whether the Kantian regards that duty as an imperfect or a perfect one. If it is imperfect, then it cannot be legally enforced. If it is perfect, it may be enforceable, but the Kantian seems to have the same problem as the consequentialist of a requirement of extensive beneficence. In advance of detailed examination of particular theories, it is not possible to make general claims about whether deontological theories of a moral requirement to rescue are compatible with a legal obligation.

I tried to show in Section 3 how difficult it is to make persuasive the minimalist's case that a requirement to rescue is an unjustified infringement of an individual's liberty. I argued that Nozick's treatment of the Lockean proviso makes it appear that Nozick is drawing an arbitrary distinction between negative duties not to interfere with certain needs and positive duties to assist in satisfying those needs. Someone who opposed a legal duty to make at least an easy rescue would also have to oppose a legal duty to pay taxes which may be used for the benefit of those in need; as, of course, Nozick would. One could deal with this point only by means of a more detailed critique of Nozick's programme.[111] However, it is worth bearing a simple point in mind. As Alberto Cadoppi points out in Chapter 3, in contemporary society, all that most good samaritans would need to do in order to fulfil their legal or moral duty is to make a telephone call to the rescue services. It is hard to see that as an unacceptable infringement of the individual's liberty.

From a consequentialist point of view, there is little difficulty in principle in turning a moral requirement into a legal one since, to put it crudely, the law may be regarded as an instrument for producing certain good consequences. There are a number of ways of bridging the gap between morality and law. For example, we could make use of Mill's principle, defended in the essay *On Liberty*.[112] Mill argued that the state could intervene to prevent harm to others. Mill thought that this principle was a liberty-maximising principle which could be justified on utilitarian grounds. I believe that Mill was committed to a moral and legal duty to rescue in virtue of his so-called harm principle. I think that Mill's discussion of the duty to warn in *On Liberty* illustrates that this was his view, but his argument has often been misunderstood as an argument for paternalism.[113]

I turn now to the second problem. The previous discussion of the consequentialist argument for a moral requirement to rescue focused on the problem of limiting the duty. If there were a convincing consequentialist argument for a legal obligation to rescue (based, for example, on considerations such as those in the previous paragraph), this would be a problem that the law would need to confront. Lord Macaulay's discussion of this problem (as a problem for a criminal code) is deservedly famous (see Section 5). Macaulay argued that it is not possible to draft a (criminal) bad samaritan statute that does not require too much. The legal evidence, such as it is, is inconclusive.

From the continental point of view, the difficulty here seems, at least in practice, to have been exaggerated. As Alberto Cadoppi makes clear in Chapter 3, Sections 4 and 5, many European and Latin American jurisdictions have broadly-drawn bad samaritan criminal statutes and seem to operate without much difficulty. However, as he also notes, the courts in some jurisdictions have expanded the duty in a way that gives point to Macaulay's worry (see Chapter 3, sections 6.2 and 8). By contrast, the common law seems to have precisely the difficulty that Lord Macaulay predicted. For example, in the area of civil law, after flirting briefly with a broadly-based duty to rescue of the kind that would be required if the consequentialist arguments considered earlier were accepted, the civil law now seems to have turned back to something very similar to the requirement that Lord Macaulay thought was the only basis for a duty to rescue. Common law civil courts now require proximity as a condition for liability in tort. Moreover, the criminal law duty is exactly as Macaulay would have had it: that is, based squarely on special relationships. These developments are discussed in detail by Alexander McCall Smith in Chapter 2.

Macaulay posed a dilemma for the criminal law: either we keep any legal obligation to rescue a narrow one based on special relationships, or we allow prosecutors and juries too much discretion. I take it that the second horn must include the potential risk of compelling the ordinary citizen to do too much to benefit others. Feinberg disagrees with Macaulay, contending that we should embrace the second horn by attempting to draw a line. We could at least create criminal liability for anyone who fails to make an easy rescue; that is, a rescue that clearly causes no unreasonable risk, cost or inconvenience to the rescuer.[114] He argues that there is no serious practical worry about this, since courts and juries are used to operating with a standard of reasonableness in criminal matters. For example, the standard of proof is proof beyond reasonable doubt; the plea of provocation requires that the provocation offered should be unreasonable. However, Feinberg does not consider the difficult question whether the test for reasonableness is objective or subjective (see Chapter 2, Sections 2.5 and 3.7).

While this approach has its attractions, I think it is clear that the discretion that would be created by Feinberg's solution is of a different order than that currently accepted in the criminal law of common law countries. It is one thing to apply the test of reasonableness once a norm has been established; it is another to use the criterion of reasonableness to establish the norm. Suppose that there is a criminal statute creating liability for failure to rescue where there is no unreasonable risk, cost or inconvenience. Jim and Joan are adult siblings. Jim has a life-threatening disease which requires a bone marrow transplant from Joan. Joan would have to suffer the pain of a bone marrow puncture, together with the minimal risk of infection and the inconvenience of hospitalisation. Is this a rescue which would not cause unreasonable risk, cost or inconvenience? Arguably, it is. However in successive (civil) cases, United States courts have refused to order siblings or other close relatives to donate tissue in life-saving circumstances.[115] Presumably, courts have been unwilling to reject the well-established principle that invasions of the physical body cannot be compelled for another's good. One can imagine, however, that this principle may come under pressure. If some future court were prepared to order a woman to undergo a Caesarean operation for the sake of her unborn foetus, that decision would establish a duty to rescue that could encompass tissue donation cases.

The question is whether one is willing to have such matters as the liability to rescue by tissue donation settled on the basis of the standard of reasonableness by judges or juries. One would have to be confident that those involved in the decision would be capable of thinking beyond the relatively simple issue: is it reasonable to be compelled to endure a few minutes' pain to save a life? There are other factors one would need to consider. One would need to take into account the less direct effects of an affirmative decision, such as the effects of a decision on the citizen's perception of the law and the medical profession. One would also need to consider the practical issues: someone, perhaps a minor, being hauled off against her will. It is arguable that these are unsuitable questions for a criminal court-room.

If one thinks that these are unsuitable questions for a criminal court, perhaps that is in part because one assumes that the stakes would be very high. There is a way of dealing with this problem. Feinberg assumes that a statute creating liability to rescue would create a result crime; that is, a crime committed only when the result of death or serious harm occurs. He furthermore may assume that the penalty would be proportional to the gravity of the result. There is the alternative of creating a specific statutory offence of failing to rescue. The offence would be committed whenever one fails to res-cue, irrespective of the result of that failure.[116] Such a crime would be what continental jurisdictions regard as a pure crime of omission (see Chapter 2, Section 2; Chapter 3, Sections 2 and 7.1). The penalty for such an offence could be relatively minor. This alternative seems in fact to be the solution adopted by many continental countries and by the state of Vermont.[117] The position in European and other legal systems is discussed in Chapter 3, and summarised in Chapter 3, Section 8.

There is one final point to be made against a criminal statute drawn so as to create a wide discretion. In Chapter 3, Sections 4.1 and 6.1, Alberto Cadoppi points out the totalitarian implications of a broad duty to rescue statute. Such broadly-drawn statutes tend to place the individual at the service of the community and the nation. As a matter of fact, bad samaritan statutes were effectively used by both the Nazis and the Italian Fascists. However, despite their origins in Nazi Germany and Fascist Italy, broad bad samaritan statutes still remain in force in those countries (see Chapter 3, Sections 6.2 and 7.1).

As it stands, Feinberg's solution is too simple,[118] but if the case for a duty to rescue is clear, then there can be no objection to attempting to find legal solutions to line-drawing problems in the criminal and in the civil law. The jurisprudence of this is undoubtedly very com-plicated, as both Alexander McCall Smith and Alberto Cadoppi ex-plain in Chapters 2 and 3. However, does advocating such an attempt create a tension in my argument? I have, for example, argued against Weinrib's account of the legal duty to rescue on the basis that the moral requirement to rescue is more extensive than the proposed conditions allow.

We are now in the area of pragmatic solutions: if the case for a legal obligation to rescue is persuasive, what is the most jurisprudentially satisfactory way to create an effective legal obligation? Given the preceding argument of this chapter, it will almost certainly be the case that no criminal statute will exhaust one's extensive moral liability. A more comprehensive approach is required. To deal more satisfactorily with one's moral requirements, we will need other legal instruments. To choose just one example, one will need an administrative law system of social welfare based on taxation. Otherwise one would be in the uncomfortable position of either prosecuting someone who does not give to a destitute beggar, or of saying that we have no legal obligation corresponding to our moral duty to help the very poor.[119] As I argued earlier, we do as individuals have extensive duties to give to the poor. The most effective way of discharging these duties is usually by means of collective solutions. The law is an important vehicle for collectively discharging our moral duties. Many systems of law do have developed administrative law welfare provisions. Laws imposing a duty to rescue are therefore more common than the absence of discrete statutes imposing a duty to rescue would indicate, as Alexander McCall Smith demonstrates in Chapter 2.

Suppose we were to take Bentham and Sidgwick, as well as Weinrib, as offering conditions for a legal duty to rescue. Their mistake in that case would be that of seeking a discrete legal obligation. The moral requirement to rescue is extensive; it cannot be encompassed by the conditions that Bentham and the others propose. So the legal obligation cannot be encompassed by those conditions either. Rather, what is required is for the legal system as a whole to take on the burden of rescue. That way we do not have to solve the false dilemma: either one is a criminal if one does not give to an indigent person, or there is no legal obligation to help those in need. Whatever the merits of Feinberg's solution in the criminal law, the legal duty to rescue cannot be co-extensive with a criminal statute (nor does Feinberg think that it is).

I might put the same point another way. Bentham, Sidgwick and Weinrib might have conceived the problem in individualistic terms: what is the individual's duty to rescue? Goodin offers a solution in collectivist terms. Both are only partially correct. Both individual and collective solutions are required. Because the burden is large, a collective response is required. So Bentham and Sidgwick were mistaken in trying to limit the burden. But because there are collective legal duties in social welfare law (such as the duty on the local authorities in Great Britain to house the homeless), it does not follow that we can do without individual duties. Even within a society that has welfare legislation, the individual is often required to act. A criminal statute might be an appropriate instrument for certain cases. It would be a different mistake to think that all that is required is a discrete criminal statute imposing a broad duty to rescue. In the absence of all the other legal instruments, criminalising failures to rescue just would not work.

Even if the particular practical difficulties that Macaulay pointed to are tractable, there are other important practical problems which must be addressed. Daniel Shuman argues in Chapter 4 that the law must have a therapeutic effect. He contends that, for example, there ought not to be a legal obligation to rescue abused children simply because the law cannot in practice achieve its goal. There are also familiar motivational questions.[120] How much can a person be compelled to do before the compulsion becomes counter-productive? There may be good reasons to compel people to do much less then we think they are morally required to do.[121] In the following chapters, we examine the jurisprudential problems in creating legal liability for a duty to rescue.

Notes

*   Early versions of parts of this chapter were presented to seminars at the Universities of Edinburgh and Amsterdam and at Dartmouth College. I am grateful to the participants for their helpful comments. I would like particularly to thank Bernard Gert and Walter Sinnott-Armstrong.

1   Alan Gewirth, *Reason and Morality* (Chicago, 1978), 217–30. Thomas Nagel, *The Possibility of Altruism* (Oxford, 1970); Onora O'Neill, *Faces of Hunger* (London, 1986), Chs 7 and 8; John Rawls, *A Theory of Justice* (Oxford, 1972), paras 19 and 51.

2   L. Bender, 'A Lawyer's Primer on Feminist Theory and Tort', 38 *Journal of Legal Education*, 33 (1978).

3   See, for example, R. Brandt, 'The Concepts of Obligation and Duty', 73 *Mind*, 374 (1965); Rawls, note 1, paras 18–19; A. John Simmons, *Moral Principles and Political Obligations* (Princeton, New Jersey, 1979), 7–16.

4   Will Kymlicka, *Contemporary Political Philosophy: An Introduction* (Oxford, 1990), Ch. 4.

5   Ibid., at 138; Charles Taylor, *Philosophy and the Human Sciences: Philosophical Papers*, ii (Cambridge, 1985), 219.

6   Kymlicka, op. cit., 140–41.

7   Ibid., at 143.

8   Ibid., at 145.

9   Ibid., at 151.

10   Locke's Second Treatise in Peter Laslett (Ed.), *Locke's Two Treatises of Government* (Cambridge, 2nd ed., 1967).

11   Onora O'Neill, *Constructions of Reason* (Cambridge, 1989), Ch. 12.

12   R. Nozick, *Anarchy, State and Utopia* (New York, 1974).

13   Kymlicka, op. cit., 103 ff.

14   Nozick, op. cit., 33.

15   Kymlicka, op. cit, 107 ff.

16   Ibid., at 118 ff.
17   Nozick, op. cit, 178.
18   Chapter 5, Section 4.
19   Mary Warnock (Ed.), *Utilitarianism: John Stuart Mill* (London, 1962). R.J. Lipkin argues that Mill's harm principle can be used to defend only a duty to make *easy* rescues, and that such a duty is consistent with individualism. See R.J. Lipkin, 'Beyond Good Samaritans and Moral Monsters: An Individualistic Justification of the Duty to Rescue', 31 *University of California, Los Angeles, Law Review*, 252, 275 ff (1983).
20   H.J. Paton (translator), *The Moral Law: Kant's 'Groundwork of the Metaphysic of Morals'* (London, 1966), 84.
21   O'Neill, op. cit., *supra*, n. 11, 132.
22   Ibid., at 133.
23   Paton, op. cit., 86.
24   O'Neill, op. cit., *supra*, n. 11, 133–4.
25   Mary J. Gregor, *Laws of Freedom* (Oxford, 1963), 195.
26   Ibid., at 194.
27   O'Neill, op. cit., *supra*, n. 1, 160 ff.
28   O'Neill, op. cit., *supra*, n. 11, 135.
29   See Howard Williams, *Kant's Political Philosophy* (Oxford, 1983), Ch. 3; Roger Scruton, *Kant* (Oxford, 1982), Ch. 5.
30   Mary J. Gregor, *The Doctrine of Virtue* (Philadelphia, 1964).
31   E.J. Weinrib considers whether a legal obligation to rescue can be defended on Kantian grounds. He argues that the obligation to preserve physical integrity could be the basis of such a duty, but the resulting duty would be unacceptably extensive and onerous. In contrast to the view I have expressed, Weinrib argues that Kant's *imperfect* duty of beneficence could be legislatively – but not judicially – enforced in the form of social welfare legislation. See E.J. Weinrib, 'The Case for a Duty to Rescue', 90 *Yale Law Journal*, 247, 329 ff (1980). Weinrib's account of the utilitarian foundation of a duty to rescue is discussed in Section 6.3.
32   O'Neill, op. cit., *supra*, n. 1, Chs 7 and 8.
33   Ibid., at 160.
34   Ibid., at 161–2
35   Ibid., at 148–52.
36   Joel Feinberg, *Harm to Others* (New York, 1984), Ch. 4.
37   Ibid., at 165–85.
38   For a discussion of the problems of causation in the law generally, see H.L.A. Hart and A.M Honoré, *Causation in the Law* (Oxford, 2nd ed., 1985). Causation in the context of a rescue is discussed by John K. Kleinig, 'Good Samaritanism', 5 *Philosophy and Public Affairs*, 382 (1975/6) – his view is in some ways similar to Feinberg's; by Eric Mack, 'Bad Samaritanism and the Causation of Harm', 9 *Philosophy and Public Affairs*, 230 (1980); and by Richard Epstein, 'A Theory of Strict Liability', 2 *Journal of Legal Studies*, 151 (1973). Negative causal responsibility is a crucial issue in Gewirth's argument for a duty to rescue (see Gewirth, op. cit., *supra*, n. 1). That aspect of his argument is criticised by Eric Mack, 'Deontologism, Negative Causation and the Duty To Rescue', in Edward Regis, Jr. (Ed.), *Gewirth's Ethical Rationalism* (Chicago, 1984), chapter 10. In his reply to Mack in the same volume (233–41), Gewirth clarifies his argument.
Much of the philosophical literature on the distinction between acts and omissions is also relevant. See, for example, Carolyn R. Morillo, 'Doing, Refraining and the Strenuousness of Morality', 14 *American Philosophical Quarterly*, 29 (1977).
39   Thomas B. Macaulay, 'Notes on the Indian Penal Code', in Lady Trevelyan (Ed.), *Lord Macaulay's Works*, Vol. 7 (London, 1866), 429.

40   The same objection figures in Judith Jarvis Thomson's argument in her 'A Defense of Abortion', 1 *Philosophy and Public Affairs*, 47, 65 (1972).

41   Feinberg, op. cit., 130–50.

42   Warnock, op. cit., *supra*, n. 19. See Mill's essay, *Utilitarianism*, Ch. V, 305 ff.

43   Feinberg, op. cit., 144.

44   Ibid., at 134.

45   Ibid., at 145–7.

46   'Duties, Rights and Claims', 3 *American Philosophical Quarterly*, 1 (1966) and 'The Nature and Value of Rights', 4 *Journal of Value Inquiry*, 243 (1970). Both are reprinted in his *Rights, Justice and the Bounds of Liberty* (Princeton, New Jersey, 1980). Subsequent page references are to that volume.

47   Ibid., at 153–4.

48   Ibid.

49   Feinberg, op. cit., *supra*, n. 36, 112.

50   Ibid.

51   Feinberg, op. cit., *supra*, n. 46, 140; and n. 36, 134.

52   Feinberg, op cit., *supra*, n. 36, 149–50. He thinks it is a very strange view.

53   Bentham, *Introduction to the Principles of Morals and Legislation*, edited by J. Burns and H.L.A. Hart (London, 1970), 292–3.

54   J. Bowring (Ed.), *Works*, Vol. 1 (Edinburgh, 1843), 164.

55   Henry Sidgwick, *The Methods of Ethics* (London, 7th ed., 1922), Book IV, Ch. 3.

56   On a certain account of the concepts, Sidgwick's view may be that there is a *duty* to rescue which overrides the principle that performing one's *obligations* maximises utility. For this sense of 'obligation', see H.L.A. Hart, 'Are There Any Natural Rights?', 64 *Philosophical Review* 175 (1955).

57   Sidgwick, op. cit., 432.

58   Ibid., at 435.

59   Ibid., at 436–7.

60   Ibid., at 437.

61   Ibid.

62   Ibid.

63   Ibid.

64   See Sections 3 and 4.

65   It might be noted that Sidgwick makes the valuable point that assistance should be given as far as possible in a way that does not weaken self-reliance; we should whenever possible provide people with the means of growing their own food rather than just with the food itself.

66   Shelly Kagan, *The Limits of Morality* (Oxford, 1989), Ch. 7.

67   90 *Yale Law Journal*, 247 (1980).

68   Ibid., at 311.

69   1 Can S. Ct. 53 (1976).

70   *Post* v. *Jones* , 60 US (19 How) 150 (1857).

71   [1988] 2 All E.R. 238.

72   This case is discussed in Chapter 2, Section 3.3.

73   At the time of writing, the case is unreported. See *The Guardian*, 30 January 1993.

74   Weinrib, op. cit., *supra*, n. 67, 314.

75   Ibid., at 325.

76   Ibid.

77   Weinrib cites *London Borough of Southwark* v. *Williams* [1971] 2 All E.R. 175 as illustrating the claim that homelessness is not an emergency. In that case, some homeless persons occupied derelict flats owned by the borough and sought to retain occupancy by arguing, unsuccessfully, private necessity. See Weinrib, op. cit., n. 67, 315.

78   Ibid., at 327.
79   Ibid., at 314.
80   See *Post* (*supra*, n. 70).
81   Robert Goodin, *Protecting the Vulnerable* (Chicago, 1985).
82   Although he does not distinguish obligations and duties, Goodin's terminology might mislead those who do. They might describe his theory as assigning the central role to duty and explaining obligation in terms of it. I shall use 'requirement' whenever Goodin means obligation or duty and whenever I fear that confusion could arise.
83   Goodin says: A has an obligation to B if and only if ....
84   Goodin, op. cit., 118.
85   Ibid., at 121.
86   Feinberg, op. cit., *supra*, n. 36, 53.
87   The reply is in private correspondence. I am grateful to Robert Goodin for his helpful comments on an early draft of this chapter.
88   Goodin, op. cit., 163.
89   A similar view was discussed in Section 4.
90   Warnock, op. cit., *supra*, n. 19; J.S. Mill, *Utilitarianism*, Ch. 5. Some of my reasons for this assertion will become clear in Section 7.
91   Peter Singer, *Practical Ethics* (Cambridge, 1979), Ch. 8.
92   Ibid., at 168.
93   For an example of this form of argument, see John Arthur, 'Rights and the Duties to Bring Aid', in William Aiken and Hugh La Follette (Eds), *World Hunger and Moral Obligation* (Englewood Cliffs, New Jersey, 1977), 37.
94   Singer, op. cit., 10 ff.
95   Note 90.
96   Bernard Williams, 'A Critique of Utilitarianism', in J.J.C. Smart and Bernard Williams, *Utilitarianism: For and Against* (Cambridge, 1973), 108–18; Bernard Williams, 'Persons, Character and Morality', in *Moral Luck* (Cambridge, 1981), 1;   Samuel Scheffler, *The Rejection of Consequentialism* (Oxford, 1982); Dan W. Brock, 'Utilitarianism and Aiding Others', in H.B. Miller and W.H. Williams (Eds), *The Limits of Utilitarianism*, (Minneapolis, Minnesota, 1982); Kleinig, op. cit., *supra*, n. 38, 396–7.
97   Williams, 'A Critique of Utilitarianism', cit. n. 96.
98   Kagan, op. cit.
99   Ibid., at 10.
100 Ibid., at 71.
101 Ibid., at 3–5.
102 Ibid., at 21 ff.
103 Ibid., Ch. 7.
104 Ibid., at 265 ff.
105 Ibid., chapter 8.
106 Ibid., at 300. Kagan's negative argument seems to assume that a bias in favour of one's own interests is simply a hindrance to promoting the good. That view is challenged by Michael Slote, 'Shelly Kagan's *The Limits of Morality*', 51 *Philosophy and Phenomenological Research*, 915, 917 (1991). See Kagan's 'Replies to My Critics' in the same journal, at 926.
107 Kagan, op. cit., *supra*, n. 66 Ch. 9.
108 See Williams, cit. n. 96.
109 Kagan, op. cit., *supra*, n. 66, 370.
110 Recent discussions of Kagan's book include: Brad Hooker, 'Brink, Kagan, Utilitarianism and Self-Sacrifice', 3 *Utilitas*, 263 (1991); Peter Singer, 'A Refutation of Ordinary Morality', 101 *Ethics*, 625 (1991); James Griffin, 'The Human Good and the Ambitions of Consequentialism', 9 *Social Philosophy and Policy*, 118 (1992); Jonathan Dancy, *Moral Reasons* (Oxford, 1993), Ch. 11.

111 See, for example, Kymlicka, op. cit., Ch. 4; Alan Brown, *Modern Political Philosophy* (Harmondsworth, England, 1986), Ch. 4.

112 Warnock, op. cit., *supra*, n. 19. Feinberg's strategy is to apply Mill's principle to the duty to rescue; see Feinberg, op. cit., *supra*, n. 36, General Introduction and Ch. 4. For a discussion of Mill's essay, see John Gray, *Mill On Liberty: A Defence* (London, 1983). It is not necessary to discuss here Mill's view that harm to others was the *only* ground for state interference with liberty; whether Mill's principle prohibits only causing harm or also prohibits failing to prevent harm. On both points, see Feinberg.

113 Warnock, op. cit., *supra*, n. 19, at 136–7. I owe this point to S.V. Laselva, 'A Single Truth: Mill on Harm, Paternalism and Good Samaritanism', 36 *Political Studies*, 486 (1988), and to Richard Bellamy who drew the article to my attention. A further difficult matter is whether Mill's view in *On Liberty* can be reconciled with his view in Ch. V of *Utilitarianism*.

114 Feinberg, op. cit., *supra*, n. 36, 150 ff. In his argument, Feinberg emphasises that liability should exist only if there is *clearly* no unreasonable risk, cost or inconvenience. In my comments, I simplify by ignoring the complication created by 'clearly', and am therefore in danger of misrepresenting Feinberg. I think that the simplification does not affect the argument which follows in the text. Adding 'clearly' to 'no unreasonable risk, cost or inconvenience' does not change the standard. It instructs the judge or jury to resolve any doubt in favour of the defendant or accused. The addition of 'clearly' is irrelevant when the judge or jury has no doubts.

115 See *McFall* v. *Shimp*, 10 Pa D & C 3rd 90 (Allegheny County Court, 1978) in which a court order to compel a family member to donate bone marrow was refused. In the similar case of *Curran* v. *Bosze* (141 Ill. 2d 473), the father of Jean-Pierre Bosze, a 13-year-old suffering from leukaemia, raised an action to compel the boy's siblings (who were living with their mother) to be tested for suitability for bone marrow transplants. The order was refused by the Illinois Cook County Circuit Court in 1990. The case was appealed to the Illinois Supreme Court, but Jean-Pierre died before a decision was reached (*The New York Times*, 30 July 1990, page A8 and 20 November 1990, page B9). See also Chapter 2, Section 2.2.

116 So A would be liable for failing to rescue B even if B were rescued by C minutes later. There could therefore be a problem here for someone who accepts that preventing harm to others is a necessary condition for creating a *legal* duty to rescue. The case could be elaborated so that it would be possible to argue that A neither causes nor fails to prevent harm to B. Rather, A fails to rescue B from a situation in which harm to B would have appeared imminent to a reasonable person. There are a number of possible solutions to the problem worth considering. First, the condition of preventing harm to others could be extended to include means necessary for the prevention of harm to others. One way of preventing actual harm is generally to discourage failures even to attempt a rescue. There is an analogy here with the creation of a statutory offence of failing to make the workplace safe and the road traffic offence of driving with excessive alcohol in the blood. Secondly, the condition of failing to prevent harm to others could be extended to include harm to persons other than the potential victim. John Kleinig has suggested that there is an analogy here with attempted crimes:

> if attempted crimes are properly subject to punishment, then omissions which could have but did not become harm-exacerbating also ought to be subject to punishment. Apart from the threat of harm there is a criminating harm involved even if the imperiled person is not its victim. It is the harm of eroding those fundamental social relations on which our individual welfare ultimately depends. (Kleinig, op. cit., *supra*, n. 38, 399)

Kleinig's suggestion leads on to matters discussed by Alberto Cadoppi in Chapter 3.

117   The Vermont statute is as follows:

> A person who knows that another is exposed to grave physical harm shall, to the extent that it can be rendered without danger or peril to himself or without interference with important duties owed to others, give reasonable assistance to the exposed person, unless that assistance or care is being provided by others. (Vt. Stat. Ann., tit. 12, para. 519)

The penalty is a fine of 100 dollars. The state of Minnesota has a similar statute: Good Samaritan Law, ch. 319, 1983 Minn. Sess. Law Serv. 2329 (West). I owe the Minnesota reference to Lipkin, op. cit., *supra*, n. 19, 253.

118   Cadoppi is more favourably impressed with Feinberg's solution than I am; see Chapter 3, Section 7.2.

119   Feinberg, op. cit., *supra*, n. 36, 158.

120   For an interesting discussion of these, see S. Levmore, 'Waiting For Rescue', 72 *Virginia Law Review*, 879 (1986).

121   Singer, op. cit., makes a similar point about the difference between one's moral obligations and what we ought to demand publicly of people.

2 The Duty to Rescue and the Common Law

ALEXANDER McCALL SMITH

1 The Background

Whether the law should impose criminal liability for failure to rescue very much depends on what one takes to be the aims of the criminal law. Supporters of a liberal, non-interventionist system of criminal justice will argue that the occasions of liability should be strictly limited and failure to rescue should not normally have legal implications. In this view, the bystander who fails to rescue one whom he sees in peril may well be morally rebuked, but not punished by the courts. Criminal law should not aim to make people perfect, or even to make them better; it should merely seek to prevent those acts which harm others. In another, purely civil context, the legal non-interventionist would hold that any moral duty to rescue should not automatically be reflected in tortious liability. Accordingly, failure to act, although reprehensible, should have no financial consequences for the non-rescuer. In practical terms, this means that the person who sees another being attacked and fails to call the police, or who witnesses a rape and does nothing to intervene, commits no offence. Nor does he or she incur liability for any damages which the victim in such a case suffers. The loss lies where it falls. As the court observed in *Malone* v. *Metropolitan Police Commissioner*,[1] 'there are many moral precepts which are not legally enforceable'.

There is an enduring belief that common law systems – those derived from English law – unequivocally endorse this minimalist vision of the duty to rescue.[2] Like many generalisations about the law, this is true to an extent, but does not paint the complete picture. Although it recognises no general duty to rescue, the common law is not implacably hostile to the notion that liability for a failure to act may sometimes quite properly be imposed. It is certainly the case that the non-rescuer is in a stronger position in common law jurisdictions than he is in those jurisdictions in the civilian (continental European) mould, but the minimalist analysis outlined above is misleading. The non-actor *may* incur liability, but only if certain conditions are met. In what follows, the nature of these conditions is scrutinised. Do they really reveal an ideological commitment to a somewhat extreme individualism, or do they point to no more than a pragmatic desire to keep liability within check? The common law has traditionally eschewed theory and the statement of broad principle, but this does not mean that its instinct for the possible and the practical cannot be justified in terms of principle. There may well be no general rule embodying a duty to rescue, but a duty to rescue may be discernible nonetheless, although admittedly only in certain clearly defined situations.

2   The Criminal Liability of the Non-rescuer

The modern discussion of the criminal liability of the non-rescuer in English law has its roots in Thomas Macaulay's influential 1837 commentary to the draft penal code of India.[3] Macaulay cites the case of a surgeon who is the only doctor in India who can perform a life-saving operation on a man who lives some hundreds of miles away. Is the doctor obliged to travel that distance, at great cost to himself, in order to save the suffering stranger? Then there is the case of the man who fails to inform the traveller that the river which he proposes to ford is swollen, although he knows that the traveller will be drowned as a result of his not receiving this advice. Macaulay asks whether in each case the man who fails to act is a murderer and concludes, not surprisingly, that he is not, and moreover that the criminal law should not concern itself with these omissions.

The omission issue has not been confined to theoretical examples; in 1964 a young woman was murdered in New York in full view of over 30 of her neighbours.[4] The shocking aspect of this case was not so much the murder itself, which unfortunately was something which had come to be expected as part of the risk of living in a city, but the fact that only one of the witnesses bothered, belatedly, to summon the police. There were, in short, no rescuers. Subsequent cases reveal the same lack of concern by passers-by over rapes and other assaults committed before their eyes, prompting a return to the question posed by Macaulay: should a failure to rescue those in danger be a criminal offence? A failure to rescue is an omission, and omissions always signal difficulties for the criminal lawyer.[5] Is there any reason why omissions should be considered special in any way from the point of view of criminal liability? Normally, criminal liability follows upon some positive act on the part of an accused: the murderer shoots his victim; the thief takes property away; the fraudster makes a misrepresentation in order to secure some advantage for himself. In all of these cases the focus of the criminal law is on what the accused *did* rather than on what he *did not* do. The overwhelming majority of criminal defendants, then, are people who have intervened in the external world in a positive way, performing physical actions which 'make things happen'. They have acted rather than omitted to act.

The explanation for this act-focused emphasis in criminal law is to be found in the fundamental concern that the criminal law has with harm and its causation. If the criminal law is mainly concerned with punishing acts rather than omissions, this is because prevailing ideas of causation see acts, rather than omissions, as being the more potent causes of harm. The reasons for this are complex. Hart and Honoré suggest that one of the explanations of the tendency to underestimate the causal significance of omissions lies in our preoccupation with the role of human manipulation of the external world: causing becomes a matter of 'pushing and pulling', and non-physical causation is correspondingly overlooked.[6] As pointed out in Chapter 1, the case for treating omissions as causes is now widely understood and supported. Yet the law reflects ordinary intuitions, and it is not altogether surprising that it should have been hesitant to confer causal status on omissions. A further reason for the criminal law's discomfort over omissions lies in the inherent difficulty involved in the selection of one particular omission out of many as being a candidate for prosecution.[7] In relation to a specific event, there are frequently many omissions which might be taken as causally relevant. For example, the death, through neglect, of a weak and elderly person may be laid at more than one door. It may be that the failure of a son or daughter to arrange for medical attention is seen as the cause of the death. It may be the failure of a social worker to detect a need which is held to be the cause. Or it may even be a neighbour's omission to check further when there was no answer to his ring on the door bell. These are all omissions which might be considered the cause of death; but there may be others, too, and the list of omissions connected with the death may eventually be rather long. The process of selecting the relevant omission will often be difficult and controversial. By contrast, where there is a positive act, and where there is a clear causal link between the act and the result, the law encounters no difficulty in identifying the actor against whom proceedings might be brought. Nor is there any difficulty in identifying the time at which the act is committed; omissions, by contrast, are more open-ended in the temporal sense, and this contributes to the uncertainty that surrounds them.

The fact that omissions present special problems for the criminal law does not preclude the attribution of criminal liability in respect of failures to act. These situations fall into two broad categories: statutory offences, where legislation creates an offence of failing to perform a particular act, and common law offences, where the failure to act forms the *actus reus* of an offence such as manslaughter (culpable homicide). Of these two categories, the first is the most common, and indeed provides the fewest difficulties. Many regulatory offences are founded upon a failure to do something which the legislature has determined shall be a duty incumbent either on everybody or on members of an identified group within the community. Tax legislation provides a simple example of this. Failure to pay a tax demand is an offence – based on an omission – as is failure to file a tax return or, in some countries, failure to report for military service on reaching a specified age. These are omissions to perform a duty which the law imposes on all those who have a certain status; they are not connected in any way with the performance of a prior act. The fact that such instances of omission liability appear relatively uncomplicated is possibly attributable to the fact that the nature of the omission is very specifically defined in the legislation. The person upon whom the duty to act rests is spelled out, as are the incidents of the duty, and it is therefore not open to the defendant to rely on an uncertainty argument. There may be injustices, of course, and insofar as these forms of omission liability involve offences of strict liability, they are open to the criticism that they fail to require *mens rea* (the mental element requirement) and therefore offend one of the basic principles of the criminal justice system. This criticism, however, is quite distinct from any criticism based on the fact that these offences involve liability for omission.

Common law offences of omission are considerably more controversial. The essential difficulty here is that the whole approach of the criminal law has been to define offences in terms of a criminal act – an approach which is understandable, given the fact that most obvious forms of criminal conduct involve action rather than inaction. In contrast to the approach adopted in civil law countries, where the 'pure omission' is a separate crime which is not defined in terms of results, omissions in common law systems have tended to be subsumed under the categories of existing offences. This is the way common law systems work: judges generally eschew the overt judicial creation of new forms of liability, but may nevertheless extend the bounds of the law by holding that certain forms of conduct amount merely to a new way of doing what is already defined as a criminal offence. Omissions may be treated, then, as another form of performing an existing crime. The clearest example of this is provided by homicide offences. Many common law systems recognise two main forms of homicide: murder and manslaughter (also known as culpable homicide). The way in which these two offences are defined varies from jurisdiction to jurisdiction, but, in the broadest terms, murder requires intentional killing or an intention to inflict serious injury; manslaughter may result from the causing of death in circumstances where, although there is a wrongful act on the part of the accused, there is neither of the intentions which would otherwise make the killing murder. There has been considerable debate as to the appropriate mental element for homicide, but much less attention has been paid to the question of what *conduct* is required for conviction, and in particular as to whether murder may be committed by an omission to act.

Classic definitions of murder are often couched in terms of 'killing'. Coke's definition, propounded in the early seventeenth century, has been particularly enduring.[8] He says that murder is committed when 'a man of sound memory and of the age of discretion unlawfully killeth ... any reasonable creature in rerum natura'. Modern writers on the criminal law also tend to talk of 'killing' rather than 'causing death', a choice of terms which suggests acts rather than omissions. A standard Australian textbook on criminal law, *Howard's Criminal Law,*[9] for example, states: 'Homicide is the killing of V by D where V is a human being and D is a human being or corporation. ' The Law Commission's *Draft Criminal Code* adopts the same approach, defining murder in the following terms: 's.56. A person who kills another [intending to kill etc] is guilty of murder.' Judicial definitions of murder are also given to emphasise the requirement of an act. The judge's instruction to the jury in the Scottish case of *H.M.Adv.* v. *Cawthorne*[10] talks of 'bringing about death' but makes it clear that this is done through action: 'In our law the crime of murder is committed when the person who brings about the death of another acted deliberately with intent to kill, or acted with intent to do bodily harm, or ... acted with utter and wicked recklessness as to the consequences of his act.' On appeal in the same case, the Court of Criminal Appeal defined murder unequivocally as 'any wilful act causing the destruction of life'. This suggests that in Scots law, at least, murder cannot be committed by omission, a conclusion which a court might be unwilling to endorse when faced with a case of sufficient seriousness.

A definition of murder in terms of 'killing' does not necessarily mean that causing death through omission cannot be murder, even if judges have in this context tended to talk in terms of acts. The essence of murder is the intentional causing of death, and this can be achieved as much through omission as through the commission of an act, provided, of course, that the causal efficacy of omissions is acknowledged. Macaulay's example of the walker approaching the cliff provides a useful illustration here. If I see a hill walker taking a route which I know will lead to his death, and if I refrain from warning him, I may do so because I want him dead and this happens to be a convenient way of achieving my ambition. If my failure to warn is seen as a cause of the death, then I may be said to have killed the hapless walker. And if I can be said to have killed the walker, and have done so intentionally, then there should be no objection in describing me as the murderer of that walker. Many people would hesitate to describe me as a murderer in such a case, but it is possible to imagine circumstances in which there would be no hesitation to describe an omission as an act of murder. For example, a nurse who is instructed to administer a drug to a patient and who deliberately fails to do so because she dislikes the patient, and wants to see him dead, might be described as a murderess because she has intentionally brought about the patient's death. What distinguishes this case from the case of the walker is the existence of a duty to act on the nurse's part. Her omission is an omission to do that which she was required to do; the walker was not required to act in quite the same way. The nurse could be prosecuted for murder; the walker could not. Both of them wanted the death to ensue, and yet only the nurse stands to attract criminal liability. Why should this be so? Whatever the moral distinction between the two may be, the legal distinction is clear: in one case there is a legal duty to act, in another there is none. The circumstances in which a legal duty to act will be inferred demonstrate those omissions which the criminal law is prepared to recognise as attracting criminal liability. Provided that it occurs within the context of one of these categories, a failure to rescue may result in criminal liability. This amounts to a limited duty to rescue, imposed only in special circumstances and not on the general public, yet even so the existence of such liability still refutes the proposition that the common law completely fails to recognise a duty to rescue. There is liability for omissions in the common law, and therefore there may be a potential duty to rescue, but such liability is generally limited to the following cases.

2.1 Where There Has Been Relevant Past Conduct on the Part of the Person Failing to Act

Where a person creates a situation of danger he may be liable for the consequences of a later omission on his part. Unlikely examples spring to mind: the pilot who bales out of his aircraft, leaving his passengers to fend for themselves; the surgeon who leaves the operating theatre, abandoning his patient to the attentions of untrained staff; both of these have created situations of danger for others and fail to take the necessary steps to avert the consequences. Their omissions are clearly culpable and, if death results may lead to conviction for manslaughter. The failure to take action to avert the consequences of the original act amounts to gross negligence in such a case, and this may give rise to manslaughter liability.

Unlikely examples apart, several cases illustrate the application of the principle. *Richard Kroon*[11] points to the responsibilities that accompany the everyday activity of driving a motor vehicle. The appellant had been convicted of causing death by dangerous driving when the truck he was driving veered onto the wrong side of the road and killed three occupants of an approaching car. It was suggested that the most likely explanation for the accident was the fact that the appellant had dropped off to sleep while driving (having completed a fairly punishing schedule). In these circumstances, the defence argued that the appellant had not been driving at the time of the accident, as driving was a voluntary act requiring consciousness. The general principle was accepted by the court that being at the wheel while asleep did not amount to driving, provided that sleep overcame the driver without warning. There will be few such cases, the court said; in most cases there will be some warning of the onset of sleep, a degree of drowsiness, and it is in these few seconds of warning that the obligation exists to stop the vehicle and rest. In such cases, then, prior dangerous conduct (driving a motor vehicle) creates an obligation to act to prevent harm to others or the commission of an offence.

R. v. Miller[12] is a case in which an omission on the part of the accused resulted in a conviction for arson. Miller had been participating in a squat in a building belonging to another. He had fallen asleep while smoking a cigarette in bed, and had then woken up to find that his dropped cigarette had started a smouldering fire in the mattress on which he had been lying. Rather than do anything to put out the fire, Miller had merely moved into another room, with the result that the fire eventually engulfed the building. Miller's conviction for arson was upheld by both the Court of Appeal and the House of Lords, in spite of his argument that there was no criminal act on his part (the fire having been started inadvertently). Two theories were used to justify Miller's conviction. One is based on the notion that the events preceding the fire were all part of a single course of conduct on Miller's part, and that his failure to do anything about the fire is to be treated as merely part of an overall act of setting fire to the building. The other theory, preferred for its simplicity and intelligibility by Lord Diplock in his House of Lords judgement, recognises that the causing of a situation of danger gives rise to a duty to act to avert the consequences of that situation.

The first of these options, in which an omission is subsumed within a more extensive series of events, is one which has been used by courts in a number of cases in which an unintentional or involuntary act follows intentional or voluntary conduct. This approach was adopted in the Australian case of *Ryan* v. *The Queen*,[13] in which the appellant's pulling of a trigger was a reflex action in response to a sudden movement on the part of the person at whom the gun was pointed. The High Court of Australia held that, even if the actual pulling of the trigger was an involuntary act, it was only part of a wider series of voluntary acts (preparing the rifle, travelling to the scene of the robbery, pointing the rifle at the victim and so on) and it was this wider series of constituent acts which made up the act of the killing of the victim. Similarly, in the extraordinary case of *Fagan* v. *Metropolitan Police Commissioner*,[14] the court held that a person who had inadvertently parked his car on the foot of a policeman committed the offence of assault, notwithstanding his defence that he was under no obligation to act and remove the car from the position in which he had stopped it. Once again, the continuing act analysis was applied, with the result that the omission was reduced to a mere component in a composite act, the general nature of which was voluntary.

As Lord Diplock pointed out in *Miller*, either approach to the issue leads to the same result, and certainly the decision in this case provides sufficient authority for the imposition of criminal liability where there is a failure to rescue in a case where the dangerous situation has been created by the non-rescuer. Returning to a hill-walking example, if A tells B that the path he is proposing to take is quite safe, and then realises that he has misinformed B, he has a duty to warn B of the danger into which he is wandering, or indeed a duty to take such steps as he can to rescue B should B be in need of rescue. Here there is no professional or other relationship which gives rise to an obligation to act, but the fact that A has created the situation of danger gives rise to an obligation to act.

There may be liability if there is an intervention which has the effect of preventing rescue being affected by another. In *R.* v. *Taktak*[15] the defendant had introduced the victim to a drug dealer. Having been summoned by an anonymous telephone caller to remove the victim from an entrance hall, he did so, finding her in a comatose state. The defendant unsuccessfully attempted to revive the victim, but then left her at the drug dealer's house and did not call for medical assistance. He was convicted of the victim's manslaughter on the grounds that he had removed her from a place where a potential rescuer might have seen her and summoned help; once he had done this, he himself had a duty to call a doctor.

2.2 *Where There Is a Relationship Between the Person in Peril and a Potential Rescuer*

This category provides the clearest instances of a legally recognised duty to rescue in common law systems. Most of the cases arise from a failure to provide medical attention or the necessities of life to vulnerable persons, but in *R. v. Russell*[16] the court was faced with a direct requirement of rescue in a case where the accused's estranged wife had leaped into a swimming pool, along with their children. The court had no difficulty in holding that the failure to rescue the children in these circumstances amounted to a criminal omission, even if there was no duty in respect of the estranged wife.

The relationship between the parties may be a family one or it may be an assumed relationship of reliance and support. There is little clear authority on the point, but it is probably the case that there is no duty to rescue all those who may claim some form of family relationship with a potential rescuer. The duty has been held to exist in respect of one's children, but in *R. v. Shepphard*[17] the court expressed the opinion that it did not apply to children who had reached majority. In relation to spouses, the position is unsettled, but it is unlikely that the courts would infer a duty to rescue a spouse in the absence of some other special factor. Some jurisdictions recognise a duty to aliment both a spouse and a minor child, and by analogy this might be grounds for arguing that there is an obligation to rescue a spouse from danger, but the thrust of legal reform appears to be in the direction of greater independence of spouses and this might count against such a conclusion.

In many jurisdictions, the duty to provide the necessities of life to children is recognised by statute, and a failure to do so will constitute a crime of child neglect. This is the case, for example, in English law, where wilful neglect of a child constitutes an offence if the neglect is liable to cause unnecessary suffering or injury to health.[18] This offence may be committed by anyone who has the 'custody, charge or care' of the child, and is therefore not restricted to parents. The equivalent provision in Canada is s.197(2) of the Criminal Code, which imposes upon parents (or equivalents) the duty to 'provide the necessaries of life' for a child under the age of 16 years. Similar statutory provisions exist in the legislation of the Australian states and in New Zealand.[19] In the United States, a wide range of child neglect statutes make it an offence for parents, or those with de facto custody of children, to fail to provide them with the basic necessities of life.

A relationship of dependence may arise even outside the direct family, and in such a case a failure to provide for the necessities of life may be an offence. An important consideration here is whether the accused has undertaken responsibility for the vulnerable person; if he has assumed this responsibility, then a failure to discharge it may be criminal. In *R. v. Instan*,[20] the accused had accepted responsibility for her 73-year-old aunt, with whom she lived. When her aunt became ill, the accused failed to summon medical attention or to provide food, and the aunt's death was brought about, or at least hastened, as a result of this failure. This was treated as a culpable failure to discharge an obligation willingly taken on, and the accused was convicted of manslaughter. Other decisions are to similar effect. In *Stone and Dobinson*.[21] Stone and his cohabitee, Dobinson, allowed Stone's sister to stay with them in Stone's house. The sister, who became anorexic, remained in her room and clearly needed medical help. Neither Stone nor Dobinson made serious attempts to arrange this and, in due course, the sister died. Both Stone and Dobinson were convicted of manslaughter in respect of their failure to attempt to save the deceased's life, and this conviction was upheld on appeal. The Court held that Stone's duty to act was based on the fact that the ill person was his sister and the fact that she was living under his roof; in the case of Dobinson, there was a duty to act on the grounds that she had willingly undertaken certain duties in respect of her welfare (she tried to wash her and she took food to her). This case is important in that it suggests that a sibling relationship may play a role in giving rise to a duty to act. It is unlikely, though, that a family relationship of this sort would be capable of giving rise to an obligation if there were not some other factor present. For example, had Stone's sister not been living with him, but had been living, say, in the next street, then even if he was aware of her condition he would be unlikely to be held to have a duty to seek medical attention for her. Here we see a practical application of the distinction between 'pale' and 'vivid' obligations developed by Kagan and discussed in Chapter 1. In these terms, there is clearly a vivid obligation to those under one's roof, while the claims of those in the next street are, by comparison, 'pale'. Then there is the question of whether Stone would have been liable if the ailing woman had been somebody to whom he was not related at all, to whom he let a room in his house. Are we more 'vividly' obliged to our siblings than we are to those unrelated to us? Most people would conclude that we are, although the extent of this obligation would vary from society to society.[22]

Dobinson's position is different again. It is unlikely that she would have been held to have a duty to act if she had not undertaken the duties in question. It is possible that a court might hold that there is a duty to act in respect of those who are 'members of the same household' as oneself, but this is a notion which is somewhat vague and there is no authority to suggest such a duty at the present. We might speculate as to what might be the case where two lodgers share the same lodgings, but are by no means on intimate terms. They may meet in the kitchen, or in the corridor, but that is the extent of the relationship. Is the mere fact of being under the same roof sufficiently strong to create an obligation to act? Such a case would certainly be weaker than a case where people share a house in the full sense – taking meals together, sharing bills, engaging in joint outings from time to time. We would certainly be readier to condemn inaction in such a case than in the case of the relatively isolated and distant lodgers in the first example. Yet why should the fact that Dobinson took food to Stone's sister create an obligation on her part to continue to act? If I give a coin to an undernourished vagrant who accosts me in the street, am I under an obligation to give him money the following day? What if he tells me that the meal that I bought him the previous day saved his life, and that he is certain to starve to death if I don't continue with my charity? To an extent, Dobinson was in a similar position. If the sole basis of her liability is that she started to act, then it would seem that I must be equally liable for not continuing my help to the desperate vagrant.

This is really an aspect of the dependence issue discussed above. The initiating of a course of action may give rise to a duty to act because of dependence, but this must be qualified if we are to avoid postulating a rule which would make me liable for the death through starvation of the importuning vagrant. The reasonableness test might work here: was it reasonable to expect Dobinson to continue to help (or at least to get alternative help) once she had involved herself in the situation by attempting to wash and feed the sister? Possibly. Is it reasonable to expect to me to continue to feed the vagrant for the rest of his days (or until he can obtain alternative sources)? Surely not. Yet why exactly is one expectation reasonable and the other unreasonable? The answer might be sought in the area of expectations. There may be cases in which the provision of help leads to an expectation of more. If I lend money to an indigent friend, he may expect me to lend him more the next time he finds himself short of funds. If I rescue my neighbour's child from the deep end of the swimming pool once, the child may expect me to be available to rescue the next time and in the assurance that this provides he may again venture forth into water which is too deep for him. Similarly, the vagrant may expect me to continue to give him money the longer I continue to do it. After three months of hand-outs at my door, he may feel quite aggrieved if I suddenly say: 'Enough's enough! I don't intend to give you any more.'

Such expectations are understandable, in the sense that we do tend to expect people to continue to treat us in the way in which they have treated us in the past. But this is quite different from saying that we have a right to be treated in the same way as we have been in the past, where there are no grounds, other than past practice, for justifying the continuation of this treatment. The fact that A always gives B a present on his birthday does not mean that B has a right to expect a present from A on his next birthday. Unless one accepts an extensive moral duty to aid others, as defended by Michael Menlowe in Chapter 1, the only grounds on which expectations of this nature may give rise to an obligation to act are where it would be unduly harsh for a cutting-off of the benefit to be brought about in circumstances which gave the recipient no opportunity to make alternative arrangements. The recipient has a claim of the donor for consideration at least, and this claim may give rise to a duty to attempt to make alternative arrangements. This duty, however, should be strictly limited. In the case of the vagrant, for example, it might be served by saying to him that the donations will shortly stop and that he should attempt to seek help elsewhere. The provision of the address of alternative sources of support would probably more than discharge any duty towards him. Dobinson might have been expected to do more. Perhaps she was under no duty to take food to the sister indefinitely, but she might have been under a duty to inform social welfare agencies or doctors of the situation, and to warn them that she was about to stop the help that she was giving.

These decisions may be explained in terms of reliance – the victim relied on the non-provider – but it is doubtful whether reliance itself provides sufficient grounds for the imposition of liability. Inaction may be justified even where there is reliance, provided that the reliance is an unreasonable one. If A willingly supports a work-shy friend B, the recipient of such assistance may become thoroughly dependent on A's aid, and indeed come to rely upon it. It would be absurd in such a case if A could not end his aid to B on any grounds that please him. There may be a relationship of dependence between the two, but A is quite entitled to discount this and to insist that B stands on his own feet. Self-reliance, after all, is an option which is open to B, and, what is more, B has no claim on A. In *Instan*,[23] it was not unreasonable for the elderly relative to be dependent on her niece, given that she appeared to have no alternative and given that she had been taken in by the niece.

The relationship cases ultimately have to be interpreted in terms of moral claims. The courts will infer a duty to rescue, it seems, where they feel that the moral claim is sufficiently strong to justify the creation of a legal obligation. Such a decision will clearly depend on a variety of factors, and it is impossible to define just when a moral claim will come into existence; certainly, as Michael Menlowe points out, the boundaries of such moral claims are notoriously difficult to identify. These factors will depend on social attitudes of the time and, as these change, so too will moral obligations change. Fairly widely accepted moral obligations may also fail to survive close inspection and may seem considerably less persuasive when analysed. For example, the duty of adults to care for their indigent parents is one such obligation which, although recognised by some, is difficult to justify in terms of reciprocity.[24] Courts of law, of course, tend not to scrutinise moral obligations too closely, but endorse such duties in broad terms. Such endorsement is based on appeals to such vague notions as 'the values of the community' rather than on any theoretical moral system. One may typically expect to see such invocations of moral expectations in cases involving public decency or pornography issues; they are rare, however, in cases involving criminal liability for an omission. This suggests that there is a fairly fundamental reluctance here to invoke moral considerations as grounds for imposing a duty to act, and that this reluctance results in a fairly narrow area of liability in reliance cases.

2.3 Where a Person Occupies a Position Which Requires Him to Act

The fact that a person occupies a particular position may give rise to an obligation to rescue. The position may be an official one (policeman, lifeguard or the like) or it may be one which arises from a contract of employment. This latter category is sometimes considered an example of reliance, but cases within it can equally well be considered from the point of view of the position occupied by the potential rescuer.

Nineteenth-century courts were initially unwilling to infer a duty to act where the position of the accused arose from private employment and was not based on statute. In *R. v. Smith*[25] the accused was a watchman who had been privately employed to warn pedestrians attempting to cross a road at its intersection with a tramway. He absented himself from his post (in spite of strict orders not to do so) and during one such absence a fatal accident occurred. The court held in this case that the accused was not guilty of manslaughter, as he was purely a private servant with no statutory duty to protect the public. By the beginning of the twentieth century, a different view prevailed, and in *R. v. Pitwood*[26] the defendant was convicted of manslaughter in respect of his failure properly to discharge his contractual duty as the keeper of a railway crossing gate. In spite of the absence of recent authority, it is likely that contemporary courts would have no hesitation in imposing criminal liability in a case where a clear contractual duty is breached and where life is lost as a result. It would therefore be manslaughter (or its equivalent) if a steward employed by a race track to protect spectators deliberately refrained from rescuing a child who had wandered out onto the track in front of him. An omission to rectify a known fault in an electricity supply might also result in the imposition of liability of an electrician who was contractually bound to rectify the fault.

The position of those who occupy public office of some sort is even clearer. Policemen have a duty to prevent harm occurring to members of the public – when they are in a position to do so – and if a failure to do this results in harm there may be criminal liability. The courts have been careful in recent years to limit the civil liability of policemen who fail to provide efficient protection for the public, but they have been prepared to convict policemen of assault for failing to prevent damage to those who are clearly under their protection. The Scottish case of *Bonar* v. *Macleod*[27] is such a decision. In this case a man who was detained in a police station was subjected to an assault by a police constable. The accused, who witnessed this assault, did nothing to prevent it and he was in due course charged with being art and part to the offence (art and part being the Scottish form of accessorial liability). Although the court did not rule out liability where two officers are of equal rank, weight was given to the fact that the officer who failed to intervene to prevent the crime was senior to the one who actually carried it out. This suggests that a special responsibility attaches to those whose rank gives them the right to intervene on behalf of another.

The fact that a person has control of some sort over another may give rise to a duty to act and therefore a duty to rescue. There are two groups of cases which explore this possibility – the 'driving cases' and the 'employee cases'. The classic driving case is *Du Cros* v. *Lambourne*[28] in which the court accepted that the failure of the owner of a vehicle to prevent dangerous driving when he was travelling as a passenger amounted to the offence of aiding and abetting the offence of dangerous driving. Later cases have endorsed this approach: in *Rubie* v. *Faulkner*[29] the supervisor of a learner driver was convicted of aiding and abetting the learner's driving without due care and attention. It was held here that the statute imposed a duty on a supervisor in such circumstances, and that a failure to prevent the commission of an offence amounted to aiding and abetting that offence. Liability in driving cases has also included liability for aiding and abetting the causing of death by dangerous driving, an offence which carries with it potentially heavy penalties.[30]

The courts have been hesitant to impose accessorial criminal liability on employers who have failed to prevent the commission of an offence by their employees and what decisions there are on the subject are somewhat unclear. Some cases suggest that the employer must have actually encouraged the employee to commit the offence, although this encouragement may take the form of inaction.[31] Other cases, however, support the view that what matters is control: once a person is shown to have control over a situation, then a failure to take reasonable steps to prevent the commission of an offence may result in a conviction for complicity. An example of this approach is afforded by the judgement in *Tuck* v. *Robson*[32] in which a licensee of a bar was convicted of aiding and abetting after-hours drinking when he failed to take sufficient steps to stop those who were on the premises from continuing to drink. The calling of 'time' and the turning off and on of the lights was not sufficient, the court held: firmer action was required.[33]

Can the principles at work in these cases be generalised to infer a duty to rescue in circumstances where the potential rescuer has control of the situation? The answer is that they can, at least where the harm threatening the imperilled person emanates from a criminal threat on the part of one under the potential rescuer's control. The cases describe the duty in terms of an obligation to stop the commission of a crime, but this may be indistinguishable from an obligation to rescue an imperilled person. The supervisor of a learner driver who sees the driver steering directly towards a pedestrian rescues that pedestrian by wresting the wheel from the learner's grip. The employer who stops an employee from assaulting a fellow employee may be said to be rescuing that person just as much as he may be said to be preventing the crime of assault from being committed. These are just those instances, one might suggest, which demonstrate how common law systems may conceal a duty to rescue in unlikely, or at least not immediately obvious, places.

There are certain important limits to the duty to prevent the commission of a crime. Although this duty may be inferred where the accused was in a position to exercise control over those about to perpetrate the offence, the situation is different where the potential rescuer has no such power. Once again the common law approaches this from the point of view of accessorial liability, the issue being whether the non-intervenor becomes an accessory to the crime committed by the principal. In essence, the rule is that, unless a person does something positive to encourage the commission of the offence, there is no duty to intervene on behalf of the victim. In one extreme example of this, *R.* v. *Clarkson*[34] two soldiers entered their barrack room to find that fellow soldiers were raping a woman. The two accused did nothing to intervene, but merely watched the offence being committed. Neither made any attempt to summon help. The Court of Appeal agreed that there was no duty to act in such a case although, had the two been non-commissioned officers or officers, it is possible that a different view would have been taken. This does not mean that inaction is always permissible: in the earlier case of *R.* v. *Coney*[35] the court pointed out that the mere spectator may aid and abet if he becomes aware that the fact of his presence is encouraging the perpetrators in their commission of the crime: 'It is no criminal offence to stand by, a mere passive spectator of a crime, even a murder ... But the fact that a person was voluntarily and purposely present witnessing the commission of a crime, and offered no opposition to it ... might under some circumstances afford cogent evidence ... that he wilfully encouraged and so aided and abetted.'

Failure to give assistance to the police when such help is requested may, in some circumstances, be an offence, although a rare one, of refusing to aid the police in the preservation of the peace. The offence is defined in *Brown*,[36] a case decided 150 years ago, but the offence has nonetheless been invoked more recently. In *Waugh*[37] a ticket collector on the underground railway was convicted when he failed to assist a policeman who was attempting to detain a suspect. There is only one other reported case since the decision in *Brown*,[38] and the continued existence of such an offence has been the subject of some criticism.[39] As the law stands, however, a member of the public who is asked by a policeman to join him in the rescue of a person who is being assaulted could be prosecuted under the heading of this offence for failing to do so without reasonable excuse.

2.4   Where the Potential Rescuer is the Owner of Property Connected With the Peril

This is perhaps an off-shoot of the control principle, but it is potentially one of the weakest of the cases for omission liability. In principle the ownership of property involves no duties to others (in the criminal context) other than those which arise from the use of the property for dangerous purposes: in such cases, liability may be imposed under the dangerous act doctrine discussed above. The owner of a house or of land is under no duty to rescue those who happen to be on his property and who are threatened in some way. There may be civil liability – depending on the circumstances – but the owner commits no criminal offence if he fails to intervene. If exceptions are to be made to this proposition, these would occur where a contractual relationship of some sort is inferred between the owner of the property and the person in need of rescue. A guest in a hotel who is pinned to the ground by a falling beam may reasonably claim an implied contractual duty incumbent on the hotel keeper to rescue him and a failure to do so may result in criminal liability. This liability, however, is not so much attributable to the ownership of property as to the contract between the parties.

The implications of this distinction between contractual and non-contractual cases may appear stark, particularly in a case such as the following. Two persons on A's premises (a large self-service store) are both heroin addicts. B, who is a legitimate customer, takes advantage of the washrooms provided for customers to inject a large dose of heroin directly into a vein. He collapses and is found by an employee, sprawled across the floor in a coma. C, who is not a customer at all, but who has come in off the street to use the washrooms for the same purpose of injecting, similarly injects an overdose and becomes unconscious. A, or his staff, have a duty to summon medical help for B, but probably not for C, with whom they have no relationship of a contractual nature. If medical help is not summoned and B dies, this could amount to manslaughter; C's death, however, would have no criminal law implications as far as A or his staff are concerned.

2.5 Problems of the Mental Requirement

Even if it is evident there will be some circumstances in which the criminal law imposes liability for a failure to act – and therefore for a failure to rescue – liability will be imposed only if the non-rescuer manifests a guilty state of mind (*mens rea*). The question of whether a rescue is reasonable or otherwise is really a question of justification: even in those circumstances where action is expected, the law does not expect it to be heroic. A parent's duty to rescue a child does not entail an obligation to sacrifice self in the process, although parents may well be prepared to do so. The making of an exceptionally risky rescue attempt is generally regarded as laudable, of course, particularly when undertaken by strangers, and may be officially recognised as such. But such responses are, from the legal point of view, more than what is required. In a case where an attempt to rescue would be considered reasonable – from the objective point of view – a person may still fail to act because he thinks that rescue is unnecessary or, in his view, excessively dangerous. A scrupulously subjective system of criminal justice would acquit in such a case, judging the situation in the light of what the accused *thought* it to be. In practice, this degree of subjectivity will not always be achieved and a failure to rescue may be punished even where the accused had not been deliberately or knowingly callous.

The problem has arisen in child neglect cases. Parents who fail to provide for their children may do so for a variety of reasons, fecklessness or limited intelligence being two. Prior to the decision in *R. v. Shepphard*[40] the courts were prepared to convict parents of child neglect as long as their conduct was such as a reasonable parent would have considered neglectful. This meant that a parent who did not summon medical aid for a child because he or she thought that such aid was unnecessary could be convicted of an offence under child neglect legislation. *Shepphard* changed this, holding that wilful neglect required an awareness of the risk of harm to the child and that, if a parent was genuinely unaware of the consequences of his omission, he could not be said to be wilfully neglecting the child. The Canadian case of *R. v. Tutton and Tutton*[41] proved to be very much more difficult, as this involved delicate issues of religious conviction. The Tuttons were members of a religious sect which believed in faith healing. Their three-year-old son, however, was diagnosed as diabetic and they were told that he would need daily injections of insulin in order to survive. The parents complied with this treatment regime for some time, but later on the mother alleged that she had received a divine message to the effect that her son had been miraculously healed. Thereafter she stopped the injections of insulin, the boy became ill, and died several days later. Both the father and the mother were convicted of the manslaughter of their son, on the grounds that their failure to furnish medical assistance amounted to criminal negligence. At the trial, the judge instructed the jury that a parent who has a reasonable excuse for not providing the necessaries of life would not be guilty of an offence; a mistaken belief that the situation was not serious would be grounds for acquittal – provided, of course, that the mistake was one which a reasonable person could have made. This point was taken up on appeal: should there be a conviction of an offence of this nature where the accused did not believe that there was a risk to the child?

Once this qualification was admitted, the situation of the Tutton parents appeared less bleak. If they believed that their son had been cured, and that he was therefore not in any danger, then they could not be said to be reckless as to any risk of harm. The objective view of recklessness, which holds that one may be reckless even without knowing of the risk, was rejected. The court was at pains, though, to emphasise that the principle enunciated in a line of earlier cases should stand: it is no defence for a parent to omit to summon medical help on the grounds that he disapproved of it on religious grounds – here the standard to be met by the parent is an objective one and he will be judged according to the standard of behaviour of a reasonable parent. Where, however, a religious belief led to an objectively mistaken belief that a child was cured, and in no danger, the *mens rea* requirement would not be satisfied and a parent might be acquitted.

The significance of the *Tutton* decision extends further than its contribution to the debate as to subjective and objective notions of recklessness in the criminal law. This case demonstrates that the value of a child's life is placed more highly in the eyes of the criminal law than the value of religious conscience. The duty to rescue in such cases, then, is a high-ranking one. A failure to appreciate that rescue is required may be excusable – at least in systems such as Canadian law, where the subjective view of recklessness is well entrenched – if the non-rescuer genuinely believed that there was no emergency, but a failure to rescue cannot be justified on the grounds that some higher consideration (such as a religious duty) relieves one of any duty to rescue.

3   Failure to Rescue and the Civil Law

Past discussion of the duty to rescue has tended to focus on criminal law issues and on the alleged absence of such a duty in common law systems. In fact, the problem is as much of an issue in civil law, although once again it surfaces in subtle ways. There are few cases dealing with the stark issue of civil liability for a failure to rescue a person in immediate physical peril, but there is an increasing number of cases which can be seen as rescue cases in the broader sense. These are the warning cases, in which the courts have considered the liability of those who have failed to warn others of some danger, physical or possibly financial. This is the rescue problem in a new, and rather interesting, guise. Before analysing these cases, though, it is useful to see how the law has treated those who do undertake rescues and then either cause harm to others in the process or are themselves harmed.

Even if the law is reluctant to impose a duty to rescue, and even if, in the criminal context, it restricts this duty to exceptional situations, the moral sympathies of the law are clearly revealed when the rescuer finds himself involved in a civil action, as plaintiff or defendant, as a result of a rescue attempt. In general, the rescuer is a privileged litigant. Although he has a duty to act with the same caution as anybody else, it will in practice be extremely difficult to establish liability on the part of a rescuer. The bystander who comes to the rescue of an injured person, and who through ineptitude exacerbates the injury, may theoretically be sued for the additional harm he caused, but any plaintiff attempting this would face formidable difficulties. The standard of care for a rescuer is always going to be defined according to that which is expected of a reasonable person in the circumstances. The reasonable person is not an expert; he or she is the reasonably competent layman who, although not expected to do anything grossly foolish, is nonetheless given considerable leeway for error. The standard of care expected of the rescuer would also be affected by the exigencies of the situation; in an emergency one is not always expected to calculate risks too finely. An ill-judged action, performed in an emergency, will not necessarily be deemed to be negligent, provided that it is an action of the sort which might be expected of one acting in such an emergency.

Not surprisingly, there are few cases in which incompetent rescuers have been sued by those whom they have attempted to rescue. In some jurisdictions, concern over legal disincentives to rescue have resulted in the introduction of statutory immunities, the aim of which is to block actions against rescuers. These statutes may focus particularly on attempts to rescue accident victims – as is the case with the United States 'good Samaritan' statutes – or they may be concerned with the position of professional rescuers and those they co-opt to assist them – as is the case with a number of the Australian statutes.

The injured rescuer who seeks compensation for damage suffered during a rescue attempt is equally favoured, although admittedly this was not always so. Earlier cases proceeded on the basis that the intervention of a rescuer was a voluntary intervention on his part for the consequences of which he was himself liable. The rescuer was therefore *volens* in respect of the risk he ran, and was therefore denied compensation. As long ago as 1921, Justice Cardozo expressed a reaction against this highly individualistic approach: 'danger invites rescue,' he pronounced. 'The cry of distress is the summons to relief ... The risk of rescue, if only it be not wanton, is born of the occasion. The emergency begets the man. The wrongdoer may not have foreseen the coming of the deliverer. He is accountable as if he had.'[42] Subsequent cases have affirmed this principle. One who negligently creates a situation of danger is liable for the injuries sustained by a rescuer.[43] The harm caused to the rescuer is treated as a foreseeable consequence of the original negligent conduct, and it is irrelevant whether the rescuer is one who is under a professional duty to rescue or whether he or she is merely one who happened to be in the vicinity at the time. In one of the important earlier cases, the rescuer was a policeman who ran out to stop a bolting horse (*Haynes* v. *Harwood*[44]); in *Chapman* v. *Hearse* [45] he was a doctor; in *Ogwo* v. *Taylor*[46] he was a fireman; and in *Corrothers* v. *Strobdian*[47] he was a passing motorist. The rescue attempt may seem unlikely, but this will not mean that it is too remote to be foreseeable. Two Canadian cases demonstrate this: in *Horsley* v. *McLaren*[48] an inept rescuer (who, as owner of a boat, was under a duty to rescue his passengers) caused the intervention of a second rescuer, for whose drowning the court said he would have been liable. In *Urbanski* v. *Patel*[49] a surgeon who negligently removed his patient's only kidney, under the impression that it was a cyst, was held liable for the damages of her father, who donated a kidney to his daughter.

There is a small number of cases in which a rescuer has sought recovery from the person whom he has attempted to rescue when that person's own negligence gave rise to the situation of peril in the first place. In one of the earlier cases to consider this point, *Chapman* v. *Hearse*,[50] the court took the view that, had he sued, damages would have been payable to a doctor who was injured when he stopped to attend to a driver injured through his own negligence. In *Harrison* v. *British Railways Board*[51] a railway guard who attempted to rescue a colleague who was trying to board a train in motion succeeded in an action against the colleague, and in *Horsley*[52] the court indicated that an injured person who was the cause of his own peril could be liable to a rescuer for the rescuer's damages.

3.1 Is There a General Civil Law Duty to Rescue?

Common law systems of tortious liability mirror the criminal law's refusal to impose a general duty to rescue others in the absence of some special factor. The fundamental duty of care in tort is that laid down by Lord Atkin in his 'neighbour principle' first propounded in *Donoghue* v. *Stevenson*.[53] Under the neighbour principle, we owe a duty of care not to harm our neighbours, our neighbours being those who might reasonably be expected to be damaged by our harmful acts. This simple proposition has been extensively discussed and a considerable body of case law focuses on the precise point of who is our neighbour. The background to this issue is the concern of the courts to limit the extent of civil liability and, to do this, the concept of the duty of care has been employed as a limiting factor. In the absence of a duty of care to another, a failure to act will have no implications for liability. If A owes no duty of care to B, then, even if A's negligence leads to loss on B's part, B will have no claim in tort. For example, a financial journalist who suggests that readers invest in a company which, had he bothered to check up on the facts, is close to bankruptcy, would not be liable to his readers for their loss.

Civil liability arises only when there is a duty of care. But when does a duty of care come into existence? This is a crucial matter for the law of tort. It is argued in Chapter 1 that any duty of care involves an extensive beneficent duty and, if that argument is correct, then the duty of care is itself potentially extensive. Yet this assumes that the courts accept an extensive moral duty (which they probably do not), and it also assumes that legally recognised duties of care reflect moral duties. For practical reasons, this is not the case, and in order to limit the extent of the duty of care the courts have invoked a variety of concepts, in particular the doctrine of foreseeability and, more recently, the concept of proximity. The foreseeability doctrine bases liability on the test as to whether the damages suffered by the plaintiff could have been foreseen at the time of the defendant's act. This appeared to work in many cases as a means of limiting the scope of liability, but its defects were always apparent; in particular, a duty of care relationship was still required to be established between plaintiff and defendant before the foreseeability test could be applied. Damage may be foreseeable by a person who has no duty to act for whatever reason, including reasons of policy. Indeed, in *Anns* v. *London Borough of Merton*,[54] a decision which was highly influential in elucidating the duty of care concept, the foreseeability test was seen as being only the first stage of a two-stage test, giving rise to no more than a prima facie duty of care. This duty of care was defeasible if policy reasons – identified in the second stage of the duty of care enquiry – dictated that there should be no liability. The foreseeability test applied in *Anns* proved to be a powerful weapon in the hands of plaintiffs who sought to shift loss onto public bodies. In a series of building inspection cases, the *Anns* rule led to building control departments becoming responsible for economic loss which would normally be recoverable only under contract.[55] The foreseeability principle was increasingly seen to create excessively wide liability, and eventually, in the case of *Murphy* v. *Brentwood District Council*,[56] the House of Lords abandoned the *Anns* test in favour of a test of proximity, now the most popular of the liability tests. Foreseeability, although still important in some contexts (particularly where it can be used to limit liability), had proved to be too unruly for the courts to contain. In a sense, it demonstrated the same instability which is seen in a number of the philosophical positions identified in Chapter 1: the recognition of any measure of liability led to the necessary recognition of a great deal more.

The proximity test has been embraced by many courts who have seen in it an answer to the elusive difficulties of the duty of care concept. Under this test, once a relationship of proximity comes into existence, there will be liability for foreseeable damage. This proposition, of course, still requires further explanation to be readily intelligible, and in order to accomplish this the courts have resorted to other concepts, including foreseeability. Proximity has therefore become something of a shibboleth, made up of many things and doing many tasks. Here, for example, is a definition from the Australian nervous shock case, *Jaensch* v. *Coffey*[57] in which the High Court of Australia defined proximity as a concept which involves 'the notion of nearness or closeness and embraces physical proximity (in the sense of space and time) between the person or property of the plaintiff and the person or property of the defendant, circumstantial proximity such as an overriding relationship of employer and employee or of a professional man and his client, and causal proximity in the sense of the directness of the relationship between the particular act or cause of action and the injury sustained'.

A factor which has been given particular prominence in establishing proximity is that of reliance. If it is evident that the plaintiff relied on the defendant for a particular benefit, and the defendant was aware that reliance was placed in him, then a relationship of proximity may be inferred. There are numerous cases illustrating this; an important instance was the decision of the High Court of Australia in *Sutherland S.C.* v. *Heyman*.[58] Here the purchaser of a house claimed damages from a local council for the council's failure to inspect the house foundations competently. The court took the view that there was no relationship of proximity between the plaintiff and defendant because there was no evidence that the purchaser had in any way relied on the faulty building inspection and had certainly not communicated any reliance to the council. Reliance may have been considered by some judges as the heart of the proximity concept, and yet it is difficult to see how it can itself give rise to liability in the absence of some other special factor in the relationship. It may be, for example, that A relies on B inappropriately. He may say to B that financial aid from him is his only hope of avoiding business ruin, and that he is therefore relying on him to help him. This may be real reliance on A's part, but it hardly gives rise to any obligation on B's part unless B has acted in a way which justifies A's having a special claim on him (as where, for example, A gives B a prior undertaking that he will help him financially should he find himself in difficulties). Nor does the unilateral reliance of the charity fund raiser on the potential donors give rise to any obligation on the part of the donors. There may be a moral obligation in such a case, but such an obligation would clearly not be accorded any legal status.

What is missing in these cases is a notion of reasonableness, and this is imported through the posing of the legal question: is it reasonable for the person relying on another to do so? This points us in the direction of a further factor which is used to determine the existence of proximity – the fact that it was 'just and reasonable' that there should be a duty of care in the circumstances. Whether or not there will be proximity will depend, then, on whether it seems just and reasonable that the defendant should have taken precautions against causing damage either by acting more cautiously or by ensuring that he did not make a harmful omission. *Smith* v. *Littlewoods*,[59] a decision of the House of Lords in a Scottish appeal, shows how the concept of what is reasonable in the circumstances may be used to determine liability for an omission. In this case, vandals had broke into a disused cinema and had caused an outbreak of fire within it. The fire had spread to neighbouring property, the owner of which attempted to recover his loss from the cinema owners on the grounds that they had failed to take steps to ensure that their property remained lockfast. Liability was rejected by the court, which held that in such circumstances the duty of ensuring that vandals were kept out of the property would impose an unreasonable burden on proprietors. Only if damage were highly probable might there be such a duty imposed on the owner of property, as in such a case it would not be unreasonable to expect affirmative action on the defendant's part.[60]

The classification of a relationship as one of proximity amounts to saying that there is a duty of care to be discharged. Yet this does not necessarily mean that there will be liability for an *omission* as well as for positive acts of negligence in relation to another; it is quite possible that there will be a duty of care to avoid harmful action while at that same time and in relation to the same defendant there is no duty to act. This distinction was emphasised by Justice Brennan's judgement in *Sutherland.*[61] Referring to the famous 'neighbour' pronouncement of Lord Atkin in *Donoghue* v. *Stevenson*, Brennan says:

> If foreseeability of injury were the exhaustive criterion of a duty to act to prevent the occurrence of that injury, legal duty would be coterminous with moral obligation ... Lord Atkin's definition of the person who is in law my 'neighbour' is not so wide; it is a person who is affected 'by my act', not by my omission. The judgment of Brett MR in *Le Lievre* v. *Gould* which Lord Atkin cites makes it clear that the general principle expresses a duty to take reasonable care to avoid doing what might cause injury to another, not a duty to prevent injury being done to another by that other, by a third person, or by circumstances for which nobody is responsible.[62]

So proximity is only the first step. If there is to be a duty to act, there must be proximity along with some other factor which transforms the relationship into one requiring affirmative action. This may be the very nature of the relationship, which makes it 'just and reasonable' that there should be liability for an omission. A duty to act, and therefore a duty to rescue, will exist where the relationship is, for example, a protective one, as is the case between the master of a vessel and his passengers, the nurse and her patient, or the schoolteacher and his charges. In such cases, a failure to rescue in the face of physical danger is clearly actionable in that a duty to protect is of the very essence of the close relationship between the parties. By contrast, the relationship between accountant and client or solicitor and client does not imply any responsibility for personal safety and the professional adviser in such a case has no responsibility for the physical safety of his client. Other forms of action may be required in such cases, however – there may be a duty to warn of a danger to property or of financial peril. Such duties are not dissimilar to duties to rescue, and the same dilemmas as to the extent of liability occur within them.

3.2   When a Civil Law Duty to Rescue Will Come into Existence

In a number of cases judges have been at pains to point out that there is no general legal duty to rescue, whatever the moral claims for such a duty may be. In *Dorset Yacht Company* v. *Home Office*,[63] for example, Lord Reid said: 'when a person has done nothing to put himself in any relationship with another person in distress or with his property mere accidental propinquity does not require him to go to that person's assistance. There may be a moral duty to do so, but it is not practicable to make it a legal duty.'[64] Similarly, in *Quinn* v. *Hill*[65] the court took a very limited view of the responsibility which was owed by one worker to another. The judge accepted that there was a general duty to give warning to others of any danger caused by one's own act, but held that this duty did not extend to warning as to dangers which were not caused by one's own action or to which one's own action had not contributed: 'Whenever one sees the other about to do something which threatens injury, has he a legal duty to warn or to prevent? Such a duty would have wide implications ... Why should it not apply to the case of two persons on a picnic together where one of them sees the other about to cross a dangerous bridge?'[66]

In spite of this unpromising starting-point, the courts have nonetheless been prepared to infer the existence of duties of affirmative action in a number of situations. The most obvious of these – and the least controversial perhaps – is where there has been a prior act on the part of the defender giving rise to a duty to prevent the occurrence of harm. This act may be at first blush an innocent one, but may be transformed by a later development, as was the case in *Iversen* v. *Purser*,[67] which, like the criminal case of *Miller*,[68] involved the dangerous habit of going to sleep with a cigarette in one's mouth. In this case a tenant had invited a guest back to his home after both had been out drinking. The tenant retired to bed, leaving the guest in another room. The guest then dropped off to sleep with a cigarette still in his mouth, and the resultant fire caused considerable damage to the plaintiff's premises. In an action for damages against the tenant, the court held that he should have inspected the room in which his guest was sitting in order to ensure that all cigarettes were extinguished – a duty which was required of him in view of the inebriated state of his guest and the defendant's knowledge of that state.

A similar readiness to impose liability for inaction is evident in a number of cases dealing with liability for damage caused to the property of neighbours. Such liability may arise either through the mere fact of ownership of property or through some act on the part of the owner. In Britain the Scottish courts provided something of a lead in this area, allowing damage in a number of cases where the inaction of owners had led to vandals coming onto property and causing damage to neighbouring buildings. In *Squires* v. *Perth and Kinross District Council*[69], for example, the owner of a building which had been clad in scaffolding was held liable for the loss caused to an adjoining jewellery shop when thieves entered the building by way of the scaffolding. English courts were very much more reluctant to allow damages in such cases, and eventually, in *Smith* v. *Littlewoods*,[70] the

House of Lords restricted the circumstances in which Scots law would impose a duty of action on the part of the owners of uninhabited premises. In the United States there has been no such reluctance, and the liability of the owners of premises for damage caused to tenants or other users of buildings by the criminal acts of third parties has been affirmed in a number of decisions. These cases are not rescue cases, of course, but they demonstrate the way in which a responsibility for the welfare of others may be attributed in an apparently individualistic legal tradition.

3.3   Should Public Officials Come to the Rescue?

In most societies, one of the most obvious sources of rescue is the police, and yet the liability of the non-rescuing police force is not a simple matter. It is likely that a policeman who, although able to act, stood and watched an assault on a member of the public would be civilly liable for his inaction. Certainly, if such a policeman can be criminally liable (as in *Bonar* v. *Macleod*[71]) then there can be no reason in principle why civil liability should be avoided. Yet the cases do not deal with such stark facts, and are more concerned with circumstances in which the danger is less focused or less immediate.

  Hill v. *Chief Constable of West Yorkshire*[72] followed upon the lengthy search for Peter Sutcliffe, a paranoid schizophrenic who committed 13 murders in the North of England between 1969 and 1980. The police investigation of the crimes was severely criticised, especially since Sutcliffe came under suspicion on a number of occasions and was, in fact, questioned by the police. The appellant in this case, the mother of the last victim, argued that the police had been in breach of their duty of care to her daughter, as a member of the public, in that their investigation had been tardy and inefficient. This claim was rejected on the grounds that very special circumstances were required before the relationship between the police and an individual member of the public became such as to allow proximity to be inferred. In addition to this, though, the court held that there were powerful reasons of public policy for excluding such liability: the potential liability of the police would be impossibly broad if every victim of a crime could argue that his loss is attributable to police incompetence. Another attempt to attribute loss to police inaction was made in the British Columbian case of *Lafleur* v. *British Columbia*.[73] Here the plaintiff was a motorcyclist who had been drinking with other motorcyclists and was causing annoyance to members of the public. The police were called, and they spoke to the plaintiff and his companions, advising them to 'sleep it off'. This advice was not followed, and the plaintiff set off on his motorcycle (in spite of his intoxication) and fairly soon thereafter became involved in a serious accident. The claim against the police was based on the assertion that they should have prevented him from riding the motorcycle, and that their failure to do so amounted to a breach of their private law duty of care towards him. Not surprisingly, the court considered the plaintiff to be the author of his own misfortune. It was accepted that Canadian law recognised a duty on the part of authorities to protect members of the public in certain circumstances, but this duty depended on the existence of a relationship of proximity which did not arise in this case. In a full review of the case law, especially those Canadian cases following the principle embodied in *Anns*,[74] the Supreme Court decided that the concept of proximity included not only notions of risk and reliance, but also the idea that a duty of care should exist only if it is 'just and reasonable' that this should be so. It was hardly just and reasonable, said the judge, that 'an affirmative duty of care be owed to a self-indulgent, grown man who did not want to be taken care of, who deliberately ignored repeated warnings not to drive, who spurned the reasonable and practicable suggestion to sleep it off, who, intent on self-gratification, was heedless of any danger to himself or others'.[75] Nor was there any evidence that the plaintiff relied on the police for protection and, even if there was, this fact alone would not have resulted in the imposition of a duty of care.

One might think, then, that courts would never find circumstances where this proximity existed, and yet a triable issue of this nature was found in *Jane Doe* v. *Metropolitan Toronto (Municipality) Commissioner of Police*.[76] The plaintiff had been assaulted by a serial rapist who had been preying on women in a specific area. The police had been aware of the danger which this rapist posed to women living in the area, but had not issued a public warning, their grounds for not doing so being that such a warning could cause undue alarm in the minds of the public. The plaintiff argued that the real reason for the failure to warn was more sinister – that she, and other women in the area, were in effect being used as 'bait' to encourage the rapist to strike again and thereby draw the police upon him. The court did not comment on the merits of this claim, but it did hold that here there was at least that degree of proximity between police and public which gave rise to a duty to act on the part of the police. Such a duty was the exception, however, the court stressing that: 'While the police owe certain duties to the public at large, they cannot be expected to owe a private law duty of care to every member of society who might be at risk. Foreseeability of risk alone is not sufficient to impose a private law duty of care ...'[77]

It is easy to understand why the police are a special case in which policy considerations (possibly expressed as questions of reasonablesness) will dictate against the inference of a duty of care to an individual member of the public. Such factors do not necessarily come to the fore when a public authority in quite another category is involved. In *Fletcher* v. *Manitoba Public Insurance Co*[78] the plaintiff succeeded in a claim for damages against a public insurance agency which had failed to draw his attention to cover that was available to deal with possible damage caused by an uninsured motorist. The court took the view that a public insurer has a duty to act in such a case on the grounds that the customer relies on the agency for such advice and protection. Knowledge of this reliance was imputed to the insurer, although it was held that it was not essential that the insurer should have known of the actual individual, as long as it knew of a limited class of persons to which the individual plaintiff belonged.[79] Such decisions suggest a fairly wide range of liability, but must be considered in the light of a more recent judicial inclination to limit the extent of the liability of public bodies. There is also authority to quite the opposite effect: in *van Oppen* v. *Trustees of Bedford College*[80] a school was held to be under no duty to inform parents of the fact that there was no scheme of personal injury insurance in place to cover injury sustained by pupils. The relationship between school and pupil, or between school and parents, is surely closer in many respects, and therefore more proximate, than the relationship between the member of the public and a public insurer. Yet requiring action on the part of schools could give rise to an impossibly broad duty.

The view has been expressed that the courts in Australia will impose liability for failure to rescue, or for negligence in the carrying out of a rescue when the defendant is a public rescue body.[81] There are no reported cases of such liability being imposed, but, since the decision of the High Court of Australia in *Sutherlandshire County Council* v. *Heyman*,[82] it has been apparent that reliance plays an important role in determining proximity and that reliance on public rescue authorities would not be difficult to establish in certain circumstances, nor would there be much difficulty in establishing that the rescuers were aware of this reliance. Thus a yachtsman setting off in Australian coastal waters might do so in the sure knowledge that the National Search and Rescue Authority has an obligation (acknowledged by the Federal Government) to provide assistance for those in peril in coastal waters. He may be said to rely on the Search and Rescue Authority in the making of his decision to set off in the first place and, for its part, the Authority knows that people like him are setting sail in this frame of mind. American yachtsmen, by contrast, should be less sanguine: in *DFDS Seacruises (Bahamas) Ltd* v. *United States*[83] it was held that the US Coast Guard has no obligation to render assistance at sea, although it may do so if it wishes to discharge what was described as its 'voluntary and permissive duty'. A failure to mount a rescue operation may therefore be no more than the legitimate exercise of a discretion; once a rescue is mounted, though, negligence in its conduct will be actionable in the normal way.

3.4   Warnings in the Private Sphere

Warnings may come not only from public officials but from private individuals. Although this area is not so sensitive to policy considerations as may be, for example, the question of police responsibilities for the safety of the individual, public issues nonetheless still play a part. The undue burdening of the professional adviser or businessmen will have consequences for liability insurance and for the smooth running of business; holding psychiatrists liable for the harmful acts of their patients may have a serious effect on medical confidentiality and the doctor's freedom to exercise his judgement in clinical matters. Questions of fairness and reasonability are therefore present, expressed or unexpressed, in proximity questions here as well.

3.5   Warnings of Crime

There is no duty to warn another of the fact that he is about to become the victim of the dishonesty of another. This proposition has been tested in a number of cases, but the courts have been steadfast in their desire to limit the shifting of this particular form of commercial loss. In these cases, all that is required is a telephone call, but this, it seems, is a telephone call that need not be made unless there is some special factor which places the parties in a relationship of proximity. *Banque Financiere* v. *Westgate Insurance* [84] is a case which demonstrates that there is no point in claiming that others should warn one of fraud. The unfortunate bank in this case had made substantial loans to a fraudster on the security of gemstones (which proved to be effectively worthless) and credit insurance policies. The defendant, an insurance company, knew that a fraudulent misrepresentation had been made to the bank by an insurance agent, but did not warn the bank of this fact. The bank, which was eager to recover its substantial loss, alleged that this failure had resulted in their falling victim to further frauds and that the insurers should therefore be liable. The House of Lords disagreed, holding that no duty to act existed in this relationship. In the world of business, then, we are not our brother's keeper.

The same rule applies to lawyers advising their clients in the course of their business transactions. While the law is clear enough on the lawyer's duty to draw the attention of his client to matters which have a bearing on his legal position or such of his transactions which are relevant,[85] this duty does not apply to third parties in general. In particular, a lawyer is under no duty to inform those on the opposite side of a transaction that they may be disadvantaged by fraudulent conduct on the part of his client.[86] This changes if there is some act on the part of the lawyer to bring himself into a relationship with the outsider. This process may occur in a variety of ways, although it will most commonly be through the giving of an undertaking or the making of some assurance. In *Allied Finance and Investments Ltd.* v. *Haddow & Co.*[87] the New Zealand Court of Appeal regarded the giving by a solicitor of a certificate to the effect that his client was fully bound by an instrument as creating a duty of care to the opposite party, who relied on the certificate. In *Al Kandari* v. *J.R. Brown & Co.*[88] the solicitors of a husband were held to have assumed responsibility for the welfare of the wife when they agreed to act as custodians of her estranged husband's passport. The wife's misfortunes were laid at their door when they negligently failed to ensure that the husband did not get improper access to the passport.

3.6   The Psychiatrist's Duty to Warn

The imposition on psychiatrists of a duty to prevent their patients causing harm to others is a new and disturbing development which, fortunately, has been largely confined to the United States. The problem first arose in the celebrated case of *Tarasoff* v. *Regents of the University of California*,[89] and action by the parents of a woman murdered by a jealous student whose affections she had not reciprocated. The murderer, Podnar, had consulted a psychotherapist over his feelings for Miss Tarasoff and had confessed his homicidal inclinations: a plot which might well have been dreamed up by Hollywood itself. The failure of the therapist to warn the intended victim of the danger she was in was held to be an actionable wrong to her, and damages were awarded. This was done in spite of the countervalent obligation of confidentiality and the duty of a therapist not to disclose confidences imparted during treatment. Later cases applied the *Tarasoff* principle not only where there was a threat made to a specific person, but also where the therapist was held to be negligent in not foreseeing danger to other persons.[90]

The hostility of the legal climate outside the United States to this extraordinary extension of liability was suspected but not tested until comparatively recently. The opportunity to consider the matter arose in the Canadian case of *Wenden* v. *Trikha*,[91] an action for damages by a woman who had been seriously injured by a mentally disordered driver, who had absconded from a psychiatric hospital. The court endorsed the decision in *Tarasoff*, the judge saying that he had no doubt that the psychiatrist in that case owed a duty of care to the person in respect of whom the patient had revealed his homicidal tendencies. Whether or not there was such a duty of care would depend on the proximity of the relationship between the psychiatrist and the person at risk. The court in *Wenden* did not decide this crucial question, as it was held that the requisite standard of care had been met in respect of the patient in question and that there had been no case for further closer supervision in the particular circumstances of the case. Yet the court's agreement with the imposition of a duty of care in *Tarasoff*, and its acceptance of the possibility that a duty of care may have existed in a case such as this, is significant. Ultimately, it would seem that the deciding factor will be the 'just and reasonable' test and that, in deciding this, the consequences of the imposition of liability on psychiatrists and hospitals would be taken into consideration. A strong argument against liability could certainly be made; the issue of breach of confidence would have to be addressed, as would the question of whether liability would make hospitals unduly cautious in their assessments as to potential dangerousness – with resulting inroads on the freedom allowed to those suffering from mental disorder.

On what possible basis is the liability of the psychiatrist founded in a case such as this? Foreseeability itself is insufficient, although it is a necessary condition before a duty of care can be inferred. The focus must therefore be on the assumption of duty which occurs when the psychiatrist takes responsibility for a patient's treatment. But why should responsibility for a patient's health include responsibility for the patient's conduct? The judge in *Wenden* was prepared to say that a psychiatrist has a duty to control a patient, but does not explain why this duty should exist. In the case of an involuntarily detained patient (which the patient in that case was not) this duty might be seen as part of the whole rationale of detention, but the same does not apply where there is no *custodial* responsibility for the patient. The mere fact that the doctor accepts responsibility for the patient's treatment should not, of itself, give rise to further responsibility for harm caused by that patient. It is difficult to see why a psychiatrist who does not have any custodial responsibility should be under a duty to warn a third party of damage which the patient might cause to him when there is no comparable duty on the part of any other person who has the same knowledge which is, however, obtained from another source. If I, a perfect stranger, am told by a mentally disordered person in the street that he proposes to cause harm to the next person who walks past him I am under no legal duty to inform the approaching victim. Why should the psychiatrist, in a non-custodial context, have any greater duty? The only reason of any weight is that the psychiatrist, even when he is not a custodian, is deemed to have a public duty to fulfil by virtue of his professional relationship.

The imposition of such a duty is a major step, and it is easy to imagine the objections which the psychiatric profession might be expected to have to their being singled out in this way. Mentally disordered persons may be dangerous, but so too are fraudsters, and in the commercial cases the courts have been at pains to establish that people such as insurers and accountants have no responsibility to warn others of the danger posed by such persons. Then there is the question of whether a similar public duty would be imposed on other doctors whose patients are a potential danger to others. Consistency would suggest that it should, and yet the consequences of doing this in the case of doctors dealing with sexually transmitted diseases would be almost entirely deleterious. If the principle of strict confidence were to be breached in such cases, then the willingness of people to consult about such intimate matters could well be affected.

3.7   The Just and Reasonable Test as a Basis for a Duty to Rescue

The duty of care issue in tort has been a source of great instability and confusion over the last two decades and it is difficult to predict with any confidence the future contours of the law in this area. The main cause of the confusion has been the fact that the law has been trying to satisfy two occasionally antipathetic goals – that of doing justice between those who cause loss and suffer it and that of keeping liability within such bounds as make it possible for people to avoid frequent and potentially crippling claims. In attempting to adopt a principled approach to this issue, the courts have had to wrestle with exactly the same sort of moral problems which have faced philosophers in their own attempts to identify the scope of our moral obligations to others. The moral element in civil liability is never far below the surface, and it frequently reveals itself once the concepts of civil liability are scrutinised. 'Proximity' may not sound like a term which carries a great deal of moral baggage, and yet many of the notions which give proximity some content are clearly normative. This is particularly so with the 'just and reasonable' test, which has emerged as an important basis for the inference of proximity and as a powerful means of reining in legal enthusiasm to compensate plaintiffs. The problem with this phrase, though, is its vagueness: it provides no guidance as to why it should be reasonable to compensate in one case and not in another. What makes a plaintiff's claim a reasonable one will inevitably depend on (possibly unexpressed) notions of foreseeability or remoteness, or indeed on considerations of policy.

The cases discussed above show that the law in common law countries is prepared to attribute liability for failure to rescue in certain defined situations where some special 'proximity-creating' factor is present. These categories are not closed, and it is quite open for courts in the future to extend the concept of proximity to include cases of failure to rescue which are not currently covered. Proximity, after all, has been shown to be a flexible concept. Is it unreasonable to expect a person to effect a rescue when the rescue can be easily carried out, when there be minimal inconvenience to the rescuer, and when the consequences of failure to rescue will be catastrophic for the person in peril? The answer is surely that it is not unreasonable to expect action in such a case, and indeed we might be inclined to use the word 'unreasonable' to describe the conduct of the non-rescuer here. It might also be possible to use the doctrine of reliance to construct a relationship of proximity in such cases. The fact that the reliance of the plaintiff may have come into existence only after the danger has materialised does not necessarily change the moral force of reliance. Reliance is not a contractual notion, requiring an offer and acceptance of help; it may come into existence unilaterally, and the person relied upon may be a reluctant party throughout.

Against any such extension of the doctrine of proximity is to be weighed the frequently repeated dicta of the judges to the effect that there is no legal obligation to rescue those in danger. These are, of course, only *obiter* – judicial remarks which do not bind subsequent courts – and it would be quite open for a court today to rule otherwise. One of the major attractions of a common law system is its flexibility; precedents can be distinguished, sometimes to the point at which they have little force left, and the law can be expanded incrementally. By this process the law may transform itself, abandoning a previous rule which was previously thought to be cast in stone. Such changes are particularly appropriate when there has been a change in the social or philosophical premises upon which a rule is based. The hostility of the law of tort to imposing duties of affirmative action is a product of an individualistic ideology which is no longer widely supported. The technical means for changing this now exist in the shape of the malleable and potentially easily expanded notion of proximity. It would do no great violence to the common law if a duty to rescue were to be imposed in certain cases. Yet, even if this is legally possible, is it desirable? Returning to criminal liability, this question requires that one measure the proposed crime against a benchmark of objectives in the criminal law. A system which endorsed legal moralism, and punished conduct which offended the moral convictions of society, may well endorse a policy of punishing non-rescue. The non-rescuer offends our sense of proper conduct; he is selfish and heartless, possibly even cruel. Yet the objection might be made that this is not enough to justify criminal punishment in a liberal system of criminal justice if harm to others is to be taken as the essential ground for the intervention of the criminal law.

Does one who fails to rescue cause harm to another? In those cases where a recognised obligation-creating relationship exists, we would probably have no hesitation in saying that inaction is the cause of harm. It does no violence to our sense of language and causation to say that the inattentive gaoler is the cause of the harm which befalls the vulnerable prisoner set upon by his fellow inmates. But what of the non-rescuing stranger? He would probably not be said to have caused the harm that befalls the person in peril, and yet many people would still consider him worth punishing. The causing of harm to an individual is an important ground of punishment, but is not necessarily the only one. There are numerous criminal offences where the harm in question is to some social interest. For example, in a jurisdiction where voting is compulsory, a failure to vote in an election harms the social interest in political participation. Perverting the course of justice is another offence where there may be no harm to a particular individual, but where society as a whole is undoubtedly weakened by the commission of an offence. A failure to rescue might conceivably be put into a similar category of wrongs. The harm suffered by the victim comes from a source other than the non-rescuer; yet the failure to rescue might still be punished on the grounds that a social interest in helpful conduct is weakened by non-rescue. We are all stronger if we know that we will be rescued by others if needs be; in a society where this assumption cannot be made, we are all considerably more vulnerable.

Even if a case were to be made out for the criminalisation of failure to rescue, the conclusion does not automatically follow that civil liability is desirable. The law of tort requires a clear causal link between the harm suffered and the defendant's conduct. The non-rescuing stranger might be expected to say: 'Your damage has got nothing to do with me. I did not cause it.' And at one level he would be right. It might be argued that his inaction comes into the causal sequence and can be regarded as a cause of the damage, but, however theoretically attractive this might be, it offends the 'common sense' notions of causation applied by the courts. The process of transferring loss is very different from the process of blaming for criminal purposes.

Ultimately, it may be argued that there is a realm of relations between persons which is best left to non-legal regulation of private individuals, and the duty to rescue could well be within such a realm. The threat of criminal prosecution does not always make people treat others better: a society with an intrusive and draconian criminal code is unlikely to be a better place to live than one which has a minimalist and non-intrusive criminal law. Nor will the threat of civil litigation necessarily make people more beneficent in their dealings with others; they may be more careful, but that does not amount to the same thing as being more concerned. Such arguments are seductive, and yet there are grounds for resisting them. What would the consequences be, for example, of abandoning legislation which makes it a criminal offence to discriminate against others on the grounds of their race? Such discrimination could become more acceptable and the educative function of the law be lost. The duty to rescue might be seen as analogous. It is perfectly possible to accept that, for the most part, the way in which people discharge their duties towards others will depend on their personal moral intuitions, and yet this need not exclude some guidance from the law. After all, a powerful means – perhaps now the only realistic means – of social denunciation of wrongful behaviour is through public legal proceedings. For this reason, the non-rescuer perhaps deserves the attention of the law rather than its disapproving neglect.

Notes

1   [1979] 1 Ch. 344.
2   The legal implications of the duty to rescue are extensively discussed in J. Ratcliffe (Ed.) , *The Good Samaritan and the Law* (London, 1966). For a comprehensive discussion of civil law duties to act and their implications, see M. Shapo, *The Duty to Act* (Austin, 1977).
3   T. Macaulay, 'Notes on the Indian Penal Code' in 7 *Works*, 494 (1897).
4   Discussed by L. Katz, *Bad Acts and Guilty Minds* (Chicago, 1987).
5   There is a voluminous criminal law literature on the subject of omissions. The following are of particular interest: A. Ashworth 'The scope of criminal liability for omissions', 105 *Law Quarterly Review*, 424 (1989); J. Kleinig, 'Criminal liability for failures to act', 49 *Law and Contemporary Problems*, 161 (1986); J. Smith, 'Liability for omissions in the criminal law', 4 *Legal Studies*, 88 (1984); G. Hughes, 'Criminal omissions,' 67 *Yale Law Journal*, 590 (1958).
6   H.L.A. Hart and A.M. Honoré, *Causation in the Law* (Oxford, 2nd ed., 1985), 38.
7   The question of identifying morally significant omissions is dealt with by Joel Feinberg in his *Harm to Others* (New York, 1984).
8   Coke, 3, *Institutes*, 47.
9   B. Fisse (Ed.), *Howard's Criminal Law,* (Sydney, 1990), 25.
10   [1968] Justiciary Cases 32
11   (1991) 52 Australian Criminal Reports, 15.
12   [1983] 2 AC 161; [1983] 1 All E.R. 978.
13   (1969) 121 Commonwealth Law Reports 205; [1966–67] Australian Law Journal Reports 488.
14   [1969] 1 QB 439; [1968] 3 All E.R. 442.
15   (1988) 34 Australian Criminal Reports 334.
16   [1933] Victorian Law Reports 59.
17   [1981] A.C. 394.
18   Children and Young Persons Act 1933, s.1.
19   For an analysis of the Australian statutes, see S. Parker, 'The Australian child support schemes', 20 *Family Law*, 210 (1990).
20   [1893] 1 Q.B. 450.
21   [1977] Q.B. 354.
22   For an interesting account of the grounds of obligation to family members, see J. Eekelaar, 'Are parents morally obliged to care for their children?', 11 *Oxford Journal of Legal Studies*, 340 (1991).
23   (See *Instan supra*, n. 20).

24   For discussion, see N. Daniels, *Am I my Parents' Keeper?* (New York, 1988).

25   (1869) 11 Cox's Criminal Cases 210.

26   (1902) 19 Times Law Reports 37. This case is further discussed by J. Smith, op. cit., *supra*, n. 5., and by H. Benyon, 'Doctors as Murderers', *Criminal Law Review*, 171 (1982).

27   1983 Scottish Criminal Cases Reports 161.

28   [1907] 1 K.B. 571. For discussion, see K. Smith, *A Modern Treatise on the Law of Criminal Complicity* (Oxford, 1991), 40.

29   [1940] 1 K.B. 571.

30   *Harris* [1964] Criminal Law Review, 54.

31   *Cassady v. Reg Morris (Transport) Ltd* [1975] Road Traffic Reports 470.

32   [1970] 1 All E.R. 1171.

33   See also the Australian case of *Dennis v. Pight* (1968) 11 Federal Law Reports 458.

34   [1971] 55 Criminal Appeal Reports 445.

35   (1882) 8 Q.B.D. 534.

36   (1841) Car & M. 314.

37   *The Times*, October 1976.

38   *Sherlock* (1886) L.R. 1.

39   D. Nicholson, 'The citizen's duty to assist the police', *Criminal Law Review* 611 (1992).

40   [1981] Appeal Cases 394; [1980] 3 W.L.R. 960; [1980] 3 All E.R. 899.

41   1985 44 Criminal Reports (3d) 193.

42   *Wagner v. International R.R.* 133 N. E. 437 (New York, 1921).

43   A. Linden, 'Rescuers and Good Samaritans', 34 *Modern Law Review*, 241 (1971).

44   [1935] 1 K.B. 146.

45   (1961) 106 C.L.R. 112.

46   [1987] 2 W.L.R. 988 (C.A.)

47   (1975) 51 D.L.R. (3d) 1.

48   [1972] S.C.R. 441.

49   (1978) 84 D.L.R. (3d) 650.

50   *Chapman* (*supra*, n. 45).

51   [1981] 3 All E.R. 679.

52   *Horsley* (*supra*, n. 48).

53   [1932] A.C. 562.

54   [1978] A.C. 728.

55   The *Anns* test was widely criticised, being described by one commentator as 'monstrous': T. Weir, *A Casebook on Tort* (London, 1992). Judges, too, disliked it: see, for example, dissenting views of *Anns* in *Peabody Donation Fund v. Parkinson* [1985] A.C. 210; *Takaro Properties* [1988] 1 A.C. 473; *Yuen Kun Yeu v. Attorney-General of Hong Kong* [1988] A.C. 175.

56   [1991] A.C. 398; [1990] 3 W.L.R. 414; [1990] 2 All E.R. 908.

57   (1984) 155 C.L.R. 549.

58   (1985) 157 C.L.R. 459.

59   [1987] A.C. 421.

60   For further analysis of this point, see J. Logie, 'Special relationships, reasonable foreseeability and distinct probabilities: the duty to prevent damage to the property of others', *Juridical Review* 77 (1988); B. Makesinis, 'Negligence, nusiance and affirmative duties of action', 105 *Law Quarterly Review*, 104 (1989).

61   *Sutherland* (*supra*, n. 58).

62   At 478.

63   [1970] A.C. 1004.

64   At 1027.

65   [1957] V.R. 439.

66 At 446.
67 73 D.L.R. (4th) 33.
68 *Miller (supra,* n. 12).
69 1986 S.L.T. 30.
70 *Smith* v. *Littlewoods (supra,* n. 59).
71 *Bonar (supra,* n. 27).
72 [1988] 2 All E.R. 238.
73 4 C.C.L.T. (2d) 78 (1990).
74 *Anns (supra,* n. 54).
75 At 115.
76 72 D.L.R. (4th) 580 (1990).
77 At 584.
78 74 D.L.R. (4th) 636.
79 For a consideration of this requirement, see *Haig* v. *Bamford* (1976) 72 D.L.R. (3d) 68.
80 [1989] 1 All E.R. 273.
81 L. Gruzman, 'Liability of search and rescue authorities for negligence', 65 *Australian Law Journal,* 646 (1991).
82 (1985) 157 C.L.R. 424.
83 (1987) 676 F Supp 1193.
84 [1990] 2 All E.R. 947.
85 *Crossan* v. *Ward Bracewell* [1988] 1 All E.R. 364.
86 *Seaway Trust* v. *Markle* 7 C.C.L.T. (2d) 83.
87 [1983] N. Z.L.R. 22.
88 [1988] 1 All E.R. 833.
89 131 Cal Reptr 14 (1976).
90 As in *Lipari* v. *Sears Roebuck Co.* 497 Fed Supp (1980).
91 (1991) 8 C.C.L.T. (2d) 138.

3 Failure to Rescue and the Continental Criminal Law

ALBERTO CADOPPI

1 Introduction

> One who does not defend against or prevent the occurrence of harm –
> if it is within his power to do so – is in the wrong just as if he had
> deserted his parents, friends or country.

Cicero[1] wrote in these terms more than two thousand years ago, yet
his words still seem to reflect the modern attitude of continental
European legislation towards the duty to rescue. It is something of a
truism among common lawyers that in civil law countries, as a rule, a
general duty to rescue persons in peril is imposed upon every citizen.
This is not the case in common law countries, where, as has already
been pointed out in Chapter 2 – with the limited exceptions of a
couple of states in the United States of America – a similar duty is
recognised only in very special circumstances.

The practical implications of this are remarkable. If a man walks
through Trafalgar Square and sees an unknown child drowning in
the famous fountains, he is not bound under English law to do anything at all. If the same person is sitting by Bernini's marvellous
fountain in Rome's Piazza Navona, he will be guilty of a criminal
offence if he does not rescue a child in a similar plight. This most
astonishing difference between the approach of the common law and
the civil law to this matter has always interested lawyers. This interest is understandable, because the sharp contrast between the two
legal traditions in this context could lead one to think that the whole
philosophy of the two systems is different: the common law would
appear to be inspired by a totally individualistic *Weltanschauung* expressed in the maxim: 'You shall *not do* to others what you do not

want them to do to you.' The civil law – on the contrary – would appear to find its foundations in a communal *Weltanschauung* and in the maxim '*Do* to others what you would like them to do to you.'[2]

The reasons for this marked difference of approach are complex. There is no simple sociological explanation as to why the two traditions are so at odds on this question. The real key to the matter is to be found in legal history, and it is to this that we must look to see how, mainly in the second half of the nineteenth century, European continental systems embraced a legally enforced duty to rescue. The historical background established, one might then look at the way in which these statutes have been interpreted and expanded, for the story of the duty to rescue is by no means over in continental jurisdictions.

2   Defining the Issue

The concept of a duty to rescue can occur in numerous different contexts. A mother has a duty to rescue her baby; a guard has a duty to rescue the person he is protecting, and so on. There are also duties to rescue which arise from particular requests of the authorities, or which come into existence on very special occasions (earthquakes, floods, commission of crimes, and so on). Finally, in many jurisdictions, everybody has a duty to rescue small children, or to inform the authorities of the finding of infants.

My concern is not with these special duties to rescue – flowing from the particular position of the *obligée*, the peculiar nature of the peril, or of the character of the person in peril. My focus, rather, is on a more *general* kind of duty to rescue – the duty that everyone has to rescue another person 'in peril'. Of course, the statutes are always more precise, and impose certain limitations on this broad duty. Yet the overall philosophy remains the same. Where a 'general' duty to rescue is imposed, the person obliged is not a 'special' person; the cause of the peril is not 'special'. Nor does the person in peril have to be somebody in particular. This is the most interesting aspect of the matter, because it is here that the imposition of a duty to rescue becomes more problematic. Special duties to rescue are imposed even in Anglo-American jurisdictions ('hit and run' statutes are an example of this). The real difference between common law and civil law systems lies in the fact that in the former – with rare exceptions – no criminal statute imposes a *general* duty to rescue; in the latter, by contrast, the rule is very much the imposition of such duties by the means of the criminal law. (As far as the notion of 'rescue' is concerned, I will deal with this problem in Section 5. 4 below.)

Another matter must be stressed. Where a bad samaritan statute exists, it does not mean that the law will automatically impose criminal liability for the *result* that may be caused by the omission, an issue that is perhaps best illustrated by means of an example. In Italy, there is just such a statute and, if Michele sees Stefano, an unknown person, in peril, he is bound by the law to rescue him. So if he does not comply with the duty and just walks by, he will be liable to a criminal penalty (of up to three months in jail) for the omission. But if the omission results in the death of Stefano, Michele will not be responsible for homicide. *Mens rea* is not the issue here. Michele might even desire Stefano's death and know that the death is likely to take place, because Stefano lies in a very remote place where nobody will presumably happen to walk by, and his physical condition is extremely serious. But he will still not be punishable for murder, or even manslaughter. This is the case in most continental countries.[3] Why is this? The reason is that there is a clear difference – at least in civil law jurisdictions – between so called 'pure', 'simple', 'proper' or 'genuine' crimes of omission, and 'impure', 'improper' or 'non-genuine' crimes of omission, also known as crimes of 'commission by omission'. The first category includes all those crimes that consist of the mere *non-performance* of an action required by the law. They are the product of an ad hoc statute, and do not presuppose the causation of any result (or 'event') as a consequence of the omission. They are normally petty offences, frequently *mala prohibita*, and the penalties provided for them are usually lenient. Examples of this category of 'pure' crimes of omission include misprision of felony, omission to file a tax return, and, of particular interest for our present purpose, not rescuing a person in peril.

Very different are the 'non-genuine' crimes of omission. They are nothing else than 'classical' offences which, although normally committed through an action, can be realised by means of an omission in particular cases. They are result crimes, in most cases *mala in se*, and the penalties provided for them are normally serious. Such crimes can usually be committed through an *action* by *anybody*, but only a *few people* can commit them by means of an *omission*. An example will clarify the matter. Murder is usually committed by means of an action, but exceptionally an omission is sufficient for the offence. If a wicked mother does not feed her baby and sadistically watches her slowly dying, all the while desiring her baby's death, she will be held responsible for murder, even if she did no more than omit to feed the unfortunate baby. A crime which may ordinarily be committed by action can be commited by omission only when a person has the *duty to prevent the occurrence of the result* of which the crime consists. The mother has a duty to prevent the death of her baby. So, if she does not feed her, she will be responsible for her death: she will commit manslaughter or murder, depending on the *mens rea* that she has demonstrated. In continental legal thought, such a person is considered to be in a so-called position of guaranty in respect of the interest protected by the criminal law. In the specific case, the mother must guarantee the life of the baby. And if she does not act in order to prevent her death, it is proper to consider her omission equivalent to the active causation of that result.[4] Only very special persons are considered by the law – or more correctly by its interpreters – to be 'guarantors' (in this sense) of legal interests. The duty to prevent the result must be founded upon a specific legislative provision protecting the relevant legal interests. In this respect continental law does not differ from the common law. The limitations suggested by Lord Macaulay in his draft of the Indian Penal Code are more or less the same as those to be found outlined in a European criminal law textbook in the field of 'commission by omission'. Only such persons as parents, soldiers, life-guards, firemen, and certain other public officers – and only in certain circumstances – are guarantors of legal interests.

When we consider the general duty to rescue imposed by civil law bad samaritan statutes on anyone who sees (or comes to know about) another person in peril, we must note that this duty is normally confined to a vague duty to help other people in distress. It is not to be intended as an obligation *to prevent* physical damage to or the death of the person in peril. The samaritan is not a guarantor of the life or limb of his neighbour in distress. The failure to comply with the law implies, as its only consequence, the penalty provided by the statute for the breach of that duty; it does not render the bad samaritan legally responsible for any result such as the death of the person in peril. Even in those countries where a duty to rescue is imposed by the law, the non-rescuing stranger will never be responsible for the *death* of his unknown neighbour in peril, although he may well be criminally liable for the breach of his statutory duty to act. This feature has to be kept in mind. I will analyse statutes that are not crimes of commission by omission, but which create pure crimes of omission, most of which are punished leniently, and are independent of any result.

There is one final point. Athough, as we shall see, some statutes limit the offence only to those cases in which a result (death or physical damage) does ensue, this does not really change the perspective, or the philosophy, of these statutes. The result here does not have the effect of transforming a genuine crime of omission into a crime of commission by omission. Even when the statute provides for a slightly increased penalty, the function of the increased penalty is only more effectively to deter the bad samaritan. Even here the penalties are anyway much lower than the ones provided for in the correlative result crimes. In civil law countries, then, the usual goal is to impose an ill-defined duty to rescue irrespective of the result. We shall now look at the history of these pure crimes of omission.

3 The History of the Duty to Rescue in Civil Law Countries

3.1 *From Ancient Times to the End of the Eighteenth Century*

According to Pufendorf the ancient Egyptians recognised a legal duty to rescue:

> Whoever found in his path a person in danger of being killed or mistreated in any way, and being able to protect him from the danger which menaced him, and who did not act, was punished by death. If one felt incapable of preventing the menace, one had at least to denounce the person who had caused the danger, and to participate in the bringing of the brigand to justice. If one failed to do this, one received a certain number of lashes and one was condemned to eat nothing for three days.[5]

Plato in his *Laws* included more than one bad samaritan statute. These were not *general* duties to rescue in the aforesaid sense, but they were nonetheless quite broad. The penalties were sometimes harsh: in one case entailing even 'Zeus' curse'. Plato also provided some rewards for good samaritans, such as the place of honour at the games or the liberation from slavery. This is a very interesting feature that will be found later on in the history of duty to rescue legislation. In Rome, by contrast, no general duty to rescue was imposed, and more generally pure crimes of omission played a limited role in Roman law.[6]

Bad samaritans were severely punished in the ancient laws of the Germans. Within the *Sippe* the motto was 'Einer für alle, alle für einem', and this implied a general duty to aid neighbours in distress. But criminal responsibility presupposed a result.[7] It is disputed whether canon law regarded such a duty as legally relevant, although it was morally binding in the view of Saint Augustine, Saint Thomas and other philosophers.[8] Some think that Pufendorf favours such a duty,[9] but a close analysis of his works belies this view. He cites – it is true – the sentence from Cicero which begins this chapter, but he stresses more than once the requirement of a special duty before criminal liability for omissions of this kind can arise. He writes:

> When one permits others to act, in the sense that one does not prevent them from acting, one does not inevitably become party to the crime

which those others commit; for this liability to occur it is necessary not only that one has sufficient resources to prevent the actions of others, but also that one has some obligation to oppose them. If one or other of these conditions is lacking, one is responsible for nothing.

More generally, Pufendorf distinguishes two different sorts of obligations, to which correspond perfect and imperfect rights. The general duty to rescue, as any other duty of benevolence, humanity and so on, belongs to the second category; that is, it is an imperfect duty and cannot be sanctioned by the law. A similar distinction is to be found in the writings of many other philosophers, such as Kant,[10] who likewise deny a legally binding general duty to help people in distress.

Criminal lawyers such as Farinacius, Clarus and others, are inclined to admit duties to rescue, but only in special situations, normally in those cases where the person in peril is the victim of a violent crime.[11] By the second half of the eighteenth century, it is possible to find in Germany laws providing for a more or less general duty to rescue. The Bavarian Code of 1751 included one of these statutes, but limited its application to cases of aggression. A broader duty is to be found in the *Constitutio Criminalis Theresiana* of 1768 (art. 3, para 14) and in the *Neue Bambergische Peinlische Gesetzgebung* of 1792/95 (paragraphs 40 ff. Abs. 3, P. I). Even clearer was the para. 782 (Teil II, Tit. 20) of the *Preussisches Allgemeine Landrecht* (ALR) of 1794: 'Who without substantial risk for himself can rescue a man from the hands of the robber or of the murderer, or from water or a fire or from another kind of peril to his life, and omits [to rescue] will, if the other man dies, suffer fourteen days of prison.' Paragraph 785 of that law provided some rewards for the good samaritan. These laws found a supporter in Winckler, a German legal scholar, who, in his doctoral dissertation *De crimine omissionis* (1776) – probably the first contribution ever written especially on crimes of omission – argues that the witholding of help (*denegatio auxilii*) violates Natural Law and deserves punishment.[12]

3.2   The Nineteenth Century

At the beginning of the nineteenth century the first criminal codes – in the modern sense of the word – appear. In the Napoleonic *Code pénal* of 1810 there is no general duty to rescue. The only provision dealing with the matter is art. 475 n. 12 of the Code, which punishes:

Those who, being capable of acting, refuse or neglect to perform those tasks or to provide such help as is requested of them in cases of accident, disorder, shipwreck, flood, fire or other calamities, and equally in cases of brigandage, pillage, flagrant crime, public affray or judicial execution.[13]

It is clear that the provision is only applicable when there is a request addressed to the bystander by the authorities.

A few years earlier, a commission was at work in Italy on a criminal code for the so called 'Regno italico' (Italic Kingdom). The commission was based in Milan and was the successor of a commission of jurists which had been sitting there for the same purpose since the last decade of the eighteenth century, a member of which was the famous Cesare Beccaria. By 1806, a draft code had been prepared. Article 368 of that draft imposes a general duty to rescue and punishes breaches of this duty with light penalties if no damage ensues from the omission, with more serious penalties if serious damage occurs, and with the penalties provided for culpable homicide if the death derives from the *denegatio auxilii*. The draft code was sent for comment to courts and to influential lawyers. Some courts seemed unwilling to impose such a harsh duty on anyone. The same opinion was held by a particularly eminent criminal lawyer of those times. Luigi Cremani, formerly professor of *ius criminale* at the famous University of Pavia, and author of an important institutional book on the same subject, criticised the provision.[14] In his opinion liability for an omission could not be imposed on anyone at any time, but needed to be imposed only on certain persons at certain times – this is a view that has always been present in European legal doctrine at least since the time of Aquinas.[15] Less critical was the judgement of the commentators on another duty to rescue provision of the same draft code. Article 209 imposed a particular duty to rescue on public medical doctors, obstetricians and chemists.

However the duty to rescue was slow to be accepted. In the draft code of 1809 no duty to rescue is to be found any more, not even one restricted to special persons. This draft code, however, never came into force in Italy. One year later, Napoleon was to impose on the peninsula his *Code pénal*, although it was not to last long outside France: the Restoration was not far off. In other countries, the imposition of a general duty to rescue was, in the first half of the nineteenth century, more or less exceptional. A statute was enacted in 1808 in St Gallen, a Swiss canton, but it covered only certain situations of peril. Another more refined example is to be found in the 'Police' Code of Würtemberg in Germany (art. 32) and in the Criminal Code of the Kanton Thurgau of 1841. But even earlier, article 689 of the Spanish Criminal Code of 1822 stated:

Every person who being able without damage or risk to himself does not give that help of which he is capable to whatever person who is wounded, mistreated, threatened by an unjust aggressor or found in any other situation of conflict which requires humanitarian aid, will be detained for a period from one to six days, or will pay a fine of ten reals to three duros; taking into account the provision in article 128 of the preliminary title.[16]

Article 128 provided for some rewards for good samaritans. This code, though, has never really been applied by the courts. The same provision was embodied in article 578 of the Bolivian Criminal Code of 1834. In 1845, a less secularised bad samaritan statute was enacted in Russia ('If he is a Christian and his heartlessness and lack of care result in the death of the person left without help, he will be subject to ecclesiastical punishment as ordained by his spiritual authorities'!). And in the Spanish Criminal Code of 1848 there is once again included a duty to rescue, although one confined to the finding of the imperilled person in a solitary place (*en despoblado*). But in this half of the nineteenth century similar statutes were still rare and scholars of the period did not always seem to favour them in their academic works.[17]

In the second half of the nineteenth century, similar statutes began to spread throughout Europe: in 1853, the Police Code of Tuscany (articles 97 and 98); in 1854, the Police Code of Modena and Reggio (articles 162); in 1856, the Penal Code of Neuenburg (a Swiss Canton) (punished, though, with the almost ridiculously slight penalty of 5 Franken). Similar provisions appeared in Denmark in 1866, in the Cantons of Oberwalden in 1870 and Ticino in 1873; in Norway in 1874, in the Netherlands in 1881, and in the Italian Criminal Code of 1889. At the end of the last century, then, probably half of the continental systems did recognise a general duty to rescue.

4 Comparative Analysis: The Development of Bad Samaritan Statutes in the Twentieth Century

4.1 Germany

The first criminal code of the newly-unified Germany adopted an individualistic approach to the duty to rescue. In the *Strafgesetzbuch* (StGB) of 1871 there was only one provision dealing with the issue, and this solved the problem in more or less the manner of the 1810 French *Code pénal*. Under paragraph 360, n. 10 of the *Strafgesetzbuch*, 'whosoever, in case of accident, or common danger, or necessity, is requested to help by a police agent or by a person representing him, and does not assist, even though he could comply with the request without fear of serious danger' was punished with a fine of up to 1500 Marks or with a term of imprisonment.

The disposition, which had been given the curious title *Liebesparagraph* (love section), did not really impose a general duty to rescue in the sense previously discussed. Under the Nazi regime this section was strongly criticised and considered the typical product of an individualistic and liberal society. In the new totalitarian and ethical conception of the state, a broader duty to rescue was required: everybody should be required to help his neighbour in distress, even if not requested to do so by the authorities. A new statute was in fact enacted in 1935:

> Whosoever, in case of accident or common danger, or necessity, does not render assistance, even though this is his duty according to sound popular sentiment and, in particular, does not comply with the request for assistance of a police agent, even though he could comply with the request without serious danger and without the infringement of other important duties, is punishable with prison for up to two years or with a fine. (Para. 330c of *StGB*)

A huge number of scholars wrote both before and after the enactment of this statute about duty to rescue (*Unterlassene Hilfeleistung*) and many authors considered the new paragraph 330c as a symbol of the spirit of the Nazi regime.[18] The category of the duty was now beginning to occupy a central role in criminal law theory (the so-called *Pflichtsgedanke*):[19] from this perspective, the criminal offence was not seen any more, as before, as the 'setback of interests' (*Rechtsgutsgedanke*) but as a 'disobedience to a duty'. This should not be a surprise: in a liberal state the harm and offence principles should be the only principles justifying criminalisation,[20] whereas in an authoritarian state any breach of duty (ethical or political) can be criminalised. This paragraph imposed the broadest duty to be found in the whole body of criminal legislation, and this explains why its enactment was so welcomed by those scholars who favoured the duty approach to criminal law. The explicit reference of the statute to 'sound popular sentiment' was consonant with another general feature of Nazi criminal law doctrine. The *gesundes Volksempfinden* was considered to be the cornerstone of the theory of crime, and it allowed courts to expand criminal law beyond the wording of the statutes.[21] Scholars even suggested the sharpening of the law in this context, through the expansion of the sphere of the duty and an increase in penalties.

After the war, the section was not expressly repealed, but courts refused to apply it and scholars considered it incompatible with the values of the new state. In 1953, the statute was amended and the new paragraph 330c (currently paragraph 323) does not contain any

reference to sound popular sentiment. The new statute is more oriented to the protection of the interests of life, or at least is interpreted
that way by scholars and the courts.[22]

4.2   France

As we have already seen, the *Code pénal* of 1810 did not provide for a
general duty to rescue, and for more than 100 years no statute was
enacted on the matter. It was only under the Vichy government, after
a reprisal in which 50 Frenchmen were executed for the killing of a
German officer, that a bad samaritan statute came into force, together
with provisions imposing a general duty to report and prevent crimes.
Article 4 of the law of 25 October 1941, stated:

> Whoever, being capable of preventing through his own and immediate
> act, without harm or risk to himself or those near to him, those crimes
> listed in alinea 1, article 2, and who refrains from doing so, is punish-
> able with imprisonment of up to five years and a fine of 500 to 5000
> francs. The same punishment is incurred by one who, in the same
> conditions, omits to give help to a person in peril if, as a result of the
> failure to help, such a person loses his life or suffers grave physical
> harm, all without prejudice to more severe penalties ...[23]

Some scholars commented harshly on the new law, which one influential academic described as 'repugnant'.[24] Other writers welcomed
it as a triumph for the Christian ideal of charity.[25] In 1945, the statute
was amended and the penalties were reduced, but the offence became punishable even if no result ensued. The statute was also
amended in 1954, when the penalties were again increased, and this
is the version still in force. The reason for the particular harshness of
the penalties will be explained later.

4.3   Belgium

In Belgium progress towards the recognition of a general duty to
rescue has been slower than in France. Until 1961, no bad samaritan
statute was ever in force, and it was only in the 1950s that the problem started to be debated and the first draft statutes appeared.
     Some scholars, Jean Constant for example, approved similar pro-
posals, pointing out that in an age of egoism there were those who
would undoubtedly be encouraged in their failure to do their moral
duty by the silence of the legislature on such matters.[26] Other authors
were firmly opposed to such proposals. They stressed an individualistic conception of criminal law, underlining the uselessness of such a
statute, and regarded the proposed law as totalitarian. For example:

'The duty to rescue is a purely moral duty; the intrusion of the law into the realm of individual conscience would soon become intolerable.'[27] Nevertheless, legislation was enacted on 6 January 1961, with the insertion of article 422 *bis* into the Belgian Penal Code (see List of Statutory Provisions).

4.4 Spain

In Spain, from 1848 to 1951, the duty to rescue was limited to those cases in which the person in peril was *en despoblado* (in a solitary place). A failure to rescue was a mere 'contravention' (that is, a petty offence) and was punished only with light penalties. In 1951, a new statute was enacted and inserted in the Criminal Code article 489 *bis*:

> Who does not rescue a person whom he finds without protection and in obvious and serious danger, when he can effect rescue without risk to himself or to another, may be imprisoned or fined between 1000 and 5000 pesetas.
> The same penalties will be imposed upon anyone who, unable to render any rescue, does not immediately ask for help from others.

Academics have generally welcomed this new law, and have stressed the importance of a similar provision for the protection of the interest of 'human solidarity'. Some commentators, though, seem excessively enthusiastic and over-state the religious dimension of this duty. Alamillo Camillas, for example, wrote:

> That which the Christian should observe is contained in the Ten Commandments. However these Commandments, in the way in which they are stated (with the exception of the first four), appear to contain only negative duties of abstention. So they were understood by their early adherents, and it was necessary to come to the Divine Master to seek interpretation of the essence of those, promulgating the law of love: 'These ten Commandments may be reduced to two: to serve and love God above all things and to value your neighbour as you value yourself.' With that the Lord would have us understand that the Law is not exclusively concerned with negative duties of abstention, without including positive duties, duties of action, since love is altruism, not egoism.[28]

More recently, in 1956, a third paragraph was added to section 489 *bis*, making an aggravating circumstance if the peril is caused by the bad samaritan. The statute has then been further extended to require the samaritan to rescue even if he does not find the person in peril; it is enough that he knows about it.

4.5   *Austria and Portugal*

In Austria, there was no tradition of bad samaritan statutes. Rather, since the Code of 1803, and even before, the practice has been of a duty to prevent the commission of certain crimes. The general continental trend towards the recognition of the duty to rescue, though, no doubt played a role in persuading the Austrian legislature to enact a good samaritan statute in 1975.

The situation in Portugal is similar. A general duty to rescue had been in force at least since 1867, but it was confined only to the Civil Code. However, in 1982, Portugal enacted a new criminal code, which followed in many respects the German and Austrian theory and legislation. As a result, the new article 219 is a bad samaritan statute that is similar to the German and the Austrian statutes. Influential Portuguese scholars have welcomed this new law.[29]

4.6   *Other Civil Law Countries*

Switzerland, Finland, Norway, Iceland, Denmark, The Netherlands, Greece, Turkey and San Marino all have bad samaritan statutes in their Criminal Codes, and most of them have had them for a long time. The situation in Sweden is different. The Swedes discussed the problem during the preparation of the Criminal Code of 1965, but they decided not to adopt such a statute. In 1972, a proposed bad samaritan statute was again rejected by the Swedish Parliament; amongst scholars, however, the question is still open to debate.[30]

In research into Eastern European codes, prior to 1989, I found that in all those states (except Albania) a similar statute was in force.[31] In Latin America, almost every country – except Colombia, Haiti, the Dominican Republic and perhaps Bolivia – provides in its penal code for the punishment of bad samaritans. These codes have their roots, in fact, in continental European codes such as the Italian Code of 1889, and also in various Spanish and Portuguese codes. In Latin American countries, one notices – with few exceptions – an increasing number of such statutes, and an evolution of broader duties to rescue. More than one code, for example, abandons the requirement taken from the Spanish codes that the person in peril must be *en despoblado*. This is the case in both Cuba and Guatemala.

5   Comparative Analysis: Seven Focal Points

Bad samaritan statutes can be lenient or harsh. They can enforce moral duties or moral ideals. They can require minimal actions of solidarity or supererogatory acts. In short, they can impose 'easy' or 'difficult' rescues.[32] There are many elements in the offence which these statutes create, and each of them plays a role in making the rescue easy or difficult. From a comparative law point of view, seven focal points should be considered:

1 the danger for the person in peril;
2 the degree of proximity between the two parties;
3 the danger for the rescuer;
4 the conduct demanded of him;
5 the possible exclusion of the duty to rescue when the action 'cannot be expected' from the potential rescuer;
6 the possible need of a result; and
7 the sanctions.

5.1 The Danger for the Person in Peril

This is a central feature of a bad samaritan statute. To impose a duty to help another person in distress without any specification of the danger would place an intolerable burden upon the average person. In some states, the duty to rescue is limited to cases of *mortal danger*: for example, Finland ('in serious mortal danger'); Norway ('a person whose life is in obvious and imminent danger'). In other jurisdictions, the danger need not be mortal, but has to be in some way qualified or serious: for example, Belgium ('a person exposed to grave peril'); Spain ('in manifest and grave danger'). Most criminal codes do not require anything more than a vague danger for the person or even less than that: for example, Italy ('a person injured or otherwise in danger'); Germany ('accident, common danger or necessity'); Ecuador ('a person who is alone, wounded, mistreated or in danger of death'). This last provision is somewhat ambiguous because it treats equally conditions which are very different from one another. The same has to be said about the Austrian provision which imposes a duty to rescue any person in 'danger of death or of substantial physical damage, or faced with damage to health'. The prospect of damage to health is much less serious than danger to life. In such cases, though, one should consider that the less serious hypothesis will be *sufficient* for the operation of the duty.

5.2 The Degree of Proximity Between the Two Parties

The degree of physical proximity between the two parties is very important because the closer the potential rescuer is to the person in peril, the easier it will be for him to perceive the necessity of his intervention. If I hear on the radio that somebody far away is exposed to a serious danger, I will not feel myself bound to help this person in distress, but if I see a wounded person at the side of the road, I will immediately feel some sympathy for him and feel bound to aid him in some way.

If a duty to rescue is to be imposed on anyone, it will mean that it is to be imposed on those who do not have any close personal relationship with the person in peril. It is important, then, that the law requires at least a physical (or topographical) proximity between the two. Nevertheless, the majority of the criminal codes considered here appear not to require any kind of proximity between the potential rescuer and the person in distress: this is so in Germany, Austria, Portugal, France, Norway, Iceland, Denmark, Greece, Brazil, Cuba, San Marino and Ecuador (where the statute seems to be more ambiguous, though). In Spain in the past the rescuer had to find (*encontrar*) the person in danger. The statute, though, has been interpreted broadly by the courts to convict doctors who refused to visit a patient in serious danger, having been called by telephone. These decisions were severely criticised by certain influential scholars,[33] and the legislature solved the problem by amending the law. There is now no need of any proximity between the two parties.

In other criminal codes there must be sensory contact between the two parties. In The Netherlands the potential rescuer must witness the danger. Elsewhere (Italy, Turkey, Argentina, Mexico, Paraguay, Panama, Peru, Guatemala, Venezuela) the person in peril must be found by the bystander. In Belgium the potential rescuer must have personally seen the peril or have received a reliable request for help. One must keep in mind that this focal point is particularly susceptible to discretionary and adventurous interpretations by scholars and the courts. In Germany, for example, although the statute does not specify the degree of proximity, academics and judges sometimes try to limit what would otherwise be the indefinite extension of the statute in this regard.[34] By contrast, in countries where the statute requires particular proximity between the two parties, courts and scholars are often tempted to extend the limits of the statute.[35] The contrasting discussion of proximity in the common law is dealt with in Chapter 2, Section 2.1.

5.3   *The Danger for the Samaritan*

This element is of course of central importance in determining the degree of difficulty of the rescue. A law that imposed on the man in the street a duty to help his neighbour in distress even if he runs serious risks in complying with that duty would be an intolerably harsh law. Even the oldest bad Samaritan statutes (see Section 3) exempted the rescuer from acting in certain cases. Nevertheless, modern codes differ in this respect. Most criminal codes exclude the offence when the rescuer runs *a risk of any degree*.[36] In some countries the responsibility is waived only if the danger is serious: Germany and Portugal (for the rescuer only) and Belgium (for the rescuer *or third parties*). In the remaining criminal codes the risk for the rescuer is ignored in the statute: this occurs only in Italy, Turkey, San Marino and Panama. The same happens in Paraguay, but, as will be seen, there the duty is limited to something less than a proper rescue. In these jurisdictions, the only possible remedy for the accused is the defence of necessity, which is usually difficult to prove as it requires something more than just a risk on the part of the rescuer.

5.4 The Conduct Requested of the Bystander

It goes without saying that the conduct requested of the bystander is a focal point in measuring the level of difficulty of the duty. If a rescuer is merely required to inform the police or a hospital, his liberty is much less restricted than were he obliged to effect a rescue on his own. A duty to inform the authorities can be, as will be shown, an appropriate substitute for a proper duty to rescue. In some countries the duty imposed is to perform a rescue.[37] In other countries the bystander is obliged either to rescue or to promote a rescue by someone else.[38] Finally, certain other criminal codes, for example the Italian code, apparently leave it to the discretion of the bystander to decide whether to rescue or to inform the authorities.[39] Generally, scholars and courts are inclined to require a rescue, leaving to the bystander the decision whether or not to inform the police only when the rescue is impossible or unnecessary.[40]

5.5 The Exclusion of the Duty to Rescue when the Action 'Cannot Be Expected' from the Samaritan (Unzumutbarkeit)

A few other countries provide for another, more general limitation to the duty to aid, the limitation that the rescue 'cannot [reasonably] be expected' from the bystander. These are cases in which the rescuer would not run any real risk (in relation to his own life or limb) in performing the rescue, but would nonetheless be seriously inconvenienced or placed in the position of violating other important duties. For example, if one can easily rescue another, instead of visiting an aged parent who is extremely ill, it would be excessively harsh to punish that person if she failed to rescue. In this, and other similar, exceptional cases, a duty to rescue cannot be imposed, even though the potential rescuer does not run any physical risk in complying with the duty.

This is an application of the German criminal law doctrine of *Unzumutbarkeit*. It is not *zumutbar*, that is, it cannot be expected of the *obligé* that he perform a duty which in the exceptional circumstances would be unduly onerous. This doctrine is particularly applicable in relation to negligence and omission. Therefore it is especially appropriate in respect of an offence such as a failure to rescue, since the duty, in this case, is to a high degree invasive of personal liberty and is not imposed by virtue of a person's special role. This limitation of the duty is provided for in Germany, Austria and Portugal, where this German doctrine has been received with particular enthusiasm. A similar defence seems to be available in Norway and Denmark where the performance of the helping behaviour is required only when this does not demand any sacrifice of the rescuer or others.

5.6   The Need of a Result

Whether or not a result is needed in order to entail criminal liability is of course another important question for a bad samaritan statute. One must bear in mind the point already discussed (Section 2), that the need of a result (death, physical damage and so on) will almost never transform the offence of failure to render assistance into a crime of commission by omission. Amongst the jurisdictions considered here, only one country, The Netherlands, requires as a result the death of the person in peril. This is in virtue of an 1881 statute, which is still in force. In some states the offence is fully completed without the result, but if a result ensues the penalties are increased.[41] In all the remaining countries the presence or absence of a result does not make any difference: it can only affect the sentencing.

5.7   The Sanctions

The sanctions imposed for a failure to rescue are normally very lenient. This feature makes such a law more acceptable and supports the idea that the breach of such a duty only implies the perpetration of a pure offence of omission – a petty offence – and not a crime of commission by omission, the penalties for which should be much more serious. In most criminal codes the penalty can be alternatively detention or a fine.[42] In numerous countries – mainly Latin American – only a fine can be imposed.[43] In Portugal and France, both detention and a fine must be imposed. In Greece and San Marino (at least according to the crime provided for by art. 162) the bad samaritan must be punished with detention: no fines are employed by the statute.

The highest penalties are provided for in France, where the minimum period of detention is three months and the maximum is five years. This is because the French statute is probably the only example of a statute whose function is not only that of creating a genuine crime of omission, but also that of enabling judges to punish people who have special duties to rescue – especially doctors – and who cause harm through their omission. In short, with article 63 of the *Code pénal*, the legislator had more in mind a commission by omission than a pure omission. This is because the French code lacked, at the time – and since 1810 – any provision comparable to, article 40, paragraph 2 of the Italian Penal Code, or paragraph 13 of the German *Strafgesetzbuch*. Both these statutes concern the problem of commission by omission, and make punishable the perpetration of a crime described by the law as a crime of commission (for example homicide) by means of an omission, whenever the agent has a duty to prevent the specified result. Rather than following these examples, France adopted a novel solution,[44] creating an offence which embodied features of both pure omission and commission by omission. This is why the penalties are high, and why the statute has been inserted in the general part of the Penal Code, that part concerning the general principles of criminal liability. Every other country locates bad samaritan statutes in the special part, that is to say, the part concerned with individual offences and penalties.

One more observation on the penalties: in some countries (Spain, Austria and Portugal) penalties are higher if the bad samaritan was the same person who provoked the danger to the person in need of rescue. This is an application of the German doctrine of *Ingerenz*, originally construed in the area of crimes of commission by omission. By this doctrine, if a person – even accidentally – put someone else in danger, he would be particularly bound to prevent further harm to the person in peril. By providing for an 'aggravating circumstance', the legislator finds a middle way between the solution of punishing this fact as a result crime (should a result ensue) or as a pure crime of omission.

5.8 Comparative Law Summary

Bad samaritan statutes in the criminal codes of western Europe and Latin America are changing in number and nature. There is a growth in number because until the 1930s important jurisdictions such as France, Germany, Spain, Portugal, Belgium and Austria did not have such a statute; in the 1950s new statutes were enacted in Germany and France, and a duty to rescue was imposed in Spain. In the 1960s a bad Samaritan law was passed in Belgium, in the 1970s in Austria, and in the 1980s in Portugal.

There is a change in the nature of these statutes in that duties to rescue – with some explicable exceptions[45] – are now both wider and sanctioned with higher penalties. A few examples will suffice. In Spain the duty was originally restricted to cases in which the person in peril was found in a solitary place, and the finding had to be by the samaritan himself (see Section 4.4.). Both these limitations have been waived by subsequent legislation, which has also provided for the aggravating factors mentioned in Section 5.7. In many Latin American statutes, as has been pointed out, the same limitation of the 'solitary place' has been removed in recent years.

In more than one country, penalties have been increased. In the nineteenth century, most of the bad samaritan statutes (for example, the Italian code of 1889) limited the sanction to a mere fine. The most recent European statutes impose detention *or* a fine, and the only countries in which the penalty is still a simple pecuniary one are Turkey and Latin American countries, whose statutes are based on the Italian, Spanish and Portuguese codes of the last century. On the other hand, the structure and significance of the duty to rescue has changed a great deal in recent years. In ancient law, the duty to rescue was mainly limited to (or confused with) the duty to prevent the commission of criminal offences (see the Egyptian example, Section 3.1). Responsibility for the violation of the duty was mainly discussed as a question of participation in the crime committed by the aggressor. In not preventing a crime, one became an accessory.[46] The question was: 'Qui prohibere potuit, nec prohibuit, an reus criminis?' ('He who could prevent, and who did not: is he guilty of a crime?').[47] Through the medium of the morally oriented Canon lawyers, the problem of duty to rescue gradually became distinct from the problem of non-prevention of a crime, although the perspective was still concentrated on the failure to prevent a harmful event: '*Qui soccurrer perituro potest, si non succurrit, occidit*' ('He who can help an imperilled person, and who does not do so, kills') – so wrote Lactantius, followed by Saint Augustine.[48]

This somewhat archaic view of the duty to rescue endured in the criminal law, both in the doctrines of scholars and in the codes. The bad samaritan statutes of the eighteenth century (see Section 3.1) all made the ensuing of a result, usually the death of the person in peril, a condition of liability. This is the case in more than one nineteenth century statute. By contrast, the modern pattern of bad samaritan laws is different. It is on the one hand wider, but on the other hand more lenient. It is wider, because the offence is fully completed even without the ensuing of a result; and it is more lenient, because it only requires of the good samaritan that he render a vague form of assistance, and does not compel him to *prevent* any harm. Thus, where harm does ensue, it does not consider the bad samaritan to be responsible for it. Only the oldest statutes still in force depart significantly from this modern pattern. The Dutch one, as we have seen, still requires the death of the person in peril before liability will be imposed.

If it is true that these statutes have grown steadily and relentlessly over recent years, it is also true in my view that they have probably reached their peak – at least in continental Western Europe. The history of the criminal law tends to repeat itself, and it is significant, therefore, that in the most advanced continental European country in the field of Criminal Law (Germany) the trend – at least among scholars – is lately towards a restriction of the duty to rescue and of its penal consequences. The same is happening in others countries, but I shall return to this issue later.

6   The Italian Experience

6.1   *The Development of Duty to Rescue from the Zanardelli Code of 1889 to the Codice Rocco of 1930*[49]

In the early stages of the long process of drafting the Italian Code of 1889, the intention was to place a bad samaritan statute in the book of contraventions (that is, petty offences). The draft code of 1868, for example, limited the duty to an obligation to inform the authorities, and imposed a fine as penalty. Supporters of such a mimimalist view of the duty to rescue predominated amongst the commissioners, but the opposite opinion eventually prevailed, and in the end the of-fence[50] was placed among the *delitti* (the notion of which is approximately comparable to the notion of 'felonies', or *mala in se*). This was in fact more for technical reasons than out of any real recognition of the seriousness of the crime. The duty was expanded to include the obligation to rescue the person in peril, although the informing of the authorities was retained as an alternative. The penalty, however, involved no more than a fine.

Under the name *indolenza colpevole* (culpable indolence), this was the first time that a bad samaritan statute either had become applicable to the whole country or had been promoted to the rank of a major crime. The only precedents in Italian law were article 97 of the Tuscan Police Penal Code of 1853 and article 162 of the Police Code of Modena and Reggio of 1854, both of which were mere police contraventions (that is, 'petty offences'). Not all Italian criminal lawyers greeted the new law with enthusiasm. Some criticised the placing of the offence in the class of the most serious crimes. Others opposed the statute vigorously, arguing, amongst other things, that bad samaritans often fail to intervene, not because they have a wicked disposition, but more out of fear, indolence or pusillanimity. One feature of the new bad samaritan law which was unanimously accepted was the exclusion of the duty if the rescuer runs any risk.

During the late 1920s, the Fascist regime began to feel the need of a new criminal code to attest to its power and legal authority. The new code was inspired by a totalitarian and ethical view of the state in which the individual is at the service of the community and of the nation. Accordingly, a strong duty to rescue must be imposed. This resulted in article 593 of the Penal Code of 1930:

> [A penalty of up to three months imprisonment or a fine of up to six hundred thousand lire may be imposed on a person] who finds a human body which is or seems lifeless or a person who is injured or otherwise in danger, and fails to render the necessary aid or to inform the authorities without delay. Where the above-mentioned conduct of the guilty person results in bodily harm, the penalty will be increased; if it results in death the penalty will be doubled.

The new offence was placed once again – notwithstanding the critics – in the category of the most serious crimes (*delitti*); the penalties were increased (from a mere fine to either a fine or detention for up to three months, or six months in case of an aggravating factor); and the defence of danger for the rescuer was deleted. This last amendment is the most noticeable one. The legislator, in the official report accompanying the enactment of the Code, stressed the importance of this change in the law and disparaged the former (1889) statute, which allowed the accused to defend himself through what were considered to be 'immoral and easy claims'. Two aggravating factors were added to the statute. The penalty was increased by up to one third if physical damage resulted from the omission; and doubled if the person in peril died. The new statute was welcomed by contemporary scholars, and even the removal of the defence of danger to the rescuer was accepted. The law was in harmony with the new Fascist *Weltanschauung*, in which duties of solidarity outranked individual liberty, and in which the criminal law reflected, not the ethical minimum, as in traditional thought, but the ethical maximum of society.[51]

It should be added that article 593 of the Criminal Code of 1930, still in force today in Italy, is not the only statute that deals with the question of the duty to rescue. Among other special duties, it is important to note article 133 of the Traffic Code of 1959,[52] applicable to drivers who fail to render assistance to victims of car accidents in which they are involved. The provision is similar to article 593 of the Penal Code, but the penalties are higher, and there is no alternative of informing the authorities.

6.2   How Does the Statute Work in Practice?[53]

Reported cases of prosecution under the 1889 Code concerned failures to effect extremely 'easy' rescues. In one case, article 389 of that Code was applied to the companions of a drunk, who fell from a handcart, and was abandoned in the middle of a quiet road. In other instances, the section was employed to punish behaviour that could possibly have been punished as homicide (manslaughter). An example: a man was drunk in an *osteria* (public house). It was late at night, and the innkeeper had to close the premises. It was December, in one of the coldest villages in the Italian Alps. The drunk man was expelled and was left outside in the snow, to die the next day. The landlady was punished under article 389, and so escaped with a mere fine. (The doctors in fact had not been able to ascertain the actual cause of death.)

Under the statute of 1930, the situation changed radically. The statute is particularly harsh, since it is applicable whatever the degree of peril for the person in danger, and whatever the risk to the rescuer in complying with the duty. From a comparative law point of view, one could rank the Italian statute among those that require the most difficult rescues. It must be said, though, that at least two features of the Italian bad samaritan law render the treatment of the rescuer less harsh. On the one hand, the statute limits the area of the duty to those cases in which the rescuer *finds* the person in peril. On the other hand, the statute requires the good samaritan either to rescue or to inform the authorities. With regard to the first of these features, it could easily be argued that mere knowledge on the part of the rescuer that a person is in peril is not enough to make him responsible for a failure to act: in fact, in this case the rescuer does not *find* the person in peril. In order to find Elisabetta, the samaritan Cosimo should find himself in a situation where sensory contact can be established with her. Cosimo finds Elisabetta only if he *sees* her, *hears* her and so on, but not if he merely knows that she is in distress, or perhaps because he has been called by Alessio seeking his help. As far as the second of these features is concerned, the statute does not specify whether the duty to rescue is satisfied only by informing the police. It could be argued that the duty to rescue and the duty to inform the police are genuine alternatives and indeed the statute has been so interpreted by comparative lawyers.[54]

Both of these features of article 593 could render it much less invasive of individual liberty. The first feature limits the duty to those cases in which the rescuer might be expected to have some inclination to rescue. The second feature leaves the samaritan free to decide whether to render aid or to inform the police, thus making obedience possible without effort or danger. In short, the alternative of informing the police makes up for the absence of statutory exclusion of the duty to rescue in those which would involve danger for the rescuer. However, the courts have more than once ignored these features of the article. In respect of the first feature, they have argued that the concept of 'finding' can be expanded to cover situations in which the rescuer only *knows* of the person in peril, perhaps because he has been telephoned by friends or relatives of the person in peril.[55] More than once the courts have convicted doctors who did not visit a patient after being called by relatives and have also convicted drivers who had been requested to carry to hospital persons lying injured nearby but not strictly 'found' by the drivers. With regard to the second feature, they have repeatedly stated that the good samaritan is allowed (and required) to inform the police only when the rescue is impossible or unnecessary. So the good samaritan does not have the choice between rendering aid and informing the police. If the judge thinks that direct intervention would have been more appropriate in the individual case, reporting of the finding to the police is not sufficient to prevent conviction. There have been convictions of those asked by the police to take people to hospital or, in the case of doctors, to visit a patient. In those cases the police were obviously already informed. Therefore these convictions mean that informing is not sufficient to escape liability if the judge thinks that the direct intervention of the rescuer was appropriate.

The courts have dealt with another point in a highly questionable way. Let us suppose that Mr Puccini arrives at the scene of an emergency when many other people are already there trying to help. Is Mr Puccini bound to render aid? The Italian courts usually make a distinction: if Mr Puccini's help is still useful, notwithstanding the presence of other people, he has a duty to take part in the collective effort. Only if Mr Puccini's aid is unnecessary will he not be bound to help. This solution is highly disputable. It obviously serves the purpose of the doctrine, which is to guarantee to the person in peril the maximum possible aid. But from the juridical point of view, it is probably wrong to impose this duty on any passer-by when other bystanders are in some way already helping the person in trouble. In fact this extension of the duty to the second passer-by could lead it to expand even more, without any clear limits. The only criterion by which one could ascertain whether the duty existed or not would be the usefulness of the aid. But this criterion would not help, because it is too vague, and because most of the time further help would of course be useful.

Last but not least, on more than one point the practical application by the courts of article 593 has been uncertain, inconsistent and contradictory. Many examples could be given here, but one will be enough. It is not clear what level and what kind of risk must be run by the person in peril: some decisions say that any degree of risk is sufficient; other decisions require a serious risk; finally, some courts restrict the scope of the duty to cases of an imminent risk of serious physical harm. In short, court decisions on the Italian bad samaritan statute have been highly unsatisfactory, but the courts are not the only culprits in this. It is probably true that the law itself is defective. It is no wonder, then, that some scholars in Italy are starting to criticise the article, and to make proposals for reform.[56]

7   A Critical Analysis of Bad Samaritan Statutes

7.1   Reasons for the Development of Such Statutes in Continental Europe and Not in Common Law Countries

Why are bad samaritan statutes so common in civil countries and so rare in the common law world? One of the reasons could be a different *Weltanschauung* of the English tradition, but this would not be entirely convincing. In late eighteenth-century England, Bentham was strongly supportive of the need for a general duty to rescue,[57] while in civil law countries more than one writer opposed such a duty.[58] The difference is much more likely to be explained by the historical development of the two legal traditions. In Britain, the criminal law has always been the common law of crimes. The creation and development of the law was mostly the work of the courts, in dealing with harms to individuals, and with the problem of finding a person responsible for these harms. It is unsurprising that, given this perspective, no general duty to rescue is to be found since such a duty might have compelled a judge to decide on his own authority that bystanders were responsible for the deaths of others. If a system is based on judge-made law – as Bentham called it – the development of a general duty to rescue is inherently less likely.

The situation of the criminal law when it is based upon a criminal code is very different. In drafting a code, a commissioner can employ many different tools. He can provide for serious harm offences and for petty offences that do not create any immediate harm; he can conceive new statutory law that could not possibly have developed through case law. A variety of duties could be sanctioned as offences of omission in the code. The transition from judge-made law to a criminal code – in the continental sense, not in the sense of a compilation of penal laws such as the codes enacted in certain common law countries[59] – creates an opportunity to rethink the whole system of crimes and punishments. As part of such a process, it is possible to create a bad samaritan statute. This probably explains why a general duty to rescue was not normally imposed in continental Europe before the great codifications of the latter part of the eighteenth and the beginning of the nineteenth century. In the common law world there has never been a real codification age. It is unsurprising, then, that no duty to rescue has been conceived, or that when such a duty has been discussed it has so far usually been rejected. It is also understandable that now, when academic discussion in common law countries seems to favour real codification of the criminal law, more than one scholar is arguing for the enactment of bad samaritan statutes.

This might also be the product of renewed interest in comparative law, that seemed lacking at an earlier stage of the development of the criminal law in common law countries. The modern English-speaking criminal lawyer is now more inclined to look to different jurisdictions in order to find new solutions to old problems. He obviously notices the bad samaritan statutes that characterise the continental criminal codes. Even in continental codes such statutes emigrated from one code to another. Commissioners, when preparing a draft code, usually looked at codes of neighbouring countries and incorporated their bad samaritan statutes in their own drafts. An example was the preparation of the Zanardelli Code of 1889 in Italy. Evidence of this is also the fact that countries with cultural and language affinities usually provide for similar bad samaritan statutes. This has already been demonstrated in Section 4: for example, the bad samaritan statutes provided for in Scandinavian countries are very alike. The same can be said of South American statutes, which are mostly copies of Spanish, Italian or Portuguese statutes. It might be added that these bad samaritan statutes, especially at earlier stages of European codification, provided for very lenient penalties. Consequently, the recognition of such a duty in a new code (or in a draft code) did not create dramatic changes in the whole philosophy of the criminal law.

Dramatic changes came only during the totalitarian experience in countries such as Germany, France or Italy. These instances really do represent a new *Weltanschauung* and a new philosophy of the criminal law. It was then that penalties were suddenly increased, and the duty was expanded far beyond its traditional scope. After the experience of totalitarianism, the fact that in many countries bad samaritan statutes remained quite harsh and demanding is probably explained by the difficulty a legislator experiences in withdrawing established laws from a criminal code. This is probably why in Italy, Germany and France such statutes remained (in Italy the Fascist Code of 1930 is, in fact, still in force). Moreover, the newly enacted statutes in other neighbouring Countries (for example, in Belgium, Spain, Portugal and Austria) are comparable with statutes in France, Italy and Germany more in virtue of the juridical affinities between those nations than as a result of radical choices in favour of a strong approach to the duty to rescue.

It is also to be stressed that a bad samaritan statute is not just another law. The recognition of a duty to rescue is obviously seen as a recognition of the role of solidarity in the social life of a country. The enactment of a bad samaritan statute, then, is particularly tempting for a legislator. When proposing a new code, its drafters can always parade the bad samaritan statute to show that the new code is inspired by the sentiment of brotherhood. But this kind of law, even though charming in a way, is also quite tricky. It has many side-effects, but they have rarely been considered by civil law legislators, whose main purpose was to adopt from neighbouring jurisdictions the most 'advanced' or 'progressive' legislation. It is easy to consider such a statute as representing progress in the criminal law.[60] It is easy to expand the law towards the goal of the positive pursuit of Good, and beyond the traditional, negative prevention of Evil. This is why European and civil law countries in general have adopted such statutes. This development has not been the outcome of rethinking the whole philosophy of criminal law; rather it has reflected the desire of legislators, who have tried to appear be as advanced and progressive as possible by adopting new solutions from other recently enacted criminal codes.

This process has been favoured by a particularly developed theoretical doctrine of the criminal law, which since at least the beginning of the last century has separated the problem of pure crimes of omission from the problem of commission by omission.[61] If from the perspective of commission by omission the recognition of a general duty to rescue would have had intolerable consequences, from the point of view of pure omission such statutes would not affect the whole system of the criminal law. The enactment of a bad samaritan statute would have the limited outcome of making it possible to sanction (with very lenient penalties) those who show reckless indifference towards the life and limb of their neighbours in distress, and who consequently increase the risk run by persons in peril. However, it must be pointed out that the introduction of such statutes has not always been unanimously supported by scholars, even in continental Europe.

What has been said so far would lead to the conclusion that the recognition and the growth of a general duty to rescue in civil law countries and not in common law countries have less to do with the philosophy that underlies the two systems than with their different juridical structures. However, it could be argued that the juridical systems themselves differ by virtue of a different political philosophy, but this is not a question that can be pursued here. In conclusion, it might be argued that the introduction of a general duty to rescue in common law jurisdictions would not *necessarily* run counter to the overall philosophy of the criminal law in these countries. At the same time, though, the critical discussions of the common law scholars about such a general duty might beneficially be taken into account in rethinking the uncritical adoption of bad samaritan statutes in European countries.[62]

7.2   Theoretical Problems

The theoretical problems of a bad samaritan statute have probably been more deeply investigated by common lawyers than by civil lawyers. Usually, at least four problems have been identified by Anglo-American writers in this respect:

1   is it acceptable to use the criminal law to enforce moral duties?
2   how is it possible to reconcile this duty with an individualistic philosophy?
3   can the law impose positive duties as distinct from negative ones?
4   is it possible to draw a line between those cases in which such a duty exists and those in which it does not?

The first problem was considered by certain writers in Italy after the enactment of article 389 of the Code of 1889. It was argued that, if people saw the duty to help their neighbours in distress as a moral one, legal recognition of it was unnecessary. By contrast, if they did not feel morally bound to discharge such a duty, legislation would still be useless, because it could not change human morals and character.[63] It is true that, if people do not recognise such a duty as a moral one, a law along these lines would not be considered legitimate and would probably be ineffective, at least in the long run. The criminal law must reflect the social norms of the community. If it does not, it becomes oppressive and may lose its deterrent effect. Having said this, one should not muddle up two different problems. On the one hand, if a law is needed for the protection of a legal interest – protection of social or individual interests should be the only goal of criminal law –[64] this law can be justified only if it comports with common morality. From this point of view the consonance between the legal and the moral norm is not against, but is in favour of, the recognition of a legal duty. If there is no relevant legal interest to protect, on the contrary, the law is injustified even if the behaviour is contrary to morality. This second perspective prevents the use of the law to enforce 'morality' as such, for which purpose the law does not seem the most suitable tool available to society.[65] If this is correct, the argument that duty to rescue is a moral duty does not decide the issue as to whether there should be a legal duty. It is rather to be ascertained whether there is a relevant legal interest that has to be protected by the law in this regard. This interest could be found if it is recognised that every citizen in peril has a right to be rescued by any unknown bystander.

The duty to rescue must confront the objections of individualistic philosophy, theories which are found both in common law countries and, not infrequently, in continental countries. It has been argued that individualistic considerations cannot come into play when the rescue is an extremely easy one.[66] The interest which the individual has in the pursuit of his own ends and in the avoidance of harm to himself is so completely outweighed by the interest which the imperilled person has in rescue that only the most extreme concept of individualism would endorse inaction. Even in an individualistic system, then, the person in peril may have a right to be rescued.[67] This matter is extensively discussed in Chapter 1, Section 3.

With regard to the third problem, the distinction between positive and negative duties – which often figures in discussions on duty to rescue – is very ancient. According to St Thomas Aquinas an omission (that is, the breach of a positive duty) is normally less morally wrong than an action (that is, the breach of a negative duty).[68] Similar arguments have been made by others.[69] It is true that positive duties are more invasive of individual liberty than negative duties. To comply with a negative duty it is sufficient to refrain from a certain action, while to comply with a positive duty normally implies a bigger effort. Moreover, to comply with a positive duty a person has to perform an action, and cannot at the same time do anything else. This means that in principle negative duties limit personal liberty much less than positive duties.[70] But this does not mean that all negative duties are acceptable and all positive duties are intolerable. There are intolerable negative duties and tolerable positive duties. It would be unacceptable, for example, to prohibit people from listening to a certain radio station (a negative duty); and it would be perfectly acceptable, and proper, to impose upon parents a duty to feed their children or to send them to primary school (positive duties). A positive duty imposed on everyone is, in fact, most of the time unacceptable, because duties are normally related to special roles played by people in society, and few roles are played by everyone. But there are exceptions (almost everybody must pay taxes, for example) and a general duty to rescue could be one of them. But this seems to be acceptable only in the case of extremely easy rescues, and not in the case of difficult ones. The example of the infant drowning in the shallow pool is an obvious instance of easy rescue, and a positive duty in such a case is perfectly tolerable and appropriate.[71] (For further discussion, see Chapter 1.)

Finally, it is not a simple matter to draw a line between easy and difficult rescues – between rescues imposed by *moral duties* and rescues suggested by *moral ideals*. Joel Feinberg, among others, has suggested a solution to this problem.[72] He divides the spectrum of hypothetical cases into three segments:

> I. Clear cases of opportunity to rescue with no unreasonable risk, cost or inconvenience to the rescuer or others (including cases of no risk, cost, or inconvenience whatever); (2) clear cases of opportunity to rescue but only at unreasonable risk, cost, or inconvenience to the rescuer or others; and (3) everything in the vast no-man's land of uncertain and controversial cases in between the extremes. To err only on the side of caution, we would hold no one in the middle (uncertain) category liable. Then we could hold everyone liable who *clearly* deserves to be liable, while exempting all those who do not clearly deserve to be liable, both those who clearly deserve *not* to be liable, as well as those whose deserts are uncertain. Careful draftsmanship of statutes could leave it up to juries to decide where reasonable doubts begin.

This might be an acceptable solution to the problem, although Michael Menlowe has expressed his reservations (see Chapter 1, Section 8).

7.3   Practical Problems

There are psychological, sociological, medico-legal and other practical problems raised by a bad samaritan statute. Psychologists have studied the question of the duty to rescue and have come to the conclusion that a failure to rescue is usually understandable, if not justifiable, from a psychological point of view. It has been pointed out that:

> apathy and indifference are the least likely primary psychic vectors in response to such an event. The sequence ... is, first, the intense emotional shock – characterized predominantly, but not exclusively, by anxiety; second, the cognitive perception and awareness of what has happened; third, an inertial paralysis of reaction, which as a non-act becomes in fact an act, and fourth, the self-awareness of one's own shock anxiety, non-involvement which is followed by a sense of guilt and intra-psychic and social self-justification.[73]

In this view, it would be wrong to label those who pass on the other side of the road as bad samaritans: from a psychological point of view they are not usually wicked.

Sociologists have made interesting studies of the duty to rescue. In Austria, Germany and the United States, amongst the students interviewed in such a study, less than 50 per cent would impose a penalty on the bad samaritan, and an even smaller percentage would put him to prison.[74] Much the same result was obtained in an Italian study, where most people seemed to consider a failure to rescue morally wrong, but only a small percentage of those interviewed would impose criminal punishment on the bad samaritan.[75] From the medico-legal point of view, it has been argued that a rescue rendered by a non-expert can make matters worse. In most circumstances the layman who finds an injured person should rather summon an ambulance. Even carrying an injured person in a private car can be dangerous, and therefore not even this minimal form of rescue should be considered a legal duty, according to this view.[76] To refrain from rescue might accordingly be the best response, as is suggested by Daniel Shuman in Chapter 4.

Let us turn now to another practical problem involved in the duty to rescue. In my view, a general duty to rescue was particularly appropriate for a rural society in the past, when the state did not (and could not) take adequate care of individuals. In the past, if Paolo was riding his bicycle from Bolzano to Trento, and found along the way Nadia, injured at the side of the road, the only way to help her was to try and rescue her by himself, or to ask a peasant nearby to carry her to the hospital in Trento on a pushcart. How could Paolo do otherwise? There were no telephones, so the only way to inform the hospital would have been to go there by bicycle. In a more technologically developed society, matters are totally different. Today, if Paolo is driving towards Trento, and finds Nadia injured at the side of the road, he should stop and immediately telephone the nearest hospital – perhaps using his car-phone.

In such a developed society, then, the law should not impose on the bystander a duty to intervene beyond summoning the appropriate rescue services. This solution seems to be imposed not (or not only) by moral or theoretical reasons, but by the practical considerations of pursuing the more efficient and less dangerous kind of rescue. In this way one overcomes the problems rehearsed in this section. Such an approach is also consistent with the need to impose on bystanders the duty to make only easy rescues. Furthermore, it solves the problems of line drawing, since informing the police does not cost any serious effort to the rescuer, except in extreme cases. It is true that in some instances – for example, the blind man who walks toward the cliff, the infant drowning in the shallow pool – direct intervention on the part of the bystander would be more appropriate. But in most of these cases the samaritan will render his help, and on the other hand a criminal statute is not meant to cover every possible form of bad behaviour. What it must do, though, is comply with the principle of clarity; that is, it must draw clear lines between what is criminal and what is not.[77]

8   Final Remarks

Civil law bad samaritan statutes are open to criticism on a variety of grounds. They sometime impose difficult rescues, as is the case with the Italian legislation, in which not even a defence of danger to the samaritan is allowed. And even when difficult rescues are not required, they tend not to contain clear-cut definitions of what sort of conduct will be unlawful. Finally, they rarely state exactly what proximity, if any, is required between the two parties. This lack of precision is evident in other regards. These statutes do not state precisely what degree of risk must be faced by the imperilled person. They are not clear enough in describing the conduct required in the individual case of the rescuer. It is true that in any case it would be hard to describe this conduct in advance, taking into account the way in which circumstances will vary. It is also true that sometimes these laws give the samaritan a choice as to how to react, but then it is not always made clear how this discretion is to be exercised. Some codes, including the Italian one, give the samaritan the alternative of calling the police rather than effecting a rescue, but it is not clear when this alternative will be available. Other codes, such as the French one, give the rescuer the choice of rendering aid himself or of procuring it through another. How much real discretion is conceded to the samaritan here? Even in those statutes which provide a defence of danger to the rescuer, it is not clear what degree of danger is to be tolerated before the defence becomes available. This problem is even more complicated if the statute excepts the samaritan from punishment when conduct 'cannot reasonably be expected' from the samaritan.

The practical application of these statutes in Europe has not produced particularly unacceptable results, but it has shown the problems inherent in such statutes, especially those drafted without proper care or expanded in order to impose difficult rescues in the name of God[78] or of a totalitarian concept of the state. The courts – at least in Italy – have shown a regrettable tendency to expand these statutes even further, and anyway to apply them in an inconsistent and expansionist way. The argument as to line drawing, discussed in the nineteenth century by Lord Macaulay, is shown to be justified when one considers the civilian experience. On the other hand, it is doubtful whether such statutes have had any real deterrent effect. The average person often does not even know that a bad samaritan statute is in force and, even if such a person does know, he may not know its precise dimensions (nor do the courts seem to be too aware of these). Cowards usually go on being cowards, brave men keep on being brave, and heroes go on being heroes.

If bad samaritan statutes are so open to criticism, should we continue to have them at all? One wonders, after all, how effective they are. Our cities are full of drunkards, drug-addicts and those whose suffering is manifested in other ways, but no one ever stops to help them: how many of these people are punished under a bad samaritan statute? Yet these statutes are well established and are unlikely to be abandoned. In these circumstances, perhaps the best approach is to attempt to reform these laws and to stop demanding too much from them. These statutes should be confined to the imposition of elementary duties to aid other people in danger, and they should also be as precise and limited as possible. In particular, they should be restricted to requiring that accidents should be reported to the police or other authorities, a solution which is clearly more compatible with the nature of a modern, technologically sophisticated society. This is a limited duty to rescue, a far cry from some of the broader claims of some examples of such legislation, but at least it makes for a realistic and enforceable law.[79]

Notes

1   *De Officiis*, I. 23.

2   The first *Weltanschauung* was mantained, for example, by Christianus Thomasius; the second one by Leibniz: see N. Bobbio, 'La funzione promozionale del diritto', in *Dalla struttura alla funzione* (Milan, 1977), 14–15.

3   For exceptions see F.J.M. Feldbrugge, 'Good and Bad Samaritans. A Comparative Survey of Criminal Law Provisions Concerning Failure To Rescue', 14 *American Journal of Comparative Law*, 630, 648 ff (1966), whose personal opinion does not seem acceptable in toto .

4   Among many others, see H.H. Jescheck, *Lehrbuch des Strafrechts – A.T.* (Berlin, 1989), 540 ff; G. Fiandaca and E. Musco, *Diritto penale - P.G.* (Bologna, 1989), 427.

5   'Celui qui trouvant sur son chemin une personne en danger d'être tuée ou maltraitée de quelque autre manière que ce fût, & pouvant la garantir du mal qui la menaçoit, ne le faisoit pas, étoit puni de mort. Que si l'on ne se sentoit pas assez fort ... il falloit du moins, dénoncer l'auteur de la violence, & se rendre partie en Justice contre le Brigand. Si on y manquoit, on recevoit un certain nombre de coups, & l'on étoit de plus condamné à ne manger rien de trois jours' (*Le droit de la nature et de gens* (ed. 1771, Basle), L. I, Ch. V, XIV, 93 ff).

6   See A. Cadoppi, *Il reato omissivo proprio* (Padua, 1988), I, 196 ff, 265 ff and references.

7   W. Huschens, *Die Unterlassene Hilfeleistung im nationalsozialistischen Strafrecht* (Freiburg, 1938), 5 ff.

8   See more recently R. Maceratini, 'Considerazioni tratte dal *corpus juris canonici* e dal *codex juris canonici* sul concetto penalistico di omissione', *Annali di Macerata*, 383, 399 ff (1982). More generally, on the history of duty to rescue, see E. Pedotti, *Die Unterlassung der Nothilfe* (Aarau, 1911), 6 ff.

9   See, for example, W. Huschens, op. cit., 12.

10   See Chapter 1, Section 4.

11   M. Gand, *Du délit de commission par omission* (Paris, 1900), 42.

12   *De crimine omissionis,* 21 et seq.

13   12. Ceux qui, le pouvant, auront refusé ou négligé de faire les travaux, le service, ou de prêter le secours dont ils auront été requis dans les circonstances d'accidens, tumultes, naufrages, inondation, incendie ou autres calamités, ainsi que dans les cas de brigandages, pillages, flagrant délit, clameur publique ou d'exécution judiciaire.

14   See *Collezione dei travagli sul codice penale pel Regno d'Italia* (Brescia, 1807), III, 267.

15   *Summa Theologiae,* XVII, II–II, q. 79, a. 3 ('Utrum omissio sit speciale peccatum').

16   Todo el que pudiendo hacerlo sin perjuicio ni riesgo suyo no prestare el socorro que esté en su arbitrio a cualquiera persona que halle herida, maltratada, acometida por un agresor injusto o constituìda en otro conflicto que requiera los auxilios de la humanidad, serà reprendido y sufrirà arresto de uno a seis dias, o pagarà una multa de diez reales de vellòn a tres duros; observàndose lo prevenido en el articulo 128 del titulo preliminar.

17   In Italy, Carmignani was generally against any crime of omission; in France, Ortolan opposed a general duty to rescue; so also De Vries in The Netherlands. In Germany, Berner favoured such a duty.

18   For example, W. Huschens, op. cit.; K. Fahlenbock, *Die unterlassene Hilfeleistung nach 330 c StGB* (Koln, 1939) and many more.

19   F. Schaffstein, *Das Verbrechen als Pflichtverletzung* (Berlin, 1935).

20   J. Feinberg, *The Moral Limits of The Criminal Law* (New York, 1984–8).

21   See P. Nuvolone, 'La riforma del art. 2 del codice penale germanico' (1938), in his *Trent'anni di diritto e procedura penale* (Padua, 1969), I, 1 (critical on this point).

22   References in A. Cadoppi, *op. cit.,* II, 1072–3.

23   Sera puni d'un emprisonnement d'un an à cinq ans et d'une amende de 500 à 5.000 francs, ou de l'une de ces deux peines seulement, quiconque pouvant empêcher par son action personnelle et immédiate, sans préjudice ni risque pour lui ou pour ses proches, l'une des infractions énumérées à l'alinéa 1er de l'article 2, s'abstient volontairement de le faire. La même peine est encourue par celui qui, dans les mêmes conditions, omet de porter secours à une personne en péril si, faute d'être secourue, cette personne a perdu la vie ou souffert une grave lésion corporelle le tout sans préjudice de peines plus fortes …

24   L. Hugueney, Preface, in A. Tunc, *Le particulier au service de l'ordre public* (Paris, 1943), 6.

25   A. Tunc, op. cit., 60 ff.

26   'A notre époque d'égoïsme exacerbè que Gustave Flaubert appelait d'une façon fort imagée le 'panmuflisme', il convient plus que jamais que le législateur étende l'action de la répression à certains devoirs moraux particulièrement impérieux: car, à défaut de sanctions pénales, bon nombre d'individus sans conscience n'hésiteraient pas à se soustraire à ces devoirs, en cherchant dans les règles de l'inertie et du moindre effort de fallacieuses justifications et dans le silence du législateur un encouragement à leur lâcheté.' ('La répression des abstentions coupables', *Revue de droit pénal et criminologie,* 199, 211) (1961).

27   C. Braas, J. Van Den Bossche and A. Fettweis, 'L'abstention de porter secours', 32 *Revue de droit pénal et criminologie,* 21, 29, (1951–2).

28   'Lo que el cristiano (y todos los hombres deben ser cristianos) debe obrar, esta contenido en los Diez Mandamientos. Pero estos Mandamientos, por el modo de su formulaciòn (excluvendo los cuatro primeros), paracen contener solamente deberes negativos, de abstenciòn. Asì lo entendieron sus primitivos guardianes, y hubo de venir el Divino Maestro a interpretarnos cuàl era la esencia de ellos, promulgando la ley del amor: "estos diez Mandamientos se encierran en dos: en servir y amar a Dios sobre todas las cosas y a tu pròjimo como a ti mismo". Quiere darnos con ello a entender el Señor que la Ley no se concretaba exclusivamente a deberes negativos,

de abstenciòn, sino que incluìa también deberes positivos, de operaciòn, porque el amor es entrega y no egoismo.' (*La solidariedad humana en la ley penal* (Madrid, 1962), 27 ff).

29   J. De Figueiredo Dias, 'Les délits d'omission dans le droit pénal portugais', in 'Infractions d'omission et responsabilité pénale pour omission', *Revue international de droit pénal* , 449, 849 (1984).

30   N. Jareborg, 'Criminal Liability for Omissions', ibid., 960 ff.

31   A. Cadoppi, op. cit, II, 1084 ff.

32   See *infra*, Section 6.2.

33   For example, G. Rodriguez Mourullo, *La omision de socorro en el codigo penal* (Madrid, 1966), 185 ff.

34   A. Schönke-H. Schröder, *Strafgesetzbuch Kommentar* (Munich, 1985), sub para. 323c, 1864.

35   See *infra*, Section 6.2.

36   For example, in Austria, France, Greece, Argentina, Brazil, Mexico, Peru, Guatemala, Venezuela, Cuba and Ecuador (only for himself); and in Spain, Finland, Norway, Iceland, Holland, Denmark (for himself *or for others*).

37   This is so in Austria, Germany, Norway, Iceland, Denmark, Greece, Guatemala, Cuba and Ecuador.

38   This applies in France, Belgium, Portugal, Spain (which is particularly precise in this respect), Finland and Holland.

39   Also Turkey, Argentina, Brazil, Mexico, Panama, Peru and Venezuela.

40   See *infra*, section 6.2. This seems to be the case, without the need of adventurous interpretations, in San Marino, where two different offences are provided for, one that imposes a duty to *rescue*, and another 'subsidiary' and less serious one that imposes only a duty to inform the authority. More ambiguous is the provision of the Paraguay Criminal Code, by which the samaritan is required to 'give shelter' (to the person in peril) or to inform the authorities or the family (of the unfortunate).

41   This is so in Austria and Norway (where death is the only result taken into account) and in Italy, San Marino and Brazil (where the penalty is increased if harm to physical integrity is caused, and still more if the person in peril dies).

42   This is the case in Italy, Germany, Austria, Belgium, Spain, Finland, Holland, Norway, Iceland, Denmark, Brazil, Mexico and Cuba.

43   Turkey, Argentina, Paraguay, Panama, Peru, Guatemala, Venezuela and Ecuador.

44   The French statute has been analysed by common lawyers: see A. Ashworth and E. Steiner, 'Criminal Omissions and Public Duties: the French Experience', 10 *Legal Studies*, 153 (1990).

45   I refer in the text to the German experience, which is different mainly because of the politically dubious origin of the bad samaritan statute. On the Italian situation see *infra*, section 6.

46   See the discussion of the matter by Pufendorf in Section 3.1.

47   A. Mattheus, *De criminibus* (ed. Ticini, 1803), I, 15.

48   M. Gand, op. cit., 42.

49   On this problem see A. Cadoppi, *Il reato di omissione di soccorso* (Padua, 1993), 7 ff.

50   Art. 389 of the Code of 1889.

51   G. Guarneri, 'In tema di omissione di soccorso', *Rivista italiana di diritto penale*, 570, 571 (1936).

52   Now article 189 of the new Road Traffic Code of 1992.

53   For references on the individual points see A. Cadoppi, op. cit., *supra*, n. 49, *passim*.

54   A.W. Rudzinski, in J. Ratcliffe (Ed.), *The Good Samaritan and the Law*, (Garden City, New York, 1966), 107.

55   Recently this traditional dictum has been overruled by the Corte di Cassazione: *Balestrero*, 31 January 1978, *Foro Italiano*, 1979, II, 374.

56   See Section 8.

57   See Chapter 1, Section 6.

58   See Section 3.1.

59   From this perspective it seems possible to understand why in the USA such a duty has never (with the recent exceptions of a couple of states, Vermont and Minnesota) been imposed: codifications in that country have never (until the Model Penal Code) followed a continental pattern. Dudley Field's New York Penal Code and its successors were more compilations of existing laws than codes in the European sense (and in the sense Bentham conceived them). See C. McClain, 'Criminal Law Reform, 3. Historical Development in the United States', in S.H. Kadish (Ed.), *Encyclopedia of Crime and Justice*, II (New York, London, 1983), 507, 508. This is also probably why Lord Macaulay did not agree to impose such a duty: he thought more of the problem of commission by omission than of pure omission in drafting a code which was again far from a code in the continental sense.

60   See, for example, the *Official Report* to the Italian Code of 1889 by the then Minister of Justice, Giuseppe Zanardelli.

61   The first author to draw such a distinction was probably A.S. Oersted, *Ueber die Grundregeln der Strafgesetzgebung* (Copenhagen, 1818), 203 and 331. The distinction was then clearly developed by H. von Luden, *Abhandlungen aus dem gemeinen teutschen Strafrechte*, II (Göttingen, 1840), 219 ff.

62   See Chapter 2.

63   A. Bianchedi, 'Alcune note sul delitto d'indolenza colpevole', 8 *Supplemento Rivista penale* , 65, 79–80 (1899/1900).

64   This is how continental criminal lawyers express a principle recognised also by common lawyers: see, for example, J. Feinberg, op. cit., *supra*, n. 20.

65   H.L.A. Hart, *Law, Liberty and Morality* (Oxford and New York, 1963). In the Italian literature, see G. Fiandaca, 'Laicità del diritto penale e secolarizzazione dei beni tutelati', in *Studi in memoria di P. Nuvolone* (Milan, 1991), I,165.

66   See, for example, H. Fingarette, 'Some Moral Aspects of Goodsamaritanship', in J. Ratcliffe (Ed.), op. cit., 213, 215.

67   J. Feinberg, 'The Moral and Legal Responsibility of the Bad Samaritan', op. cit., *supra* n. 66, 56, 59 ff.; R.J. Lipkin, 'Beyond Good Samaritans and Moral Monsters: An Individualistic Justification of a General Duty to Rescue', 31 *University of California Los Angeles Law Review* , 252, 287 ff (1983). A right to be rescued has been recognised also by Italian philosophers: see S. Cotta, *Diritto persona mondo umano* (Turin, 1989), 247 ff.

68   *Summa Theologiae*, XVI, II–II, q. 79, a. 4 ('*Utrum peccatum omissionis sit gravius quam peccatus transgressionis*').

69   See F. Cordero, *Criminalia. Nascita dei sistemi penali* (Bari, 1985), 218 ff.

70   See, for example, N. Bobbio, 'Norma giuridica', *Novissimo Digesto italiana*, XI (Turin, 1965), 331.

71   See J. Feinberg, op. cit., *supra*, n. 67, at 56, 67.

72   Ibid., at 56, 65.

73   L.Z. Friedman, 'No Response to the Cry for Help', in J. Ratcliffe (Ed.), op. cit., 171, 176 ff.

74   See H. Ziesel, 'An International Experiment on the Effects of a Good Samaritan Law', in J. Ratcliffe (Ed.), op. cit., 209 ff. for further details.

75   E.U. Savona, 'Criminalità o devianza? Confronto tra reazione "ufficiale" e reazione dell'opinione pubblica', 3 *Sociologia del diritto*, 107, 134 (1980).

76   A. Sacerdote, 'Appunti medico-legali sui reati di omissione di soccorso e di fuga previsti dal nuovo codice della strada', 1 *Giustizia penale*, 10, 12 ff (1960).

76 In English, on such continental doctrine, see my 'Recent Developments on Italian Constitutional–Criminal Law', 28 *Alberta Law Review*, 427, 432 (1990).

78 See the example of the Russian Code of 1845, in Section 3.2. See also the comments by some Spanish authors, in Section 4.4.

79 See A. Cadoppi, op. cit., supra, n. 49 at 177 ff, where a proposal for a new bad samaritan statute has been put forward. The statute (which will be simply reported where and not commented upon in detail) would be drafted as follows:

Whosoever finds himself or comes in presence of an abandoned or lost child of an age below 10, or of a person in imminent and obvious danger of life, is punished, if he fails to report it to any Authority without delay, with detention ... or a fine ...

No omission is committed in any of the following cases:

(1) if the reporting would have caused physical danger to the accused or to another person, or anyway if the compliance with the duty could not be fairly expected from the accused;

(2) if the accused renders or procures, or tries to render or procure reasonable aid to the child or the person in peril;

(3) if someone is already present before the accused, except if it is obvious that the present people are incapable of complying with the duty;

(4) if, in case of simultaneous presence of more than one person, someone is obviously capable of reporting or rendering the aid in a quicker and more proper way than the accused;

(5) if another anyway complies with the duty with the same effectiveness and speed that would have been possible for the accused.

List of Statutory Provisions

Belgium: Criminal Code (statute added in 1961)

Article 422 bis. Sera puni d'un emprisonnement de huit jours à six mois et d'une amende de 50 à 500 francs ou d'une de ces peines seulement, celui qui s'abstient de venir en aide ou de procurer une aide à une personne exposée à un péril grave, soit qu'il ait constaté par lui-même la situation de cette personne, soit que cette situation lui soit décrite par ceux qui sollicitent son intervention.

Le délit requiert que l'abstenant pouvait intervenir sans danger sérieux pour lui-même ou pour autrui. Lorsqu'il n'a pas constaté personnellement le péril auquel se trouvait exposée la personne à assister, l'abstenant ne pourra être puni lorsque les circonstances dans lesquelles il a été invité à intervenir pouvaient lui faire croire au manque de sérieux de l'appel ou à l'existence de risques.

[A person is punishable ... if he fails to come to the aid of, or procure aid for a person exposed to grave peril, whether he himself observes the situation or whether his attention is drawn to the situation by those asking for his help.

The offence requires that the person failing to act could have intervened without serious danger to himself or another. Where he personally does not observe the situation of danger, the person failing to help will not be punishable if the circumstances in which his help was invited are such as to make him believe that the appeal was serious or to believe that the risks were real.]

Guatemala: Criminal Code (1973)

Quien encontrando perdido o desamparado a un menor de diez años; a una persona herida, invàlida o amenazada de inminente peligro, omitiere prestarle el auxilio necesario, segùn las circunstancias, cuando pudiere hacerlo sin riesgo personal, serà sancionado con multa de veinticinco a doscientos quetzales.

[One who, encountering a child under ten who is lost or abandoned, a wounded person, or a person who is disabled or who is facing imminent danger, fails to give him the help which is necessary in the circumstances, when he could do so without personal risk, will be punishable with [penalty]]

Italy: Criminal Code (19)

Article 593. (Omissione di soccorso). Chiunque trovando abbandonato o smarrito un fanciullo minore degli anni dieci, o un'altra persona incapace di provvedere a se stessa, per malattia di mente o di corpo, per vecchiaia o per altra causa, omette di darne immediato avviso all'Autorità, è punito con la reclusione fino a tre mesi o con la multa fino a lire seicento mila.

Alla stessa pena soggiace chi, trovando un corpo umano che sia o sembri inanimato, ovvero una persona ferita o altrimenti in pericolo, omette di prestare l'assistenza occorrente o di darne immediato avviso all'Autorità.

Se da siffatta condotta del colpevole deriva una lesione personale, la pena è aumentata; se ne deriva la morte, la pena è raddoppiata.

[Whosoever, finding an abandoned child of less than ten years, or another person incapable of providing for himself through physical or mental illness, through old age or for other cause, omits to inform the authorities immediately, is punishable ... [penalty]

The same penalty may be imposed on one who, finding a human corpse or a person who appears to be dead, or an injured person or a person in danger, omits to give immediate assistance or to inform the authorities without delay.

If the person affected by the conduct of the accused suffered a personal injury, the penalty is to be increased; if death results, the penalty is doubled.]

Turkey: Criminal Code (1926)

Article 476. Whoever finds an infant below the age of seven left unattended, or a person unable to care for himself owing to a mental or bodily defect, and fails to notify the office concerned or a government official, shall be punished by [a fine]

Whoever comes upon a wounded person, or in danger, or a dead body or one appearing to be dead, and fails to render any possible aid or fails to notify the proper office or a government official immediately, shall suffer the same punishment.

Cuba: Criminal Code (1979)

1   El que no socorra o preste auxilio debido a una persona herida o expuesta a un peligro que amenace su vida, su integridad corporal o su salud, sin que ello implique un riesgo para su persona, es sancionada con pravaciòn de libertad de tres a nueve meses o multa hasta doscinetes setenta cuotas o ambas.
2   Si el hecho se comete por quien tiene el deber de socorrer o auxiliar a la víctima, por razòn de su cargo o profesiòn, la sanciòn es de privaciòn de libertad de tres meses a un ano o multa de cien a trescientas cuotas o ambas.

[1   Whosoever does not help or provide the required aid to a wounded person or to one exposed to a danger which threatens his life, bodily integrity or health, when there would be no risk to his own person, is punishable ... with a prison sentence of three to nine months and a fine, or both]
2   If the offence is committed by one who had an obligation to help or provide aid to the victim on the grounds of his duty or profession, the penalty is [a prison sentence of three months to one year and a higher fine than in (1) above.]]

Finland: Criminal Code (1889)

Whosoever knowing that another is in serious mortal danger, refrains from giving or obtaining help which can be provided without endangering himself or any other shall be sentenced for neglecting an act of rescue to a fine or to imprisonment for at the most six months.

Germany: Criminal Code (1950)

Article 323c.   Wer bei Unglücksfällen oder gemeiner Gefahr oder Not nicht Hilfe leistet obwohl dies erforderlich und ihm den Umständen nach zumuten, insbesondere ohne erhebliche eigene Gefahr und ohne Verletzung anderer wichtiger Pflichten möglich ist, wird mit Freiheitsstrafe bis zu einem Jahr oder mit Geldstrafe bestraft.

[Whosoever does not provide help in the event of an accident, general peril or necessity, although it may be expected of him to do so in the circumstances, particularly where it is possible for him to act without causing danger to himself or injury to another, is punishable [with imprisonment of up to a year or with a fine]].

4 The Duty of the State to Rescue the Vulnerable in the United States

DANIEL W. SHUMAN*

1 Introduction: The Wrong Question

The debate over the duty to rescue has been eclipsed by concerns about the obligations of private citizens,[1] yet, with the possible exception of privately employed emergency medical personnel, few private citizens regularly encounter people threatened with immediate and substantial harm by disasters of natural or human origin who look to them for rescue. Rather, it is from the state, through its law enforcement, fire fighting and social service agencies, that those in peril regularly seek assistance. Thus any discussion of the duty to come to the aid of another in peril that did not address the duty of the state to rescue vulnerable members of society would be incomplete.

The discussion in Chapters 1 and 2 focuses on the arguments that underlie the common law rule on failing to recognise a duty to come to the aid of another in peril. These arguments deal with the problems inherent in defining the extent of a duty to rescue and, in the view of some, render a duty to rescue impracticable. If tort law were concerned only with autonomous individuals it might be justified in recognising a duty to avoid intentionally or negligently injuring others and not recognising a duty to rescue. But our society is comprised of autonomous and non-autonomous individuals and tort law must address both. Whatever force these arguments have against a duty to rescue autonomous individuals, they do not adequately address the specific problem of vulnerable and dependent persons who may have a claim on the state, even if they have no claim on other private citizens.

131

In what follows, I look at the problem of one vulnerable group in society, abused children. Although there is an understandable inclination to recognise a duty to rescue abused children, there are dangers with this. Even if the analysis in Chapters 1 and 2 supported a general duty to rescue, this analysis ignores the therapeutic dimension of the duty to rescue. Rescue proceeds on the assumption that it will be therapeutic; we encourage rescue because we think it will be beneficial to the physical or emotional health of the person rescued. If legal intervention on behalf of abused children lacks a likely therapeutic outcome, then a duty to rescue may leave children worse off than if no intervention had occurred.

2   The Traditional Rule

2.1   *The Odds Always Favour the House*

It is not particularly surprising that the state which creates the law, albeit democratically, has not chosen to impose upon itself a duty to come to the aid of its citizens. The state is, in the final analysis, interested in the perpetuation of the state. In the United States the state[2] has the right, but not an inherent duty, to come to the aid of vulnerable populations.

The absence of an inherent duty of the state to come to the aid of vulnerable populations has its roots in the failure to recognise an inherent structural or constitutional obligation on the part of the state to provide for the health or economic security of its citizens. The United States Constitution is a written document that establishes the contours of the relationship between the state and the individual. It limits the powers of the state over the individual, but imposes no affirmative burden on the state to aid the individual.[3] The state is not obliged, for example, to provide health care, housing or payments for unemployment, old age or disability. These programmes do exist, but the decision to provide for them is controlled by democratic politics rather than constitutional mandate. This results in a patchwork of programmes and services that provide for people who fit various unco-ordinated categorical limitations. For example, while there is no national health insurance in the United States, there are separate health care programmes for the poor, the elderly, veterans and Native Americans.[4] The scope and extent of these programmes are a function of the financial fortunes and largesse of the state at a given time.

The constitutional or structural limitations imposed on these programmes are proscriptive, not prescriptive. The state need not act to aid its citizens, but if it chooses to do so there are proscriptions that limit its actions. Equal protection and due process considerations largely define the scope of these proscriptions. For example, if the state chooses to provide programmes for dependent populations it may not deny the benefits of those programmes to members of a disfavoured minority.[5] And, although the state need not create a public benefit programme, if it does so it may not withdraw benefits without timely notice and a meaningful opportunity to be heard.[6] State tort law has not recognised a non-constitutionally derived duty to come to the aid of vulnerable citizens, although it has recognised a state's voluntary assumption of a duty to aid its citizens.[7] However, even when a state has voluntarily assumed a duty to aid its citizens, several obstacles stand in the path of a plaintiff seeking recovery for injuries from a breach of that voluntarily assumed duty.

In many states, under the public duty doctrine, whatever duty the state has assumed is construed to be owed to the general public and not to any particular member of the public. This doctrine has been traced to Cooley's 1877 treatise, *Liability of Public Officers*[8] and has been carried forward in his treatise on torts:

> If the duty which the official authority imposes upon an officer is a duty to the public, a failure to perform it, or an inadequate or erroneous performance, must be public, not an individual injury, and must be redressed, if at all, in some form of public prosecution.[9]

The public duty doctrine distinguishes duties owed by a public official to the general public, which can only be enforced by the general public through public prosecution, and duties owed to specific members of the public, which can be enforced by those specific individuals. The public duty doctrine posits a rigid hierarchical distribution of political power; the public may seek redress for public wrongs by public officials only through other public officials. Since statutory duties to provide police and fire protection, for example, are addressed to the public at large, rather than any person in particular, under the public duty doctrine the failure of the police or fire department to provide protection does not give rise to a duty enforceable in tort law by an injured plaintiff.[10] Although the actions of the state may in some instances create a special relationship that narrows the obligation owed to the public to an obligation to a specific individual,[11] other sets of hurdles face a plaintiff seeking recovery for a breach of that duty.

States may not be sued for their torts without their consent.[12] Although most states have abrogated sovereign immunity, the abrogation is limited to ministerial acts and specifically excludes the exercise of discretionary governmental functions.[13] This limitation is based upon a concern that courts not substitute their own discretion for the government's exercise of discretion under the guise of adjudicating tort claims. Thus, for example, the decision to create a programme in which prisoners are paroled is a discretionary governmental function immune from challenge in a tort action arising out of an injury caused a private citizen by a parolee.[14] Many states have also limited the amount of recovery against the state in any tort action,[15] and many recognise a good faith immunity for official acts.[16]

Although state tort law may support a duty to rescue based upon a special relationship when the state has voluntarily undertaken to engage in a particular activity, the decision to recognise a duty ultimately rests with the state. Because state tort law recognises a duty only when the state voluntarily undertakes an activity, the state can obviate any duty simply by refusing to undertake any effort to rescue.[17] The capacity to decide for whom it should intervene is defined by the state's *parens patriae* power. The right of the state to intervene directly on behalf of the vulnerable and dependent under its *parens patriae* power[18] encompasses the authority to act for the benefit of those who are unable to care for themselves because of age, illness or circumstance. A partial list of these populations includes incapacitated decision makers like Nancy Cruzan[19] and Karen Ann Quinlan,[20] the mentally disabled,[21] unborn foetuses[22] and abused children. [23] I have chosen the case of abused children as a vehicle to examine the state's duty to rescue, for two reasons.

First, abused children clearly do not fit the construct that might be used to justify the no duty to rescue rule. Abused children are not competent adults capable of caring for themselves.[24] The cases of Nancy Cruzan and Karen Ann Quinlan also involve incapacitated decison makers, but are distinguishable. They present the duty of the state *not* to rescue. In those cases the state is an uninvited rescuer; the legal issue presented is the right of the person to refuse to be rescued by the state from the consequences of that person's own decision or lack thereof. In the cases involving abused children the state is an invited rescuer; the legal issue presented is the right of the person to be rescued by the state from the abuse of a third party. What these cases do have in common is the question whether rescue by the state is ultimately therapeutic. Will state intervention be beneficial whether or not it is sought? It is certainly possible to reconstruct the issue presented in cases like *Cruzan* and *Quinlan* to ask whether these individuals have a right to be rescued from themselves or their surrogates, yet this reconstruction so broadens the concept of a duty to rescue as to shift the focus from the issue of rescue to the issue of autonomy. Retaining the focus on the case of abused children avoids the interjection of an interesting but confounding issue in this discussion.

Second, a recent decision of the United States Supreme Court, *DeShaney v. Winnebago County Department of Social Services*,[25] presents a controversial ruling on the duty of the state to rescue abused children in a compelling context.

2.2 *DeShaney* v. *Winnebago County Department of Social Services*[26]

DeShaney presented to the United States Supreme Court a civil rights claim of a young boy who was severely beaten by his father following an unsuccessful intervention by the defendant social service agency. Joshua DeShaney's parents were divorced when he was an infant and he was awarded to the custody of his father. Following the divorce, the defendant social service agency received numerous complaints that Joshua was being physically abused by his father. Finally, after Joshua was admitted to a hospital with bruises and abrasions, the agency obtained an order removing Joshua from the home temporarily, but subsequently returned him when an interdisciplinary child protection team concluded that there was insufficient evidence of abuse to retain custody. The agency did, however, obtain an agreement, in conjunction with Joshua's return, that the father would participate in a counselling programme, make changes in family living arrangements and enter Joshua in a pre-school programme (Head Start) to monitor his condition. Joshua's father did not fulfil the agreement, the complaints of abuse continued and Joshua made frequent trips to the emergency room for traumatic injuries. The agency made numerous ineffectual inquiries, but did not again seek to remove him from the home. Finally, Joshua's father inflicted injuries on his four-year-old son so severe that Joshua sustained permanent irreversible brain damage requiring life-long care in an institution for the profoundly retarded. Joshua's mother then instituted a federal civil rights claim, as Joshua's guardian, against the social service agency for depriving him of his liberty in violation of the Fourteenth Amendment of the Constitution by failing to protect Joshua.

The Supreme Court affirmed the rulings of the district court and court of appeals rejecting the civil right claim against the county social services agency. It reasoned that Joshua was not constitutionally entitled to protection from the state to prevent abuse by his father. The Court ruled that the Due Process Clause of the Fourteenth Amendment creates no general duty to protect children from parental abuse. The Court rested its doctrinal analysis on the proposition that the constitution guarantees no governmentally insured minimum level of safety or security. Because the physical abuse occurred at the hands of Joshua's father, and the Court characterised the state's role as failing to act to avert that abuse, the majority opinion found no violation of a constitutional duty.

The argument on behalf of Joshua's guardian suggested that there was little dispute, in the abstract, about the existence of an affirmative constitutional obligation to protect children from parental abuse. Joshua's guardian argued that there was an enforceable constitutional duty of protection based upon the existence of a special relationship between the state and Joshua arising out of the state's abortive efforts on Joshua's behalf. In prior opinions involving harm following failed efforts by the state, the provision of medical care to prisoners[27] and involuntarily institutionalised retarded citizens,[28] the Court had recognised a constitutional obligation to provide these persons with a minimum level of care. A number of federal courts of appeal had relied upon these decisions to find a special relationship in circumstances similar to Joshua's triggering a constitutional duty to protect children from abuse in these limited circumstances.[29]

The *DeShaney* majority distinguished the Court's prior decisions and rejected the claim that a special relationship between the state social service agency and Joshua triggered a duty to protect Joshua from abuse by his father. It held that a special relationship between the state agency and the individual triggers a duty to protect the individual only when the state takes a person into custody and holds that person involuntarily. Because the state had released Joshua to his father before the final batterings, Joshua could not meet the custodial requirement imposed by the Court to establish a special relationship. Unnecessary to the holding and therefore not discussed was another hurdle that the plaintiff would have had to overcome even if the Court had recognised the plaintiff's claim: good faith immunity.[30] The Court was careful to point out that the state's undertaking the abortive rescue might render it liable under state tort law. Because the validity of state tort claims do not fall within the jurisdiction of the Supreme Court, and in any event were not raised in this case, they were not pursued further in this opinion. What the Court was careful not to point out was the likely reason that this claim was brought as a federal civil rights action rather than a state tort claim.

Plaintiffs often choose federally based civil rights claims rather than state tort claims to avoid the immunity, damage cap and limited duty hurdles, noted earlier, that exist under state law. Wisconsin imposed a ceiling of $50 000 per claim in its limited abrogation of sovereign immunity.[31] Wisconsin also retained immunity for discretionary governmental functions. Typical of the claims that might be brought are those involving negligence in the operation of a state-owned motor vehicle, which do not involve the exercise of governmental discretion.[32] Thus it was highly unlikely that in Wisconsin, where this case arose, a state tort claim would be brought. Many states have enacted good faith immunity for all official acts of child protective service workers.[33] Under the public duty doctrine, other states have interpreted the state's duty as owing to the general public but not any particular member of the public.[34] Most importantly, either by resurrection of sovereign immunity or refusing to remain in the child abuse rescue business, the state can prospectively obviate any tort liability for failure to rescue abused children. Federal civil rights claims, however, are grounded on federal constitutional law and may not be rejected as a matter of state law.

Both the facts that gave rise to *DeShaney* and the court's austere response to these facts are troubling. The court's response is a stale formulaic doctrinal analysis based largely upon an action/inaction dichotomy.[35] There is a temptation to respond to this approach and to criticise the decision on its own terms. Most critics of *DeShaney* have not resisted this temptation and have argued that the creation of the child protection agency and response to the complaints of abuse take this case out of the category of inaction or non-feasance.[36] Others have pointed to the history surrounding the adoption of the Fourteenth Amendment as an affirmative response to slavery to criticise the Court's interpretation that it constitutes only a negative limitation on the states.[37] It is important to avoid the temptation to be drawn into the debate on these terms for it has not and is not likely to yield any new insights or analysis. The debate is mired in a doctrinal rut. Rediscovering constitutional history or reconceptualising causation distinguishing action and inaction may strengthen criticisms of the Court's reasoning, but seem likely to accomplish little else. This debate devolves into a zero-sum game pitting those who seek to protect child victims of abuse against those who seek to protect the constitutional rights of the accused.[38] A new approach with new insights is needed to re-energise that debate. One approach that offers new insights into this problem is therapeutic jurisprudence.

3   Therapeutic Jurisprudence

3.1   *A Therapeutic Once-over*

Therapeutic jurisprudence is a mode of legal analysis that considers the law's potential as a therapeutic agent.[39] It posits that, whenever it is possible to do so without offending other important normative values, legal rules should encourage therapeutic outcomes. Therapeutic jurisprudence calls for a systematic empirical examination of the therapeutic dimension of the law,[40] and, while the inquiry suggested by therapeutic jurisprudence has certainly been undertaken previously without that label, the advantage of therapeutic jurisprudence is that it sharpens the focus of this legal lens.

For an example of this analysis, consider an application of therapeutic jurisprudence to another area in which the state has chosen to exercise its authority to come to the aid of a vulnerable population –

civil commitment of the mentally disabled. There is a body of research indicating that voluntary hospitalisation is more effective in
treating the mentally disabled than involuntary hospitalisation.[41] A
therapeutic jurisprudence analysis would suggest that, unless other
important normative values would be offended, the state's interest in
treatment of the mentally disabled should be advanced by encouraging voluntary treatment and permitting involuntary treatment, if at
all, only after efforts to encourage voluntary treatment have failed.[42]
It is particularly appropriate to examine the duty of the state to come
to the aid of abused children from the perspective of therapeutic
jurisprudence. The debate over the duty to rescue has been dominated by doctrinal analysis devoid of empirical inquiry.[43] While the
doctrinal analysis is necessary, alone it is not sufficient. The argument
in favour of a duty to rescue, specifically in the context of child abuse,
is therapeutically driven: it implicitly assumes that the reason for
rescuing abused children is a therapeutic outcome – safer and healthier
children. Yet it infrequently goes beyond merely assuming that things
will improve if we just do something. If a duty to rescue abused
children is therapeutically driven, then it is reasonable to rephrase
the inquiry to ask when rescue will be therapeutic and only then, if at
all, to consider a duty to rescue.

The proponents of a duty to rescue abused children assume an easy
and successful rescue. They would have us believe that the existence
of abuse is invariably clear, that the goal of intervention is acknowledged by all, and that the result of the process will be safer and
healthier children. Remarkably, both the majority and the dissent in
DeShaney give scant attention to the reality exposed by the facts of
that case. The social service agency did not ignore the reports of
abuse of Joshua DeShaney. It responded by seizing Joshua and returning him only after an interdisciplinary team concluded, albeit
wrongly with the benefit of hindsight, that the evidence did not
justify retaining custody. And it responded with a proposal for a
counselling programme for Joshua's father, a change in living arrangements at Joshua's home, and a pre-school programme for Joshua
to monitor his situation. Whether the social service agency was inac-
curate, indifferent or inadequate is unclear from the record. What is
clear is that trying is not enough, and that it may make things worse.

3.2   The Harm in Trying

Creating chaos out of order   Successful rescue of abused children turns
on the satisfaction of two requirements: the ability to identify abuse
and the ability to respond appropriately. To rescue an abused child
successfully there must first exist the ability to make an accurate
determination that abuse has occurred and the ability to make an

accurate identification of the source of that abuse – who needs to be rescued and from whom? Determining the existence of abuse and the identity of the abuser in the case of child sexual abuse frequently pits the testimony of a child against the testimony of an adult. When the sexual abuse consists of penetration, the physical evidence of abuse is less demonstrable than lay expectations might suggest.[44] But, when the sexual abuse consists of inappropriate touching, rather than penetration, no physical evidence of abuse may exist and, in any event, the identity of the abuser is not likely to be subject to non-testimonial proof.

The research literature does not reveal accurate tests to identify victims of sexual abuse or sexual abusers. We must proceed cautiously:

> Child abuse research has grown geometrically over the past 2 decades, leading to a major expansion of our knowledge base. However, the quality of research designs and methods has not advanced in proportion to the quantity of the studies. Consequentially, many questionable research findings have found a life of their own and are often treated as 'established facts' despite being based on methodologically inadequate studies.[45]

One popular subject of testimony by some child abuse professionals to aid in identifying children who have been sexually abused is the child sexual abuse accommodation syndrome, a pattern of behaviour thought to be common in children who have been victims of sexual abuse.[46] This pattern of behaviour is thought to include secrecy, helplessness, accommodation, unconvincing and delayed disclosures, and recantation of disruptive disclosures.[47] One problem with the use of this syndrome as a forensic tool to identify children who have been sexually abused is that a critical review of the published research does not reveal that children have common reactions to sexual abuse.[48]

Meta-analysis of the research reveals that children react in diverse ways to sexual abuse, depending upon a number of variables that include the age and developmental level of the child, the frequency of abuse and the time period over which it occurred, the relationship of the abuser to the child, the manipulation or control of the child by the abuser, the reaction of family and friends to the revelation of abuse, and the degree of violence involved.[49] The syndrome does not distinguish the effects of other stressors in the child's life, such as a divorce of parents, change in residence or problems at school.[50] Thus confidence that a child's behaviour is a reliable indicator of sexual abuse is unfounded. Compounding the problem of our limited knowledge about behaviour that identifies sexually abused children is the problem of the reliability of allegations of sexual abuse. For example, 'professionals often believe that allegations [of abuse] that arise in divorce/custody disputes are less likely to be true'.[51] The concern that parents and others may play a role in encouraging children's complaints of abuse raises the question of children's memory and suggestibility that has been a particular concern in cases of sexual abuse. 'How good, in both absolute and relative terms, is the memory of children for eye-witnessed or experienced events? How do the child's memory functions change with age? How is a child's recall of events best facilitated and least contaminated? ... Unfortunately, the state of [psychology] is such that we do not answer with one voice.'[52]

The extent of the problem may be best illustrated by a report of researchers whose work most strongly supports children's resistance to suggestion:

> Children do not make up facts often, both studies agree, but ... we can conclude that children are especially likely to accept an interviewer's suggestions when they are younger, when they are interrogated after a long delay, when they feel intimidated by the interviewer, when the interviewer's suggestions are strongly stated and frequently repeated, and when more than one interviewer makes the same strong suggestions.[53]

At best, there is much with which to be concerned as adults with their own agenda play a role in asserting, denying and investigating allegations of child abuse. Accordingly, judges and juries are often concerned whether to believe the child who claims to have been abused rather than the adult who denies the abuse.[54] Here again some child abuse professionals have offered their expertise on yet another form of syndrome evidence, the battering parent syndrome. The battering parent syndrome is a cluster of traits thought common in adults who physically abuse children. [55] These traits include low self-esteem, a short temper, high blood pressure, social isolation, lack of trust, inadequate child development knowledge and parenting skills, and having been abused as a child.[56] The use of this syndrome in identifying battering parents poses two problems. First, the rules of evidence exclude the use of character evidence when offered to show conformity and have therefore resulted in exclusion of this evidence when offered to identify the defendant as an abuser.[57] Second, there is substantial disagreement in the research literature about these traits thought common in adults who abuse children. [58] One researcher has opined that 'the ability to separate out a distinct group of parents (or future parents) who will physically abuse or serious [sic] neglect one or more of their children will probably never be possible'.[59]

Putting aside the evidentiary limitations on the use of character evidence to show conformity, both the potential inaccuracy and accuracy of this syndrome is troubling. If the battering parent syndrome inaccurately describes child abusers, then it suggests the lack of an accurate basis for determining the identity of abusers. We may be punishing or treating the wrong person. Accordingly, not only is it unlikely that intervention will be therapeutic, but the child may be placed at increased risk owing to the false sense of security that the danger has been abated. If the battering parent syndrome accurately identifies abusers, then it suggests an anti-therapeutic consequence of intervention. The dynamic described by the battering parent syndrome is that of a person with poor impulse control and lack of social support systems who responds to stress with displaced aggression towards a child.[60] An accusation of child abuse directed at a person described by that dynamic can be expected to increase the stress that precipitated the abuse and, correspondingly, increase the risk of inappropriate anger or resentment. The irony is that, if the battering parent syndrome accurately identifies the behaviour of child abusers, the very act of rescue from abuse is likely to increase the risk of abuse for that child or other members of the family unless great skill and effort are utilised.[61]

Yet another syndrome, the battered child syndrome,[62] offers assistance in identifying children who have been physically abused. 'Although the findings are quite variable, the syndrome should be considered in any child exhibiting evidence of possible trauma or neglect (fracture of any bone, subdural hematoma, multiple soft tissue injuries, poor skin hygiene, or malnutrition) or where there is a marked discrepancy between the clinical findings and the historical data as supplied by the parents.'[63] The breadth of the battered child syndrome suggests that it may be useful as a clinical tool for health care providers in a case like *DeShaney* to identify cases in which further investigation of abuse is appropriate, but that it is not particularly useful as a forensic tool to identify cases in which abuse has occurred. Moreover, abuse can mimic organic and psychosocial diseases and organic and psychosocial diseases can mimic abuse.[64]

Although the use of misinformed myths, referred to by one author as 'ordinary common sense',[65] may lead to the conclusion that the existence and source of abuse will ordinarily be clear, a careful review of the research reveals that confidence in our ability to make accurate determinations of these questions is misplaced. Our facile constructs of what abuse and abusers look like reinforces convenient but erroneous myths. In our desire to simplify and control, we have deluded ourselves into believing that there is an order to the chaos.

What does the dog do after it catches the car it was chasing?   The second requirement for successful rescue of abused children by the state is the ability to respond appropriately. Even if we could accurately determine who has been abused by whom, we are faced with the proverbial problem of the dog who chases cars. 'No conflict has caused greater dissention [*sic*] among professionals working on behalf of abused children than the use of criminal prosecutions as a response to child abuse.'[66] There is sharp disagreement amongst professionals within the field between the inconsistent goals of treatment and punishment that is highlighted when the abuser is related to the child victim. The dominance of one approach over the other seems to vary over time.[67]

Those who argue in favour of treatment as the goal of intervention point to the role of family systems and the need to break the intergeneration cycle of abuse.[68] 'In working with the family it is essential to change both interactions to prevent or ameliorate abuse, and also to understand the specific meanings, beliefs, and realities of the family which connect with the abusive behaviour. Each member carries such realities, whether the family continues together or not, and these also require change.'[69] The familial denial that frequently surrounds abuse may increase and the willingness to participate in treatment may decrease when abuse is categorised as a criminal act. Punishment of the abuser may exacerbate familial tensions, including the financial repercussions of incarceration of the abuser whose support is lost. Even when a parent has sexually abused a child, the child may experience guilt over the parent's confinement,[70] and incarceration may leave the abuser in the criminal justice system without treatment.

Even if there were agreement upon the goal of treatment, however, that would not end the inquiry. There is not a professional consensus on the cause of child abuse.[71] In the case of both physical[72] and sexual abuse[73] of children multiple models or theories exist. Given the disagreement on aetiology, it is hardly surprising that, in general, treatment has not been a panacea.[74] Even the most highly touted programmes reveal a decrease in abuse in only 40 per cent or less of the families treated.[75] Moreover, there is a risk that treatment inappropriately visits responsibility for the abuse on non-abusing members of the family.[76] Those who argue in favour of punishment as the goal of intervention point to the need to protect the child and other vulnerable members of society from abuse and to send a strong deterrent message that child abuse will not be tolerated. They challenge a distinction in the punishment of strangers, but not family members who engage in similar acts with children[77] and they argue that children should not be treated differently from other victims of violence.

They also point out that punishment vindicates a sense of fairness and serves an educative function.

Yet, at least as a specific deterrent, the benefits of punishment alone are limited: 'Incarcerating the offender, without treatment, is only a temporary solution.'[78] While punishment does not perforce preclude treatment, it has anti-therapeutic consequences. From the perspective of the child, punishment of the offender may require that the child confront the abuser in court and be subjected to rigorous cross-examination.[79] In theory, a child's testifying against an adult abuser has the potential to be an empowering, therapeutic act. In practice, however, critics have charged that abused children are twice victimised, once by the abuser and a second time by the legal system.[80] Consequentially, a large percentage of cases are dropped because of the reluctance of the child to testify.[81]

Other anti-therapeutic consequences of punishment result from certain facets of the criminal justice system that reinforce common cognitive distortions in sex offenders that deny or minimise the inappropriateness of their conduct. Restructuring these cognitive distortions is an important part of the treatment process.[82] Plea bargaining dominates criminal adjudication and the cases of sex offenders are no exception.[83] The plea bargaining process may reinforce sexual offenders' denial or minimisation of their actions by accepting no contest (*nolo contendere*) pleas without an admission of guilt.[84] These cognitive distortions may also be reinforced by the way in which individuals identified as child sexual abusers are treated by fellow prisoners. Moreover, research on the efficacy of prison treatment programmes reveals that, when they are available, they may change behaviour within the institution, but there is scant evidence that they reduce the rate of recidivism upon release, and they show less promise than community-based treatment programmes.[85]

3.3   Zen and the Art of Rescue

Those who address the duty to rescue abused children often behave as if they were writing the script for an old Hollywood western in which the classification of the good folks and the bad folks is clear and calling in the cavalry guarantees that the good folks will be successfully rescued from the bad folks. The lessons of history should temper that zeal. The classification of the good folks and the bad folks has often changed with an historical perspective, and calling in the cavalry has often done more harm than good.[86]

Proponents of a duty to rescue proceed on the assumption that intervention is generally preferable to non-intervention, yet we know little about the consequences of this choice: 'The impact of intervention has not been measured. There is virtually no longitudinal research measuring the impact of various types of intervention and no research comparing intervention to nonintervention.'[87] We are quick to forget that 'the real purpose of the scientific method is to make sure nature hasn't misled you into thinking you know something that you actually don't know'.[88]

There are numerous known limitations on intervention. Our capacity to identify the abused and the abuser and to agree upon and effectuate the goals of treatment or punishment will often be unsuccessful even with optimal efforts. We operate with imperfect knowledge and, far too often, with inadequate resources. In addition, there are 'several well known and consistently identified barriers to accurate judgment that negatively impinge upon the reliability and validity of human decisionmaking generally and clinician's decisionmaking particularly and [suggest] that judgments of experienced clinicians are in many cases more susceptible to error than those of trainees and sometimes even lay decisionmakers'.[89] The judgemental errors, or heuristics, identified by cognitive psychologists are availability, representativeness and anchoring. Availability refers to the tendency to give undue weight to an event based upon the ease with which it can be recalled. Thus a particularly vivid characteristic of an abused child may be remembered by a child protective service worker to the exclusion of other less vivid but more numerous characteristics when generalising about the characteristics of abused children. Representativeness refers to erroneous associations with a larger organisational structure that ignore such considerations as base rates and sample size. Thus a child protective service worker who sees a particular characteristic in a large number of abused children may assume that this trait distinguishes abused children from non-abused children, without examining other explanations for these characteristics, such as ethnicity or socio-economic status, or comparing the frequency of that characteristic in a controlled study of large numbers of abused and non-abused children of differing ethnicity and socio-economic status. Anchoring refers to the tendency to make a final decision based upon initial impressions rather than subsequent information. For example, a child protective service worker who meets early in the investigation an alleged abuser who makes a favourable impression is more likely to discount subsequently received evidence pointing to that person as the source of the abuse than if the worker meets that person late in the investigation having received all other available evidence of abuse.

The capacity of child care professionals to make accurate determinations of abuse and abuser is limited.[90] Perhaps more perplexing, however, is the fact that child care professionals, like other professionals, often profess their competence to reach accurate conclusions in the face of overwhelming research to the contrary. In our rush to do good we embrace an omniscience that obscures the complexity of the problem and increases the likelihood of unsuccessful rescue. And unsuccessful rescue of abused children entails more than simply not obtaining the desired positive result. It risks dissuading others from assisting, and also poses numerous anti-therapeutic risks.[91] As noted above, unsuccessful rescue may exacerbate the stress that precipitated the abuse and increase the risk of inappropriate anger or resentment towards the child or other family members. Thus unsuccessful rescue may increase the probability and severity of physical abuse. In addition, unsuccessful rescue risks hardening both the physical and sexual abuser to treatment.

Research on individuals who sexually abuse children reveals a series of cognitive distortions to deny or minimise responsibility for their actions.[92] 'I did not touch the child,' 'It was the child's idea,' or 'It was enjoyable to the child' are typical of child sexual abusers' cognitive distortions.[93] An important part of the treatment process is restructuring these cognitive distortions. Research on caregivers who physically abuse children reveals that they often feel justified by children's defiance of their authority.[94] When intervention founders because of insufficient evidence to conclude that abuse occurred or because of insufficient resources to pursue the case it risks reinforcing the abuser's denial, minimisation or justification. *DeShaney* provides a powerful example of this risk. Joshua was temporarily seized by the social service agency and then returned to his father because of insufficient evidence of abuse, although the agency did advance a therapeutic programme. The actions of Joshua's father in continuing to abuse Joshua and in failing to comply with the therapeutic programme raise the troubling question as to whether the return based upon insufficient evidence of abuse reinforced the denial, minimisation or justification of his actions and overshadowed the agency's message that there was a serious problem for which he needed, and the agency offered, help.

Thus, if a duty of the state to rescue abused children should be recognised only when rescue will be therapeutic, it will rarely be possible to justify such a duty. Our knowledge and ability to address child abuse seriously lag behind our humanitarian instincts. Tell the cavalry to stand down. It may be best to assist by not rescuing. 'Judicious non-intervention' has been suggested by Edwin Schur in the context of juvenile delinquency to minimise judicial intervention in specific cases.[95] Rather than intervene in individual cases of delinquency, Schur argues that our efforts should be directed toward voluntary programmes that address the underlying problems that foster delinquency. Notwithstanding the differences between delinquency and abuse, the logic of non-intervention in individual cases can also be advanced in the case of child abuse. If a duty to rescue individual abused children should be recognised only when rescue will be therapeutic, then limits on our knowledge of who, when and how to rescue that thwart therapeutic results should limit recognition of a duty to rescue individual children. It might be argued that, rather than abandon the concept of a duty to rescue abused children, that duty should be reconstructed. Research consistently reveals a correlation between poverty and physical abuse of children. [96] While physical abuse of children exists in rich and poor families, poverty undoubtedly adds to the emotional burden of any family. One commentator explains the dynamic between poverty and abuse as resulting from an 'inability to participate in the economic process of society, their own feelings of inadequacy, and [that] society is reluctant to bear the responsibility for effectively meeting their needs'. [97] At least as a response to physical abuse, broad-based voluntary social programmes designed to address the issues that underlie poverty – employment, health care, education and housing – may maximise the therapeutic consequences for the greatest number of children and minimise the anti-therapeutic consequences of ineffective intervention in specific cases. [98]

The attractiveness of this solution must, however, ultimately be tempered by the enormity of the task and the political realities. Not only is it difficult to articulate meaningful criteria for a state duty to eradicate poverty, but, at least in the United States, the political trends suggest that such an effort is unlikely to be fruitful in the foreseeable future. Moreover, it is unlikely that efforts directed towards rescuing individual abused children will be abandoned. Thus, while a therapeutic jurisprudence analysis may not support a duty to rescue in specific cases, the certainty that such efforts will continue calls for an analysis of ways in which the anti-therapeutic effects of the existing legal regime might be minimised. Inappropriate termination of attempts to rescue abused children are anti-therapeutic. In addition to terminating the rescue and leaving the child vulnerable to continued abuse, inappropriate termination risks making matters worse than if no rescue was attempted, by exacerbating tensions and reinforcing the abuser's cognitive distortions surrounding abuse. One way that the law can play a therapeutic role in avoiding inappropriate termination of attempts to rescue abused children is by minimising the difference between investigative standards for child abuse and adjudicative standards for termination of parental rights or criminal conviction for abuse. [99]

One investigative statutory duty that applies in all states to those who work with children, and in many states to everyone, is the duty to report child abuse. [100] The difference between investigative standards for mandatory reporting of child abuse and adjudicative standards for prosecution and/or termination of parental rights may play an unrecognised anti-therapeutic role in initiating rescues that will be terminated for failure to satisfy the adjudicative standard. It also floods the system with inappropriate cases so that investigation and prosecution of appropriate cases is frustrated. Society's response to the problem of child abuse, beginning in the mid-1960s, has been to pass increasingly vague and over-broad laws that mandate the reporting of child abuse.[101] Although the adjudicative standard requires proof beyond a reasonable doubt of a past act of abuse in criminal cases and proof by clear and convincing evidence in termination cases, investigative standards often require only reasonable cause to suspect that an undefined harm to a child's health or welfare is threatened.[102] Moreover, it is far from clear that the vague and over-broad reporting laws have been aimed at the appropriate cases. While common sense might suggest that these laws result in identifying more cases of abuse, the resulting number of false positives and false negatives is alarming: some 60 per cent of reported cases are not substantiated by child protective services and over 60 per cent of abuse remains unreported.[103]

These vague and over-broad reporting requirements have resulted in a geometric increase in the number of reported cases.[104] In practice, however, 'the epidemic of reporting has not been matched by a rise in appropriate services to the child and family'.[105] As reporting rises at an astounding rate, funding for child protective services has not kept pace. The low threshold of reporting has resulted in a system that is inundated with reports of insubstantial or unproven risks and thus is often unable to respond effectively when real danger exists.[106] Twenty-five per cent of child deaths from abuse and neglect occur after reports have been made to child protective service agencies.[107] Good intentions have brought the system to its knees. *DeShaney* stands as a glaring example of this problem. Moreover, child protective service workers are overworked and suffer from low pay and high turn-over.[108] In short, the difference in the investigative and adjudicative standards may well be anti-therapeutic and there appears to be good reason to crystallise the standards[109] and narrow the gap by raising the investigative standard for mandatory reporting of child abuse.

The duty to report child abuse should be crystallised through a practical articulation of the specific types of behaviours required to be reported and those not required to be reported. Reporting of inappropriate cases takes precious time from child protective services and threatens to bring about the anti-therapeutic consequences discussed previously. To crystallise and close the gap between investigative and adjudicative standards requires consideration of the magnitude of the harm required to be reported, its nature (that is, physical, sexual or emotional harm) and the relevant time frame (past or future harm). The greater the harm, the more it is limited to physical and sexual abuse, and the more it is limited to past harm, the narrower becomes the gap between the investigative and adjudicative standards.

Another potential anti-therapeutic consequence of the duty to report child abuse occurs when a patient discloses abuse to a therapist who is then required to report that abuse. Consider the case of a parent in treatment for issues not thought to be related to abuse who tells the therapist about an incident one year ago when the parent lost her temper and used excessive force to discipline her child. It is unlikely that this incident will result in termination of parental rights or criminal prosecution, yet the therapist is probably under an obligation to report the incident to the authorities. Accepting the limitations on the efficacy of therapy noted above,[110] given that the state is likely to offer nothing better than the treatment that the parent has already instituted and may well offer worse, keeping this person in treatment with her current therapist may be the best that we may hope for to reduce the risk of her abusing again. Therefore, when the abuser is already in treatment and termination or prosecution is unlikely, reporting should not be mandatory if it impedes treatment. Therapists often regard mandatory reporting of child abuse as a threat to treatment.[111] Although the effect of the fear of disclosure on treatment is far from clear,[112] therapists often perceive disruption of their ability to help and the poor quality of child protective services as justifying non-reporting.[113] When the abuser is already in treatment there is a compelling reason to consider recognising an exception to the reporting requirement so long as there is no reason to believe that the abuse is continuing and treatment of the child and the family is adequately addressed.[114] There is no evidence that therapists provide a unique fund of evidence of abuse that is not otherwise discoverable, and this exception would have no application to anyone other than the therapist. Therefore, if the abuse is continuing or has risen to a significant level, others who are not excepted from the reporting requirement, such as teachers and primary care physicians, will still be required to report the abuse.

It seems unlikely that child protective service agencies will receive a substantial increase in funding at any time in the near future and it is not clear that funding directed to the reduction of child abuse would best be put to that use in any event. The therapeutic role that the law can play is to reduce over-reporting and unsubstantiated cases of abuse that dilute the efforts of child protective services. The law should assist in permitting child protective services to focus maximal effort on serious cases of abuse that are not otherwise being adequately addressed. Perhaps then they will have the capacity to respond appropriately to tomorrow's Joshua DeShaney.

4   Conclusion

Duty is not some magical incantation or a concept 'sacrosanct in itself, but only an expression of the sum total of those considerations of policy which lead the law to say that the particular plaintiff is entitled to protection'.[115] It is difficult to construct a vision of a caring society in which children are not entitled to protection from abuse. Thus there is an understandable desire to recognise a duty of the state to rescue abused children. This desire may affirm our sense of humanity, but it ignores the empirical evidence that intervention in specific cases will not necessarily make things better and may make things worse. Our knowledge of who has abused whom, and when and how to intervene is woefully incomplete. Charging in with good intentions but inadequate skills or resources risks causing significant harm. Viewing the duty of the state to rescue individual abused children through the lens of therapeutic jurisprudence leads to the conclusion that, because the evidence in favour of rescue being therapeutic is not persuasive, a duty of the state to rescue individual children cannot be justified.

Intervention in specific cases of abuse may be the least effective way to realise the vision of a caring society in which children are entitled to protection from abuse. Recasting the duty to rescue abused children as a broadly based duty of the state to eradicate the poverty that precipitates much physical abuse could reduce physical abuse more effectively while minimising the anti-therapeutic consequences of intervention in specific cases. This duty, however, seems impracticable as a specific duty in tort law and as a political reality. Perhaps the most therapeutic change in the duty to rescue that may be achieved to permit child protective services to focus limited resources on serious cases of abuse is narrowing and crystallising the requirements for intervention.

The role of the law in changing behaviour also cautions against a duty of the state to rescue abused children in specific cases. The failure of a private citizen to effect an easy rescue in the paradigmatic case of the child drowning in a shallow pool[116] may well turn on the private citizen's motivation. The only barrier to successful rescue in this paradigm is the willingness of the private citizen to act. Thus, if tort law plays a role in the actions of private citizens,[117] recognition of a duty to rescue increases the likelihood of a successful rescue of the drowning child by a private citizen.[118] The failure of the state to rescue an abused child successfully is not similarly an easy rescue whose success turns only on the motivation of the rescuer. The problem cannot similarly be categorised as a function of our not wanting to rescue, rather than not knowing how. Unlike the citizen who walks past the child drowning in the shallow pool, there is evidence in the positive law of every state that it has the motivation to rescue abused children. Every state in the United States has a mandatory child abuse reporting law and child protective service agencies to respond to cases of suspected child abuse. The potential of tort liability for failing to act on a report of abuse would only increase the risk of perfunctory removal with cursory investigation leaving the issue of return to the court, thereby insulating the workers from liability.[119] Rather than motivation, what stands in the way of successful rescue of abused children in specific cases is a multitude of factors that include methodologically sound research on the identification and treatment of abuse, adequate funding and staffing of well trained childcare professionals, and a directed, narrowly focused charge. Recognition of a duty to rescue does not adequately address the considerations that make successful rescue of abused children in specific cases by the state more likely.

Notes

*   Research on this chapter was supported by a grant from the M.D. Anderson Research Foundation. Barbara Atwood, Joel Dvoskin, Thomas Mayo, Marjorie Moyers and David Wexler provided insightful comments on an earlier draft.

1   James B. Ames, 'Law and Morals', 22 Harvard Law Review, 97 (1908); Frances Bohlen, 'The Moral Duty to Aid Others as a Basis of Tort Law', 56 *University of Pennsylvania Law Review*, 217 (1908); Saul Levmore, 'Waiting for Rescue: An Essay on the Evolution and Incentive Structure of the Law of Affirmative Obligations', 72 *Virginia Law Review*, 879 (1986); Ernest J. Weinrib, 'The Case for a Duty to Rescue', 90 *Yale Law Journal*, 247 (1980).

2   The term 'state' has multiple meanings in the United States. It may refer to the 50 states that comprise the United States and it may also refer to the government – federal, state and local – in its entirety. The unique nature of federalism in the United States involving a sharing of power between the federal and state governments and the distinct roles each plays in social welfare programmes renders the distinction one of consequence. However, given the space and scope limitations of this chapter, I have chosen to lump the federal and state governments together in my use of the word 'state' and treatment of the duty to rescue except where I have explicitly indicated otherwise.

3   Although scholars have challenged this negative view of the constitution, the courts have maintained its viability. See Susan Bandes, 'The Negative Constitution: A Critique', 88 *Michigan Law Review*, 2271 (1990). See also Catherine Mackinnon, *Feminism Unmodified* (Cambridge, 1987), 207, advancing a feminist critique of the negative constitution.

4   Health Services for the Homeless, 42 U.S.C.A. § 256 (West 1991); Health Services for Residents of Public Housing, 42 U.S.C.A. § 256a (West 1991); Health Services for Aged and Disabled, 42 U.S.C.A. §§ 1395–1396ccc (West 1991); Hospital, Nursing Home, Domiciliary, and Medical Care, 38 U.S.C.A. §§ 1701–1764 (West 1991 & Supp. 1992); Indian Health Care Improvement Act 25 U.S.C.A. §§ 1601–1682 (West 1983 & Supp. 1992).

5   *Yick Wo* v. *Hopkins*, 118 U.S. 356 (1886).

6   *Goldberg* v. *Kelly*, 397 U.S. 254 (1970).

7   W. Page Keeton *et al.*, *Prosser and Keeton on the Law of Torts* (St. Paul, 5th ed., 1984), § 56.

8   Thomas Cooley, *Liability of Public Officers* (St. Louis, 1877).

9   Thomas Cooley, *A Treatise on the Law of Torts, or the Wrongs Which Arise Independently of Contract* (Chicago, 4th ed., 1932), 385.

10   *Williams* v. *State*, 34 Cal.3d 18, 664 P.2d 137, 192 Cal. Rptr. 233 (1983); *Cuffy* v. *City of New York*, 69 N.Y.2d 255, 505 N.E.2d 937 (1987); *Chapman* v. *Philadelphia*, 290 Pa. Super. 281, 434 A.2d 753 (1981).

11   *Schuster* v. *City of New York*, 154 N.E.2d 534 (N.Y. 1958).

12   Both the states and the federal government must compensate owners of property for public takings. *Chicago, Burlington & Quincy Ry. Co.* v. *Chicago*, 166 U.S. 226 (1897).

13   *Brasel* v. *Children's Services Div.*, 56 Or. App. 559, 642 P.2d 696 (1982).

14   *State* v. *Silva*, 478 P.2d 591 (Nev. 1970).

15   Or. Rev. Stat. Ann § 30.270 (1991) ($50 000); Wis. Stat. Ann. § 893.80 (West Supp 1989) ($50 000).

16   Mo. Ann. Stat. § 210.135 (Vernon 1983); Ill. Ann. Stat. ch. 23, para. 2059 (Smith-Hurd Supp. 1992); N.Y. Social Services Law § 419 (McKinney Supp. 1992); Fla. Stat. Ann. § 415.511 (West Supp 1992); Minn. Stat. Ann. § 626.556, Subd. 4 (West Supp. 1992): N.C. Gen. Stat. § 7A-550 (1991); N.D. Cent. Code § 50-25.1-09 (1989); S.D. Codified Laws Ann. § 26-8A-14 (1992); Wyo. Stat. § 14-3-209 (1986).

17   See, for example, *Indian Towing Co., Inc.* v. *United States*, 350 U.S. 61, 69 (1955) (Coast Guard not obliged to maintain lighthouse service, but if it represents that it maintains a particular lighthouse it is obliged to use due care in maintaining it in good working order).

18   See *Hawaii* v. *Standard Development Co.*, 405 U.S. 251 (1972); *Falkland* v. *Bertie*, 23 Eng. Rep. 815 (Ch. 1696). 'Under this doctrine the sovereign has both the right and the duty to protect the persons and property of those who are unable to care for themselves because of minority or mental illness. In England, the guardianship of those under legal disability was originally intrusted to the feudal lords, but was taken over by the Crown in the 13th century and delegated to the Lord Chancellor. In this country, the royal prerogative was inherited by the individual states and has been held to constitute part of the original jurisdiction of equity courts' (Hugh A. Ross, 'Commitment of the Mentally Ill: Problems in Law and Policy', 57 *Michigan Law Review*, 945, at 956–7 (1959) (citations omitted)).

19   *Cruzan* v. *Director*, Missouri Dept. of Health, 110 S. Ct. 2841 (1990).

20   *In re* Quinlan, 335 A.2d 647 (N.J. 1976).

21   Samuel J. Brakel *et al.*, *The Mentally Disabled and the Law* (Chicago, 1985), 24–5.

22   *Roe* v. *Wade*, 410 U.S. 113 (1973).

23   *Santosky* v. *Kramer*, 455 U.S. 745, 766 (1982); *Stanley* v. *Illinois*, 405 U.S. 645 (1972).

24   Robert Burt, 'Forcing Protection on Children and Their Parents: The Impact of *Wyman* v. *James*', 69 *Michigan Law Review*), 1259 (1971).

25   489 U.S. 189 (1989).

26   Ibid.

27   *Estelle* v. *Gamble*, 429 U.S. 97 (1982).

28   *Youngberg* v. *Romeo*, 457 U.S. 307 (1982).

29   Benjamin Zipursky, 'DeShaney and the Jurisprudence of Compassion', 65 *New York University Law Review*, 1101, at 1107 n. 58 (1990).

30   *Harlow* v. *Fitzgerald*, 457 U.S. 800 (1982).

31   Wis. Stat. Ann. § 893.80 (West Supp. 1989).

32   Wisconsin would render government conduct immune from tort claims unless it involved wilful and wanton conduct or a ministerial act, as contrasted with a

discretionary function. *C.L.* v. *Olson*, 422 N.W.2d 614 (Wis. 1988); *Yotvat* v. *Roth*, 290 N.W.2d 524 (Wis. Ct. App. 1980).

33   See authorities cited *supra*, n. 16.

34   See, for example, *Nelson* v. *Freeman*, 537 F. Supp. 602, 610–11 (W.D. Mo. 1982) (federal court sitting in a diversity action applying Missouri law rejects under Missouri's public duty doctrine a claim that child protective service was liable for failing to investigate a report of sexual abuse of a child).

35   Aviam Soifer, 'Moral Ambition, Formalism, and the "Free World" of DeShaney', 57 *George Washington Law Review*, 1513 (1989).

36   Jack M. Beerman, 'Administrative Failure and Local Democracy: The Politics of DeShaney', *Duke Law Journal*, 1078 (1990); Thomas A. Eaton and Michael L. Wells, 'Government Inaction as a Constitutional Tort: DeShaney and Its Aftermath', 66 *Washington Law Review*, 107 (1991); Laurence Tribe, 'The Curvature of Constitutional Space: What Lawyers Can Learn From Modern Physics', 103 *Harvard Law Review*, 1 (1989).

37   Akhil R. Amar and Daniel Widawsky, 'Child Abuse as Slavery: A Thirteenth Amendment Response to DeShaney', 105 *Harvard Law Review*, 1359 (1992).

38   Madelyn S. Milchman, 'Professional Controversies in Child Sexual Abuse Assessment', 20 *Journal Psychiatry and Law*, 45, at 50 (1992).

39   David B. Wexler and Bruce J. Winick, *Essays in Therapeutic Jurisprudence* (Durham, 1991); David B. Wexler, *Therapeutic Jurisprudence: The Law as a Therapeutic Agent* (Durham, 1990), vii.

40   Wexler and Winick, op. cit., xi. This inquiry into the therapeutic dimension of law can be analysed from four perspectives. First, the law may play a role in producing psychological dysfunction through discouragement of necessary treatment, encouragement of unnecessary treatment and encouragement of sick behaviour or absence of responsibility; ibid., at 19–24. Second, legal rules may explicitly seek to promote therapeutic consequences as in the case of a right to treatment; ibid., at 24–30. Third, legal procedures may play a therapeutic role in the parties' psychological response to the legal process, as contrasted with the outcome; ibid., at 30–33. Fourth, the roles played by attorneys and judges may have therapeutic consequences for the other actors in the legal process; ibid., at 33–7.

41   Mary L. Durham and John M. LaFond, 'A Search for the Missing Premise of Involuntary Therapeutic Commitment: Effective Treatment of the Mentally Ill', 40 *Rutgers Law Review*, 303 (1988); Leonard I. Stein and May Test, 'Alternative to Mental Hospital Treatment: I. Conceptual Model, Treatment Programme, and Clinical Evaluation', 37 *Archives of General Psychiatry*, 392 (1980); Bruce J. Winick, 'Competency to Consent to Voluntary Hospitalization: A Therapeutic Jurisprudence Analysis of *Zinermon* v. *Burch*', in Wexler and Winick, op. cit., 83.

42   Brakel *et al.*, op. cit., 178 n. 10.

43   See articles cited *supra*, n. 1.

44   When penetration is alleged to have occurred, the ability to ascertain whether abuse occurred from a physical examination of the hymenal orifice diameter of girls or perianal examination of boys or girls is of questionable validity. Jan E. Paradise, 'Predictive Accuracy and the Diagnosis of Sexual Abuse: A Big Issue About a Little Tissue', 13 *Child Abuse & Neglect*, 13 (1989); John McCann, 'Perianal Findings in Prepubertal Children Selected for Non Abuse: A Descriptive Study', 13 *Child Abuse & Neglect*, 179 (1989).

45   Erich Mash and David A. Wolfe, 'Methodological Issues in Research on Physical Child Abuse', 18 (1) *Criminal Justice & Behavior*, 8 (1991). *See also* Jeffrey J. Haugaard and Robert E. Emery, 'Methodological Issues in Child Sexual Abuse Research', 13 *Child Abuse & Neglect*, 89 (1989).

46   David McCord, 'Expert Psychological Testimony About Child Complaints in

Sexual Abuse Prosecutions: A Foray into The Admissibility of Novel Psychological Evidence', 77 *J. Criminal Law & Criminology,* 1, at 9 (1986).

47   Roland C. Summit, 'The Child Abuse Accommodation Syndrome', 7 *Child Abuse & Neglect,* 177 (1983).

48   In addition, the research that purports to identify this syndrome is plagued by methodological flaws. It often fails to compare matched samples of abused and non-abused children and thus fails to account for differences in socio-economic status or race, for example, that may produce the effects seen. See Mash and Wolf, op. cit., *supra,* n. 45, at 17.

49   Lucy Berliner, 'Clinical Work With Sexually Abused Children', in Clive R. Hollin and Kevin Howells (Eds), *Clinical Approaches to Sex Offenders and Their Victims* (New York, 1991), 211; Angela Browne and David Finkelhor, 'Impact of Child Sexual Abuse: A Review of the Literature', 99 *Psychological Bulletin,* 66 (1986); Suzanne M. Sgroi, 'Child Sexual Assault: Some Guidelines for Intervention and Assessment', in Ann W. Burgess *et al.* (Eds), *Sexual Assault of Children & Adolescents* (Lexington, 1978), 134–5.

50   Mash and Wolf, op. cit., *supra,* n. 45, at 17.

51   Lucy Berliner and Jon R. Conte, 'The Process of Victimization: The Victim's Perspective', 14 *Child Abuse & Neglect,* 29 (1990). See also Nancy Thoennes and Jessica Pearson, 'A Difficult Dilemma: Responding to Sexual Abuse Allegations in Custody and Visitation Disputes', in Douglas J. Besharov (Ed.), *Protecting Children From Abuse and Neglect: Policy and Practice* (Springfield, 1988), 93–4.

52   John Doris (Ed.), *The Suggestibility of Children's Recollections* (Washington, DC, 1991).

53   Gail S. Goodman and Alison Clarke-Stewart, 'Suggestibility in Children's Testimony: Implications for Sexual Abuse Investigations', in John Doris (Ed.), *The Suggestibility of Children's Recollections* (Washington, DC, 1991), 103.

54   Gail S. Goodman *et al.,* 'When a Child Takes the Stand: Jurors' Perceptions of Children's Eyewitness Testimony', 11 *Law & Human Behavior,* 27 (1987); Michael R. Leippe, 'Children on the Witness Stand: A Communication/Persuasion Analysis of Jurors' Reactions to Child Witnesses', in Stephen J. Ceci *et al.* (Eds), *Children's Eyewitness Memory* (New York, 1987). But see David F. Ross *et al.,* 'The Child in the Eyes of the Jury: Assessing Mock Jurors' Perceptions of the Child Witness', 14 *Law & Human Behavior,* 5 (1990).

55   Thomas Bulleit Jr., 'The Battering Parent Syndrome: Inexpert Testimony as Character Evidence', 17 *Journal of Law Reform,* 653 (1984).

56   Audrey M. Berger, 'The Child Abusing Family (Pt I)', 8 *Am. J. Family Therapy,* 53 (1980); William N. Friedrich and Karen K. Wheeler, 'The Abusing Parent Revisited: A Decade of Psychological Research', 170 *J. Nervous & Mental Disease,* 577 (1982).

57   Daniel W. Shuman, *Psychiatric and Psychological Evidence* (Colorado Springs, 1986), 314–16. At best this character evidence describes increased behaviour of the type studied in the target group as compared with the general population, but says nothing about the behaviour of a particular person on a particular occasion. Consequentially the use of character evidence to show conformity is generally inadmissible unless the defendant chooses to open the door to this evidence (Fed. R. Evid. 404 (a)). The nature of these data gives clues to their possible misuse. For example, while retrospective studies suggest that many abusive parents were abused as children, prospective studies reveal that most parents who were abused as children do not abuse their children. Mash and Wolf, op. cit., *supra,* n. 45, at 15. Juries may be insensitive to the risk of false positives in utilising this evidence.

Thus thoughtful researchers who claim to have developed accurate instruments to identify abusers tout their devices as screening tools to identify individuals in need of help and not for forensic use to determine retrospectively that someone abused a particular child on a particular occasion. Joel S. Milner, 'Physical Child Abuse Perpetrator Screening and Evaluations', 18 (1) *Criminal Justice & Behavior*, 47, at 50 (1991).

58　See for example, William A. Attemeir *et al.*, 'Prediction of Child Abuse: a Prospective Study of Feasibility', 8 *Child Abuse & Neglect*, 393 (1984). This prospective study used the characteristics of the battering parent syndrome to determine their accuracy in predicting abuse in a population of 1400 expectant mothers at Vanderbilt University Hospital. Using these criteria it was predicted that 273 would abuse their children. In a two-year follow-up using the child abuse reporting registry it was discovered that 6 per cent of 273 predicted to abuse did abuse and that 1 per cent of 1127 predicted to be non-abusers abused. As 2 per cent of the population studied abused, a prediction of non-abuse would be 98 per cent accurate. See also Ben Bursten, 'Detecting Child Abuse by Studying Parents', 13 *Bulletin of the American Academy of Psychiatry & Law*, 273 (1985).

Even in the case of the Child Abuse Potential Inventory, a psychological test thought to be highly accurate in predicting potential for abuse, prudent researchers have noted that 'psychologists using the CAP and similar instruments should be especially careful to ensure that legal and social service agencies do not substantiate allegations of abuse merely on the basis of such tests'. Gary B. Melton and Susan Limbers, 'Psychologists' Involvement in Cases of Child Maltreatment: Limits of Role and Expertise', 44 *American Psychologist*, 1225, at 1231 (1989).

59　Ray Helfer, 'Basic Issues Concerning Predictions', in Ray Helfer and C. Henry Kempe (Eds), *Child Abuse and Neglect: The Family and the Community* (Cambridge, Massachusetts, 1976), 363.

60　This relationship is supported by the research linking life events, stress and lack of social support with abuse. Dorothy C. Howze and Jonathon B. Kotch, 'Disentangling Life Events, Stress and Social Support: Implications for the Primary Prevention of Child Abuse and Neglect', 8 *Child Abuse & Neglect*, 401 (1984).

61　It might be suggested that Sherman and Berk's research on the effects of arrest for simple domestic violence rebuts this suggestion, but that conclusion is not supported by their research. Lawrence W. Sherman and Richard A. Berk, 'The Specific Deterrent Effect of Arrest for Domestic Assault', 49 *American Sociological Review*, 261 (1984). Sherman and Berk found that the likelihood of future domestic violence decreased when police arrested the suspect rather than ordered the suspect to leave or offered advice. Even apart from the methodological flaws in this research and the absence of parallel aetiologies for spousal abuse and child abuse, this research reinforces rather than rebuts the suggestion that botched rescues may increase the risk of child abuse. Sherman and Berk's finding is not that intervention, just doing something, necessarily makes things better. Rather it is that there is an appropriate response, and that some responses are much better than others.

62　C. Henry Kempe *et al.*, 'The Battered Child Syndrome', 181 *Journal of the American Medical Association*, 17 (1962).

63　Ibid., at 24.

64　Katherine K. Christoffel *et al.*, 'Should Child Abuse and Neglect be Considered When a Child Dies Unexpectedly?', 139 *Am. J. Dis. Child.*, 876 (1985); Robert H. Kirschner and Robert J. Stein, 'The Mistaken Diagnosis of Child Abuse: A Form of Medical Abuse', 139 *Am. J. Dis. Child.*, 873 (1985).

65　Michael Perlin, 'Pretextuality, Psychiatry and Law: Of 'Ordinary Common Sense', Heuristic Reasoning, and Cognitive Dissonance', 19 *Bulletin American Academy of Psychiatry & Law*, 131 (1991).

66　James Peters *et. al.*, 'Child Abuse is a Criminal Offense', in *Children and the Law* (Washington, DC, 1988), 161.

67　Douglas J. Besharov, *The Vulnerable Social Workers: Liability for Serving Children and Families* (Silver Springs, 1985). Besharov opines that 'most Americans believe that child maltreatment is primarily a social and psychological ill and that treatment and rehabilitation, not punishment and retribution, are the best means of protecting children'. Douglas J. Besharov, '"Doing Something" About Child Abuse: The Need to Narrow the Grounds for State Intervention', 8 *Harvard Journal of Law & Public Policy*, 539, at 553 (1985).

68   Noel Lustig *et al.*, 'Incest: A Family Group Survival Pattern', 14 *Archives of General Psychiatry*, 31 (1966).

69   Arnon Bentovim, 'Clinical Work With Families in Which Sexual Abuse Has Occurred', in Clive R. Hollin and Kevin Howells (Eds), *Clinical Approaches to Sex Offenders and Their Victims* (New York, 1991), 189.

70   Jeffrey J. Haugaard, 'The Use of Theories About the Etiology of Incest as Guidelines for Legal and Therapeutic Interactions', 6 *Behavioral Sciences and the Law*, 221, at 232 (1988).

71   Sandra T. Azar, 'Models of Child Abuse: A Metatheoretical Analysis', 18 (1) *Criminal Justice & Behavior*, 30 (1991); Richard I. Lanyon, 'Theories of Sex Offending', in Clive R. Hollin and Kevin Howells (Eds), *Clinical Approaches to Sex Offenders and Their Victims* (New York, 1991).

72   The theories advanced to explain physical abuse can be grouped according to assumptions regarding defect, deficiency, disruption and mismatch: Azar, op. cit., *supra*, n. 71, 34. An example of a defect theory is that abuse results from biologically triggered aggression. A deficiency theory views abuse as learned behaviour. Disruption theorists view abuse as responsive to some external stress such as a financial strain. Mismatch theorists suggest a transactional disparity.

73   The theories to explain child sexual abuse include psychodynamic theories (such as Oedipal complex), behavioural theories (such as learned behaviour), and biological theories (for example hormonal or chromosomal make-up): Jon R. Conte, 'The Nature of Sexual Offenses Against Children', in Clive R. Hollin and Kevin Howells (Eds), op. cit., 37–39.

74   Anne H. Cohn and Deborah Dar, 'Is Treatment Too Late: What Ten Years of Evaluate Research Tell Us', 11 *Child Abuse & Neglect*, 433, at 440 (1987).

75   Laille Gabinet, 'Child Abuse Treatment Failures Reveal Need for Redefinition of the Problem', 7 *Child Abuse & Neglect*, 395, at 396 (1983); Gordon Hall and Richard Hirschman, 'Sexual Aggression Against Children: A Conceptual Perspective of Etiology', 19 (1) *Criminal Justice & Behavior*, 8, at 9 (1992); Keith L. Kaufman and Leslie Rudy, 'Future Directions in the Treatment of Physical Child Abuse', 18 (1) *Criminal Justice & Behavior*, 82 at 83 (1991).

76   Jan Hindman, *Just Before Dawn* (Ontario, 1989), 38.

77   Scott Harshbargar, 'Prosecution is an Appropriate Response in Child Sexual Abuse Cases', 2 *J. Interpersonal Violence*, 108 (1987).

78   Reuben Lang *et al.*, 'Treatment of Incest and Pedophilic Offenders: A Pilot Study', 6 *Behavioral Sciences & the Law*, 239, at 251 (1988).

79   But see *Maryland v. Craig*, 110 S. Ct. 3157 (1990) (confrontation clause does not impose an absolute requirement of a face-to-face meeting between the defendant and a six-year-old victim of child abuse if the court determines that the child would experience serious emotional trauma such that the child could not reasonably communicate).

80   Eli H. Newberger, 'Prosecution: A Problematic Approach to Child Abuse', 2 *J. Interpersonal Violence*, 112 (1987).

81   *State v. Shepard*, 484 A.2d 1330, 1333 (N.J. Super 1984) (one prosecutor's office estimated that 90 per cent of its child abuse cases were dropped for this reason).

82   See infra, notes 92 and 93, and accompanying text.

83   Jeffrey A. Klotz, *et al.*, 'Cognitive Restructuring Through Law: A Therapeutic Jurisprudence Approach to Sex Offenders and the Plea Process', 15 *University of Puget Sound Law Review*, 601, at 604 (1992).

84   David B. Wexler and Bruce J. Winick, 'Therapeutic Jurisprudence and Criminal Justice Mental Health Issues', 16 *Mental Disability Law Reporter* , 225, at 229 (1992).

85   Derek Perkins, 'Clinical Work With Sex Offenders in Secure Settings', in Clive R. Hollin and Kevin Howells (Eds), op. cit., 173.

86   Dee A. Brown, *Bury My Heart at Wounded Knee: An Indian History of the American West* (New York, 1970).

87   Michael S. Wald, 'Thinking About Public Policy Toward Abuse and Neglect of Children: A Review of *Before the Best Interests of the Child*', 78 *Michigan Law Review*, 645, at 691 (1980).

88   Robert Pirsig, *Zen & the Art of Motorcycle Maintenance* (New York, 1975).

89   Donald N. Bersoff, 'Judicial Deference to Nonlegal Decisionmakers: Imposing Simplistic Solutions on Problems of Cognitive Complexity in Mental Health Law', 46 *Southern Methodist University Law Review*, 329 (1992).

90   Stephanie Ladson *et al.*, 'Do Physicians Recognise Sexual Abuse?', 141 *Am. J. Dis. Child.*, 411–15 (1987).

91   One anti-therapeutic risk I will not explore in detail given the scope of this chapter is the impact of intrusion by the state upon the parent–child relationship. To those who see the importance of an adequate psychological relationship between the child and parent as requiring parental autonomy unbroken by state intrusion, rescue, successful or unsuccessful, is detrimental to the child's development. Joseph Goldstein *et al.*, *Before the Best Interests of the Child* (New York, 1979), 8–10.

92   Derek Perkins, 'Clinical Work With Sex Offenders in Secure Settings', in Clive R. Hollin and Kevin Howells (Eds), op. cit., 168.

93   Gene G. Abel *et al.*, 'Complications, Consent, and Cognitions in Sex Between Children and Adults', 7 *International Journal of Law & Psychiatry*, 89, at 98–101 (1984); Nathan Pollock and Judith M. Hashmall, 'The Excuses of Child Molesters', 9 *Behavioral Sciences & Law*, 53, at 57 (1991).

94   Dorothee Dietrich *et al.*, 'Some Factors Influencing Abusers' Justifications of their Child Abuse', 14 *Child Abuse & Neglect*, 337, at 343 (1990).

95   Edwin M. Schur, *Radical Nonintervention: Rethinking the Delinquency Problem* (Englewood, 1973), 155.

96   US Dept of Health & Human Services, Study of National Incidence and Prevalence of Child Abuse and Neglect, 7-7 (1988).

97   Sanford Katz, *When Parents Fail* (Boston, 1971), 26–7.

98   See Leroy H. Peterson, 'Child Abuse and Neglect: The Myth of Classlessness', 48 *American Journal of Orthopsychiatry*, 608 (1978).

99   Because of the strong concern with perpetuation of the family, termination is permissible only upon a showing of abuse, neglect or abandonment by clear and convincing evidence. *Santosky v. Kramer*, 455 U.S. 745 (1982). Criminal prosecution of child abuse requires proof beyond a reasonable doubt. *In re* Winship, 397 U.S. 358 (1970). The duty to report abuse, however, is typically triggered by reasonable cause to suspect abuse. 42 U.S.C. §§ 5101–07 (1982).

100   Margaret H. Meriwether, 'Child Abuse Reporting Laws: Time For a Change', 20 *Family Law Quarterly*, 141 (1986).

101   Douglas J. Besharov, 'The Need to Narrow the Grounds for State Interventions', in Douglas J. Besharov (Ed.), *Protecting Children from Abuse and Neglect* (Springfield, 1988), 72. Although these statutes were initially narrowly focused, addressing only physicians who were required to report serious physical injury or non-accidental injury, the class of reporters and the kinds of conditions required to be reported has quickly expanded.

102   The Federal Child Abuse Prevention and Treatment Act, 42 U.S.C. §§ 5101–07 (1982), currently requires reporting physical or mental injury 'under circumstances which indicate that the child's health or welfare is harmed or threatened thereby'. In addition to the problems of ambiguity concerning what is intended by physical or

mental injury, the act is not limited by its terms to serious injury. The sufficiency of evidence to trigger this standard is 'reasonable cause to suspect' abuse.

103　American Association for Protecting Children, *Highlights of Official Child Neglect and Abuse Reporting* (1985); United States Dept. of Health and Human Services, *Study Findings, National Study of the Incidence and Severity of Child Abuse & Neglect* (1981); Besharov, op. cit., *supra*, n. 101.

104　Barbara J. Nelson, *Making an Issue of Child Abuse* (Chicago, 1984).

105　Holly Watson and Murray Levine, 'Psychotherapy and Mandated Reporting of Child Abuse', 59 *American Journal of Orthopsychiatry*, 246, at 249 (1989); Select Committee on Children, Youth and Families U.S. House of Representatives, *Abused Children in America: Victims of Official Neglect*, H.R. Doc. No. 164, 100th Cong., 1st Sess. (1987).

106　Besharov, op. cit., *supra*, n. 101, at 48.

107　Lorene F. Schaefer, 'Abused Children and State Created Protection Agencies; A Proposed 1983 Standard', 57 *University of Cincinnati Law Review*, 1419, at 1419 n. 1 (1985); Region VI Resource Center on Child Abuse & Neglect, *Child Deaths in Texas*, 26 (1981); Mayberry, 'Child Protective Services in New York City: An Analysis of Case Management', 109 (May 1979) (unpublished manuscript).

108　George E. Fyer *et al.*, 'The Child Protective Service Workers: A Profile of Needs, Attitudes and Utilization of Professional Resources', 12 *Child Abuse & Neglect*, 481 (1988).

109　Murray Levine *et al.*, 'Informing Psychotherapy Clients of the Mandate to Report Suspected Child Maltreatment' paper presented at the American Psychology Law Society, San Diego, California (14 March, 1992); Robert F. Schopp, 'The Psychotherapist's Duty to Protect the Public: The Appropriate Standard and the Foundation in Legal Theory and Empirical Premises', 70 *Nebraska Law Review*, 327 (1991).

110　See notes 74 and 75.

111　Fred S. Berlin *et al.*, 'Effects of Statutes Requiring Psychiatrists to Report Suspected Abuse of Children', 148 *American Journal of Psychiatry*, 449 (1991); Robert Weinstock and Diane Weinstock, 'Child Abuse Reporting Trends: An Unperceived Threat to Confidentiality', 33 *J. Forensic Services*, 418, at 421 (1988); Gail L. Zellman, 'Linking Schools and Social Services: The Case of Child Abuse Reporting', 12 *Education Evaluation & Policy Analysis*, 41 (1990). But see Watson and Levine, op. cit., *supra*, n. 105, 252. Watson and Levine studied the records of 65 cases in which a psychotherapist at a child and adolescent outpatient psychiatric clinic made a report of abuse. In one-quarter of the cases the disclosure had a therapeutic benefit, in one-quarter of the cases the patient left therapy after the report, and in one-half of the cases there was no detectable difference in therapy.

112　Daniel W. Shuman and Myron F. Weiner, *The Psychotherapist–Patient Privilege: A Critical Examination* (Springfield, 1987).

113　Gail L. Zellman, 'Child Abuse Reporting and Failure to Report Among Mandated Reporters', 5 *J. Interpersonal Violence*, 3, at 21 (1990).

114　See Berlin, op. cit., *supra*, n. 111, at 450, describing an attempt to recognise such an exception in Maryland that was rejected as politically inexpedient after one year of operation.

115　*Smith* v. *Alameda Co. Serv. Agency*, 90 Cal. App. 3d 929, 935, 153 Cal. Rptr. 712, 715 (1979) (citation omitted).

116　Fowler v. Harper and Fleming James Jr., 3 *The Law of Torts* (Boston, 2nd ed., 1986), § 18.6, at 718 n. 9.

117　Daniel W. Shuman, 'The Psychology of Deterrence in Tort Law'; forthcoming: 42 *Kansas Law Review* (1993).

118　See Saul Levmore, 'Waiting for Rescue: An Essay on the Evolution & Incentive Structure of Affirmative Obligations', 72 *Virginia Law Review*, 879 (1986).

119   Besharov, op. cit., *supra*, n. 101, 83; Peter Schuck, *Suing Government: Citizen Remedies for Official Wrongs* (New Haven, 1983), 75.

5 Rescue Across State Boundaries: International Legal Aspects of Rescue

STEPHEN C. NEFF

1 Introduction

Altruism is not, to put it mildly, commonly thought of as a feature of international political life. Expressions such as 'national interest', 'balance of power', '*raison d'état*' or 'state sovereignty' come more readily to mind than do ideas such as humanitarianism or the rescue of persons in distress. Contrary to common belief, however, there is a centuries-long strain of thought in international law on the subject of the rescue of persons or of countries in distress. Legal doctrine in these areas, in fact, goes much further back in time than the more recent positivist conceptions of national interest, state sovereignty and non-intervention.

We shall explore four major areas of international law in which ideas about a duty – or sometimes merely a right – to rescue have been advanced. Each of these areas has been the subject of legal debate and speculation since at least the Middle Ages. In addition, there has been a broadly similar evolution of thought concerning each one. Stated in very general terms, this evolution has been from an early natural law mode of thought, with strongly humanitarian overtones, to a later positivist frame of mind, in which the stress has been on the sovereign rights of states. Medieval natural law thought was strongly influenced by the doctrines of the Catholic Church. It had a distinctly humanitarian flavour and was accordingly highly receptive to the general idea of a duty on the part of more fortunate and powerful parties to lend assistance of various kinds to their less favoured fellows. The ideal medieval knight was the obvious exemplar of this ethos. Don Quixote may have been a caricature, but he represented a very recognisable, and noble, ideal.

It should be noted that early natural law thinking was not particularly centred on the conduct of states or princes. Rather, it was concerned with the articulation of general and universal standards of conduct and morality. It was not until the age of Machiavelli and Hobbes that there began to be a systematic theory of statecraft based on principles peculiar to the conduct of states as such. That development, more than any other, signals the inauguration of the positivist era in international legal thought. The positivist view evolved gradually through the seventeenth and eighteenth centuries, reaching its fullest flower in the nineteenth. Its hallmark, for present purposes, was the insistence that the central concern of international law was the rights and duties of individual states as such. International law was not, on this view, the mere application to states of general ideas of morality; rather, it was a body of rules scientifically crafted, and applicable uniquely to nation-states.

The central tenet of positivism in the international law sphere was – and remains – the principle of the sovereign equality of states. Where natural law thinking had been oriented, on the whole, towards the *duties* of states and the promotion of the general well-being of the world community at large, the positivist outlook was centred on the *rights* of states, seen as isolated and autonomous corporate entities. Positivism accordingly laid great stress on the principle of non-intervention by states into the affairs of one another.[1] It was consequently far less receptive by nature to ideas about duties of rescue. Indeed, our story, in each of the four areas with which we are concerned, is broadly the same: a sympathetic view of the concept of a duty of rescue in the early natural law period, followed by a turning away from the idea in the later positivist period.

The first subject which we shall consider concerns the question of the rescuing of *states* from aggression by other states. The source of this duty was the obligation of states, and of persons generally, under natural law to combat evil by taking the side of the just party in an armed conflict. In the positivist era, this duty to come to the rescue of victim states was firmly rejected in favour of a right of each state to follow its own national interest as it saw fit – even if that meant standing stonily aloof while neighbouring countries fell prey to aggression. In modern times, the ideas of collective security embodied in the League of Nations Covenant and the United Nations Charter have entailed a revival, to a significant extent, of the older just war ethos. The result is that a legal duty for states to assist victims of aggression *can* arise – but only if the UN Security Council chooses to exercise its right to impose one.

The second problem that we shall consider is of a different character, in that it concerns the *economic* 'rescuing' of foreign countries through the provision of economic assistance of some kind. In this case, the medieval natural law heritage posited both a duty of charity on the part of affluent persons and a right of self-help on the part of the poor. Modern, positivist-based law has discarded both of these. As a result, there is scarcely any scope for arguing for a legal duty on the part of states to grant foreign aid to poor countries. The third area of study will concern the question of the duty of states to provide asylum in their own territories to victims of distress, or of oppression, who turn up on their frontiers seeking entry. The early concern in this regard had been with victims of armed conflicts and also with mariners in distress. These are still pertinent problems, but they have been joined in the twentieth century by the concern with refugees; that is, with persons fleeing from persecution in their home countries, whether in time of peace or war. Here we shall see early support by natural law writers for the idea of a duty by states to admit persons in distress into their territories. We shall also see a firm rejection of this idea by modern international law, tempered, however, by a certain artfully circumscribed liberality in favour of genuine refugees.

Finally, we shall discuss a fourth issue: the question of rescue of persons suffering from either danger or oppression in a foreign country. These potential victims might be either nationals of the rescuing country or nationals of the state in which the oppression or danger is occurring. The danger or the oppression might be caused or deliberately aggravated by the policy of the government concerned, or it might be caused by, say, lawless elements in the country. This fourth area is more fraught with controversy than almost any other topic in the whole of international law. It is also importantly different in character from the other three, in that the concern here has never been, strictly speaking, with the *duty* of a state to rescue, but rather with the *right* of a state to rescue. The reason for this difference in focus may be stated very simply. Since (by hypothesis) the rescue operation is to be carried out by the rescuing state in the territory of another country, some infringement of that other state's normal sovereign rights must inevitably occur. This type of case, then, cannot be one of rescue in a 'pure' form. It must entail a delicate balancing of the rights of the rescuing state against those of the state on whose territory the oppression or danger exists. Nevertheless, the general evolution of thinking in this area parallels those in the other three fields. We find an inclination on the part of early natural law writers to accept the principle of humanitarian intervention, followed in the later positivist period by the gravest doubts on the question.

2   Rescuing Victim States from Aggression

Going to war for the purpose of rescuing others is the very prototype of the just war in the medieval Christian tradition. Augustine, in his discussion of the matter, rejected dogmatic pacifism as a requirement of Christians but at the same time cautioned that the real evil of warfare was rooted, not in the use of force *per se*, but rather in the intention animating the resort to force. Warfare was evil if resorted to out of love of violence for its own sake, or out of a spirit of mere vindictiveness, but resorting to arms for the purpose of advancing the cause of justice was another matter.[2] Warfare for this purpose was not merely permissible; it could even be a moral duty. 'It is the injustice of the opposing side,' Augustine posited, 'that lays on the wise man the duty of waging wars.'[3] The implication of this line of thinking is that the use of force to defend other persons is more easily justified morally even than self-defence, since rescue is more obviously a selfless act than self-defence. In this sense, Augustine's thinking bears a striking similarity to the modern collective security ethos (and, as will be seen presently, to arguments in support of humanitarian intervention).

This basic idea of using force in the general public interest, as contrasted to private quarrels, received its definitive scholastic statement with Aquinas in the thirteenth century. Aquinas famously laid down three principal criteria for a just war: that it be authorised by 'due authorities' (that is, that it be a concern of the public at large, as distinct from a private quarrel); that the cause fought for be a just one; and finally that the intention of those waging the war be to promote good and to avoid evil (rather than to engage in violence as mere sport).[4] The second of these criteria – the justness of the cause – is the one that seems most obviously relevant to the concept of a just war. It emphasises the close similarity between warfare and litigation. Indeed, the medieval concept of the just war was, in essence, that it was a permissible (and regrettable) resort to force as a last resort, for the purpose of rectifying a legal wrong. A just war, in other words, was fundamentally a struggle for the promotion of good against evil, ultimately for the benefit of the wider human community. War was not to be waged for the mere private material advantage of the combatants.[5]

This medieval conception of the just war had a number of significant implications. One of the most important was that the neutrality of third parties was seriously frowned on. Medieval theologians were not so naive as to suppose that right would inevitably triumph over wrong in the natural course of human affairs. On the contrary, the just party in a conflict might often require the assistance of others. This realisation led naturally to the general belief that, in principle at least, third persons were required to assist the just party in his (by definition) righteous case. Note that this was not a duty peculiar to the law of nations. Rather, it was simply the application to international affairs of the general duty of all good Christians to further the cause of good against evil.[6] When Right was in contention against Wrong, there could be no such thing as an 'innocent' bystander. Those who stood aside were shirking their moral duty. This required assistance to the just party might take a variety of forms. At the most extreme, it could amount to full-fledged entry into the war on the side of the just party. But it could also take lesser forms, such as providing economic aid to the just party, or hiring out a body of troops to it, or allowing its forces the right to march across its territory or to use its territory as a base of operations in the war. The essential point, though, was that third parties were not to sit aside and indifferently watch the outcome of the struggle. Nor, by the same token, were they to fatten their own purses by engaging in war profiteering with both sides.

In due course, this medieval Christian just war system broke down, for reasons that are not difficult to fathom. Medieval rulers, like their modern counterparts, were often disposed to give a higher priority to their own political concerns than to the furthering of righteousness in general. Machiavelli was an important pioneer in this regard, with his insistence on statecraft as a scientific, cold-bloodedly rational promotion of the national interest, to which traditional ideas of morality did not apply.[7] Indeed, this focus on the primacy of the self-interest of the nation-state was to become a central tenet of positivist legal thought, which would frankly stress the primacy of a state's duties to itself over its duties to mankind at large.[8] One sign of this gradual shift from natural law to positivism was an increasing acceptance of the thesis that a war could be just on both sides – in other words, that it was possible to have an armed conflict in which there was no moral reason to prefer either party's cause. During the Middle Ages, this idea had been rejected. It was no more possible, went the reasoning, for a war to be just on both sides than for both parties to a lawsuit to win the case. Gradually, however, this strict view of things broke down. Hugo Grotius, in his seminal work of 1625, *On the Law of War and Peace*, provided an instructive illustration of the way legal thought was gradually coming to terms with new realities. Grotius posited that, strictly speaking, a war could not be just on both sides, in the sense that, in terms of the disputed subject matter *per se*, only one side could be in the right. Nevertheless, he added, it was possible for each side to be free of *personal* moral blame, if it sincerely and reasonably believed in the justice of its own cause.[9] It may be noted, though, that Grotius, in this regard, was rather on the cautious side. In 1598, the Italian writer, Alberico Gentili, had already taken the step of forthrightly holding that a war could be just on both sides.[10] This admission that a war could be just on both sides led directly to a new attitude towards neutrality. If there was no moral distinction between the combatants in a war, then it was obvious that there would be every reason for third parties to stand aloof rather than to plunge into the fray. Here again, Grotius exemplifies the hesitant acceptance of new ideas on the part of natural lawyers. His recognition of the status of neutrality was decidedly half-hearted. He held to the old just war view in his insistence that neutrals had a duty to take care that they did not assist the unjust side in the conflict or in any way impede the cause of the just side. At the same time, though, he took account of the *fact* of neutrality by conceding that neutrals had a right to be free from attack by the warriors, provided that they refrained from aiding one side against the other.[11]

The wave of the future was ever more strongly in the positivist direction in the period after Grotius wrote. Warfare, according to this new view, was not a conflict between good and evil, but rather a clash between mundane rival national interests. It was waged for the good of the state, as that good was assessed by its rulers. Warfare was, accordingly, the supreme manifestation of the philosophy of *raison d'état*, having no transcendental ethical character. Armed conflict was now to be likened not to litigation, as before, but rather to the art of duelling. It was a decision on the part of the parties concerned to settle a quarrel by resort to arms, on the understanding that the winner of the contest would dictate terms of settlement to the loser.[12] The logical consequences of this new view of warfare are as obvious and significant as the old view. For one thing, there was now a strict legal equality between parties to an armed contest, since there was now no reason – whether moral or legal – to hold one party's cause superior to the other. Therefore, the rules concerning the *conduct* of the contest were now seen as strictly even-handed. This even-handedness of the law concerning the conduct of war (*jus in bello*) remains today one of the cardinal principles of the law of armed conflict.

In addition, the status of neutrality achieved firm recognition as a fundamental sovereign right of states. Just as one state might deem its national interest to be furthered by the waging of a war, so another might equally conclude that its interest lay in staying carefully neutral. In the course of time (primarily from the seventeenth to the nineteenth centuries), this status of neutrality came to be bolstered by an elaborate set of laws protecting neutrals from oppressive acts by belligerents and safeguarding their right to carry on their lives with as little disturbance as possible from the belligerents.[13] Closely connected with this continuous development of the law of neutrality was a new outlook towards neutrality in general. Neutrals were no longer seen as shirkers of their moral responsibilities, but rather as rational and peace-loving states whose forbearance from violence was to be applauded rather than condemned. Safeguarding, and indeed expanding, the rights of neutrals came to be equated with promoting enlightenment and civilisation. Some visionaries even saw the infinite expansion of policies of neutrality as the way forward to world peace. After all, if all states were to become permanently neutral, how could there ever be war?[14] In this kind of atmosphere, it is hardly surprising to find that violations of the law of neutrality were looked upon very seriously in international law and that one of the most heinous acts possible was to mount a deliberate and cold-blooded attack on a neutral state. We need only recall the world-wide condemnation of Germany in 1914 for its cynical violation of Belgian neutrality to appreciate the truth of this proposition. (It might be noted in this connection that Britain's entry into the First World War was, to some extent, a rescue mission on behalf of Belgium.)[15]

Even during the high tide of positivism in the nineteenth century, there was some disquiet about a system of international law which was so largely devoid of moral content. In this regard, too, the attitudes towards the law of neutrality are a key indicator. One noted dissenter from the positivist mainstream was the Scottish writer, James Lorimer. He was a clear spiritual and intellectual heir of the medieval natural lawyers in his insistence that the states of the world constituted an integrated, interconnected world community in the true sense. He went on to argue that, in consequence, the members of this community must have some responsibility for one another and for the well-being of the community at large – meaning that they must be prepared to intervene in quarrels of other nations when the interests of the wider community were at stake. Not surprisingly, he condemned neutrality as mere 'international apathy', scorning it as a 'cowardly and ignoble shrinking from international duty'.[16] A kindred figure was the Swedish lawyer, Richard Kleen. As the author of the supreme codification of the customary law of neutrality, and with a wide reputation as a champion of the rights of neutrals, he nevertheless forthrightly believed that neutrality was a highly dubious status from the moral standpoint. The foremost duty of a neutral state, he insisted, was to do its utmost to bring about the advent of peace. Neutrality, as a simple staying out of trouble, was to be condemned as mere egoism.[17] Another like-minded international lawyer was the English writer, John Westlake. Anticipating the later collective security era, he called for a principled co-operation with one another of the states of the world for the furtherance of international peace and justice.[18]

This community-oriented outlook of Lorimer, Kleen and Westlake clearly foreshadowed the philosophies of the League of Nations and of the United Nations (UN) in the twentieth century, just as clearly as it recalled the moralistic spirit of the medieval natural lawyers. The most explicit expression of this new – and old – philosophy is found in article 11(1) of the Covenant of the League of Nations, drafted in 1919 and annexed to the Treaty of Versailles.[19] It stated that 'any war or threat of war, whether immediately affecting any of the Members of the League or not, is hereby declared a matter of concern to the whole League.' Even more striking (and controversial) was article 10, in which the League members undertook 'to respect and preserve as against external aggression the territorial integrity and existing political independence' of all other member states. The League of Nations was the nearest thing yet devised in world history to an *automatic* device for ensuring the rescue of states that are victims of aggression by fellow League members. Only the general outline of the apparatus need concern us here. The basic strategy was to require states engaged in disputes to resort to peaceful methods of settlement. States which declined to do this, or which resorted to war in defiance of a definitive finding against their case, were to be deemed to be waging war contrary to the Covenant of the League – waging, in effect, an unjust war. It should be noted that the League of Nations system did not contain a blanket ban against waging war. Instead, it provided for the identification of the wrongdoing party in the event that war did break out, and provided for the (supposedly) automatic imposition of sanctions against that lawbreaking by the other members of the League. In this regard, the League system was squarely in the spirit of the medieval just war system.

The League had two sets of sanctions to employ against such a wrongdoing state. Neither of them was military in character, since the drafters of the League Covenant realised that member states would be reluctant to confer military power on the organisation. One of the sanctions consisted of a policy of isolating the unjust party. To this end, there was a general commitment on the part of the League members that they would not go to war against a party which complied with its obligations under the Covenant (article 15(6)). In other words, it was permissible (but not compulsory) for League members to go to war on the side of the law-abiding power, but not on the side of the wrongdoer. The general feeling was that, if the wrongdoing state was compelled to fight alone, it would be unlikely to triumph. The other major sanction was, in theory at least, more drastic: economic sanctions by all members of the League against a state resorting to war in violation of the Covenant (article 16(1)).

This return to the general spirit of the medieval just war was intensely controversial. In the United States, especially, a fierce debate raged among international lawyers as to whether this whole collective security ideal was a good one in principle or not. Answering this question in the affirmative were Charles Fenwick, Quincy Wright, Ellery Stowell, Clyde Eagleton and Henry Stimson. [20] Their arguments were clearly reminiscent of the natural law tradition. Quincy Wright, for example, explicitly favoured a return to the outlook of Grotius.[21] Stimson, in his famous 'punctilio speech' of 1932, clearly invoked the just war ethos in his plea that all nations must be concerned at the outbreak of any war: 'When two nations engage in armed conflict [he contended] either one or both of them must be wrongdoers .... We no longer draw a circle about them and treat them with the punctilio of the duellist's code. Instead we denounce them as lawbreakers.'[22] Newton Baker, in this same spirit, denounced neutrality in words worthy of the most passionate medieval moralist, excoriating it as 'a sort of indifferentism based on the theory that one is not obliged to imperil one's interests by espousing the cause of another, however innocent the victim or vicious his assailant'.[23]

A number of international lawyers vigorously attacked this idea, holding that it was a bad idea in principle to have a system in which every state's quarrel automatically became the concern of the entire world. The effect of such a system could only be to threaten peace, they argued, not to promote it. The leading figures in this attack were Edwin N. Borchard and John Bassett Moore (a former judge on the World Court).[24] They argued that a collective security regime tended, by its very nature, to expand conflict. Moore contemptuously dismissed collective security advocates as 'shallow dupes' who would have the United States 'blindly don the imported livery of "world service"'.[25] For those such as Moore, the positivist system was far preferable, because the essential idea behind it was to confine and contain conflict as strictly and narrowly as possible to the combatants themselves, by means of the law of neutrality. Borchard was the most outspoken in his opposition to collective security and his support for the traditional law of neutrality as the most effective means of preserving and promoting peace. He contemptuously dismissed the idea of collective security as 'doctrinaire ... political theology'.[26] In pleading for the retention of the traditional law of neutrality, he appealed to 'the instinct of self-preservation and the necessity of limiting the area and the destructive effects of war'. He lauded neutrality as 'a peace-preserving institution – one of the beneficent achievements of a long struggle with barbarism.'[27] In more blunt terms, he asserted that 'the philosophy of minding your own business has not yet been improved upon as a way to peace, sanity and tolerable life.'[28]

In the event, the automatic mechanism of the League of Nations failed to work as planned (or hoped), for a variety of reasons, of which two may be specifically noted. One was that, as the Covenant itself acknowledged, the peaceful-settlement processes could not be guaranteed to produce a definitive result. In such an event, the Covenant simply left it to each member state to take whatever action it thought necessary 'for the maintenance of right and justice' (article 15(7)). The other major problem lay in deciding who was to determine whether a member state had or had not 'resort[ed] to war in disregard of its covenants' (article 16(1)). It might seem logical that some League organ should make that crucial determination and that all member states would then proceed to implement the stipulated economic sanctions. The member states chose, however, not to entrust any League body with that crucial determination, but instead to permit each state to make up its own mind on the matter.[29] The effect, obviously, was seriously to weaken the impact of the sanctions element of the system. The failure of the League did not, however, put an end to the very idea of collective security. Far from it. The experience of the 1930s led to a general view that an effective collective security apparatus was more imperative than ever. In addition, the crusading spirit that prevailed during the Second World War exerted a powerful force on the side of commitment and community service, as distinct from neutrality and isolation. In 1944, Ellery Stowell gleefully pronounced the death of the 'sterile doctrine' of neutrality and the triumph of the collective security view that, even in international affairs, 'we are our brother's keeper'.[30] The following year, the world made its second attempt at a global collective security apparatus which (it was hoped) would correct some of the defects of the earlier League of Nations system.

The UN differs importantly from the League in having at its heart, as the League did not, a general prohibition against 'the threat or use of force against the territorial integrity or political independence of any state …' (article 2(4)). At the same time, however, the Charter expressly acknowledges two important exceptions to this principle, both of them involving the rescuing of states that are the victims of aggression. One exception is the express preservation (in article 51 of the UN Charter) of the right of self-defence – including, significantly, the right of *collective* self-defence (the right of states to come to the rescue of other states which are the victims of attack). In effect, then, the UN Charter permits defensive alliance arrangements, of which the best known is the NATO Treaty of 1949.[31] Three points should be noted about this right of collective self-defence. One is that it clearly is a *right* of third parties to assist victims of aggression, rather than a duty. The second point is that certain criteria have been laid down by the World Court for the invoking of this right. The victim country is required to state that it is the target of an armed attack and also to request assistance. The assisting states, in other words, are not allowed to decide unilaterally to go to the rescue.[32] The third point is that the right of self-defence (whether individual or collective) is intended to be only a stop-gap measure, to operate until the Security

Council is able to step in. Action by the Security Council constitutes the other express exception to the general ban on the use of force. This is the collective security element of the UN, set out in Chapter VII of the Charter. It resembles the League's collective security system in the general sense of being based on the idea that the maintenance of world peace is a community concern of the world at large, transcending the parochial national interest of the individual nation-states. The strategy adopted for implementing this ideal, however, differs significantly from that of the League. The drafters of the UN Charter abandoned the idea of an automatic system, opting instead for an arrangement that must be consciously invoked by a political organ (the UN Security Council) on a case-by-case basis. There is no general and permanent obligation on the part of member states to take the side of the victim in a dispute or to impose sanctions against aggressors. Instead there is only an obligation to carry out such orders as the Security Council may choose to issue in the cases in which it decides to act.[33]

That choice of whether or not to act in a given case is a political, rather than a legal, one, since the Security Council is a straightforwardly political organ. It is dominated both de jure and de facto by the five major powers: the United States, Britain, France, China and Russia (as the successor of the former Soviet Union). These five countries have two special privileges: permanent membership of the Security Council and the right of veto. The other ten seats on the Council are filled by states that are elected by the General Assembly for two-year terms. The Security Council invokes its enforcement powers (if at all) by formally designating a situation as either a threat to the peace, a breach of the peace or an act of aggression (article 39). When it does that, it thereby arrogates to itself immense powers under Chapter VII of the Charter to do whatever is necessary to resolve the matter. It can, for example, order states to impose economic sanctions (article 41). If economic measures prove insufficient to deal with the crisis, then the Security Council can go still further (under article 42) by taking, or authorising, military action (something that the League of Nations Covenant had not provided for).

It should be noted that the function of the UN Security Council is not – or at least not explicitly – the rescuing of victim states *per se* from aggressors. Instead, the primary function of the Council is to 'decide what measures shall be taken … to maintain or restore international peace and security' (article 39). That is to say, the UN's purpose is the safeguarding of *general* world peace and security, rather than the rescuing of single victim states. In most cases, presumably, the rescuing of a victim of aggression and the restoring of international peace would be the same thing. But it should be stressed that, in principle, the two might be different. (The Security Council might, for example, conclude that, in the interest of overall world peace, a victim state should simply accept its unfortunate fate.) In any event, the UN Security Council's actual record as a rescuer of states in distress has been, to put it mildly, disappointing. No Security Council action was taken when British and French troops moved into Egypt in 1956, or Indian ones into Goa in 1961, or Indonesian ones into West Irian in 1963, or Vietnamese ones into Cambodia in 1979, or Soviet ones into Hungary in 1956 and Czechoslovakia in 1968, or Israeli ones into Lebanon in 1978 and again in 1982, or American ones into Grenada in 1983 or Panama in 1989–90. These are only the most obvious examples where action might, in theory, have been taken. In addition, there have been countless examples of short-term raids by one state into the territories of others, primarily by Israel and South Africa, together with many cases of the harbouring of insurgents or terrorists by one state to operate against others. The history of the UN is, for the most part, a dispiriting catalogue of inaction.

There have, in fact, really been only two instances in which the Security Council has gone with military force to the rescue of victims of aggression, and in neither of these cases did the Security Council itself take command of the rescue missions, or require its member states to contribute to them. Instead, it took the more limited step of *authorising* its member states to use force in defence of the victim states. Neither case, therefore, was one in which UN members had a true legal *duty* to spring to the rescue. The first of these cases was the defence of South Korea in 1950 against aggression from North Korea (aided later by substantial numbers of Chinese 'volunteers'). In that case, the Security Council made a formal finding of a breach of the peace and then recommended that member states contribute contingents of troops to a unified force under the command of the United States.[34] Some 16 states made such a contribution. The second instance was the rescue of Kuwait in 1990–91 from forcible annexation by Iraq. To a certain extent, the two cases were similar. In the Kuwait crisis, as in the Korean one, the Security Council made a finding of a breach of the peace.[35] The next step was not military action, but rather the imposition of economic sanctions against Iraq.[36] The crisis then moved into a military phase. But, in contrast to the Korean case, the Security Council did not take the step of recommending that member states contribute armed forces to the liberating of Kuwait. Instead, it contented itself with, in effect, endorsing the effort of collective self-defence which was mounted, largely under American leadership, on behalf of Kuwait. Initially, this collective self-defence effort was focused on the protection of Saudi Arabia from a possible further thrust by Iraq. Before long, however, it became clear that the coalition states wished to use their forces to eject Iraq from Kuwait itself. The UN Security Council gave its approval to this policy in

November 1990.[37] Upon the expiry of a 15 January 1991 deadline which the Council gave to Iraq, the coalition proceeded to use force on Kuwait's behalf – with resounding success in the event.

The rescuing of Kuwait from the clutches of Iraq, then, was justifiable legally as a mixture of the two forms of permissible force under the UN Charter: collective self-defence and Security Council enforcement action. Some have maintained that the role of the Security Council was legally superfluous and that the entire operation could have been justified on the basis of collective self-defence alone. There is some doubt on this point. It is probably safe to say that, if the Security Council had not acted at all, the coalition's actions would have been justifiable as collective self-defence. But some question remains as to whether the entry of the Security Council into the picture may not have vitiated the self-defence right.[38]

The modern position on the rescuing of victim states from aggression may be summed up as follows. There is no *general* obligation on the part of countries of the world to go to the rescue of victims of aggression, either by military aid or by the use of non-military sanctions. In this regard, the UN represents a step backwards from the position under the League of Nations Covenant. There are, instead, two *mechanisms* for rescuing victim states. One is the right of collective self-defence, by means of which countries can lawfully spring to the defence of a state that is the victim of an armed attack (provided that the victim state requests such assistance). The other is the collective-security machinery that is in the hands of the Security Council. Neither of these mechanisms, however, is automatic. States are not legally obliged to engage in collective self-defence: they are merely authorised to do so. Nor is there a legal duty on the part of the Security Council to take action in any given case. The Council must make a conscious choice to that effect. But if it chooses to act and to issue legally binding orders pursuant to its powers under Chapter VII of the Charter, then – but only then – a duty to rescue will arise on the part of the UN member states.

3   Duty to Provide Economic Assistance

The concern in the present section is with the duty (or lack of one) to provide assistance to persons in foreign countries, or to foreign countries as such, who are suffering from economic distress of various kinds. The concern is with foreign aid given to such persons *in situ*. An alternative method of assisting such persons – allowing migration from poor countries to wealthy ones – will be discussed in the following section.

The natural lawyers of the Middle Ages had a most intense concern with questions of economic deprivation, particularly when it took its most severe and all-too-common form of famine. Writing as they did from a Christian background, the idea of charity towards the less fortunate came naturally to them. So did an intense hatred of profiteers and speculators who made large private fortunes by charging high prices in times of shortage.[39] From these beliefs, the conclusion came naturally that a person (or state) in possession of a surplus had a duty to make that surplus available to other persons at a reasonable price.[40] There was always, alas, the possibility that a property owner might fail or refuse to discharge this duty. The theologians, naturally, would consign such a person to hell for his wicked ways. But there were some who posited the existence of a more earthly solution to the problem: a right of self-help on the part of the destitute person, in the form of an actual property right of the destitute person in goods necessary for his survival. This property right would normally lie dormant, but in the special case of extreme necessity it would revive.

Hugo Grotius devoted careful atttention to this question of necessity and the rights to which it gave rise. He founded it upon a quasi-legendary conception of the origin of the institution of private property. This idea, like so much else in the natural law tradition, was set down by Augustine and reiterated as late as the eighteenth century. In prehistoric times (the thesis had it), all of the fruits of the earth had been common to all persons, with no one having private property rights over anything. The Biblical account of the Garden of Eden was an obvious source of inspiration for this belief. This age of primitive communism, or 'primitive user' as it was sometimes termed, was superseded in the course of time by the man-made institution of private property, but this institution of private property, being merely man-made, could not wholly abrogate the primitive user that God (or the law of nature) had ordained. Under certain circumstances, that right of primitive user would reassert itself. The special condition was shortage, when suffering persons acquired a legal right, by virtue of their extreme need, to the use of goods necessary to their survival. Grotius explained the matter with some care. He stressed that what was really at stake here was a specific form of *property right* on the part of the needy (that is, a right *in* the goods of other persons) to the extent necessary to relieve the distress. The right of primitive user, then, was a latent or dormant right, which would reawaken, like the Sleeping Beauty, when touched by the kiss of extreme necessity.

There were, according to Grotius, certain conditions and limitations attached to this self-help right. One was that the right only arose in extreme cases, when the necessity was truly dire. Another caveat was that the right did not arise if the owner of the goods in question was himself in equal need of them. Finally, there was a duty to restore the goods to the original owner, if possible, once the state of necessity had come to an end. If restitution in kind was not possible, then the owner was to be compensated for the taking.[41] It would clearly be quite wrong to characterise this argument as one in support of charity on the part of the affluent party. Rather, it was a right of self-help on the part of the destitute person. This theory had an obvious attraction to persons who were (or might become) destitute. A starving person who 'stole' bread was, on this view, in reality exercising his normally latent primitive-user right in the bread, and hence was doing no legal wrong. The original owner of the bread, correspondingly, had a legal duty to acquiesce in the starving person's exercise of that right. Whether this could fairly be described as a duty to rescue on the part of the bread owner could be the subject of some debate. It would seem fairer to regard it as a duty to recognise a right of self-help on the part of another.

This point was appreciated by Samuel Pufendorf, who dealt with the question in his magisterial treatise, *On the Law of Nature and Nations*, of 1672. He was critical of Grotius's property right approach to the question, preferring instead to analyse the question in terms of personal rights. He conceded that a state of necessity gave rise, on the right of the destitute person, to a right to take what he needed to survive – but he insisted that this was a personal right of self-help and not an assertion of a property right in the goods themselves. Corresponding to this personal right of self-help on the poor person's part (Pufendorf posited) was a personal duty of charity on the side of the affluent party. But there was an important element of asymmetry: the duty of charity was only an 'imperfect duty': that is to say, it was only a moral obligation, not enforceable by formal legal process. The result would seem to be that, strictly speaking, the affluent person would have a legal right to resist the taking of his goods by the poor person, while at the same time (and somewhat paradoxically) the poor person, would be acting within his rights in attempting to appropriate them.[42] With the passage of time, this asymmetry was eliminated by reducing the poor person's right of self-help to a mere 'imperfect' one – that is, to a moral 'entitlement' not backed by any legal enforcement mechanism. The result, then, was that lawyers came to deny that there was either a legal duty of charity on the part of the affluent or a legal right of self-help on the part of the poor. This newer, and harsher, state of affairs was crisply summed up by Vattel in his treatise on *The Law of Nations* of 1758:

If I, improperly and without good reason, refuse to sell you what you have need of at a fair price [he explained], I violate my duty; you may make complaint, but you must put up with it, and you can not undertake to force me without attacking my natural liberty and doing me an injury. Hence the right to buy things one has need of is only an *imper-fect* right, like that of a poor man to receive alms from a rich man; if the latter refuse to give them, the poor man has reason to complain, but he has not the right to take them by force.[43]

The legal position regarding charity by affluent states appears to be, for all intents and purposes, the same as that applying to private persons – that no legal duty to assist poorer states exists. This is the view taken by the World Court in the case of *Nicaragua* v. *United States* in 1986. One of Nicaragua's complaints was that the United States had cut off foreign aid to it. But the court stated that the giving of economic aid is essentially of 'a unilateral and voluntary nature'. Consequently, there could be no legal claim for an aid cut-off, save in (unspecified) 'exceptional circumstances'.[44] One such exceptional circumstance would presumably be a case in which there was a treaty-based duty to provide the assistance. Apart from this clear case, we are left, so far, to speculate. It is possible that it would be unlawful to cut off an existing aid flow in a precipitate and disruptive fashion, resulting in unreasonable damage to the erstwhile recipient state. Note, however, that affluent states would still be left entirely free to decline to provide aid in the first place.

Even if there is no *legal* obligation to extend foreign assistance to poor countries, there have been various contentions that wealthy countries ought to furnish economic assistance to poor ones on various other grounds. There is, for example, an argument based on a moral principle of restitution: that the wealthy countries acquired their riches in part by exploitation of poor countries, and that consequently there is a duty on their part to remit some of their gains to their victims. This argument comes in a variety of forms, one of which is 'unequal exchange' theory. The details of this theory are not of concern here, save for the general point that it posits that economic relations between rich and poor countries have been inherently unequal, with the result that the rich countries have acquired more than their rightful share of the world's resources.[45] The implication, then, is that there is an obligation on the part of the affluent countries to redress the situation, either by restructuring international economic relations in general, or by compensating the poor countries for past injustices. This argument is reminiscent, to a certain extent, of the Grotian one about the revival of the right of primitive user in cases of necessity, in that it posits that the entitlement of the affluent countries to their riches is, for various reasons, provisional rather than absolute in character. Underlying much of unequal exchange theory seems to be the old natural law thesis that the products of the world belong, ultimately, to all persons equally and that, consequently, any private property right claims are always liable to be overridden by community-based concerns. The difference, of course, is that this new thesis is rooted, not in Biblical mythology, as Grotius's theory was, but rather in insights (or claimed insights) into the 'dismal science' of modern economics. It is difficult for a non-economist to pronounce with confidence on the validity of unequal exchange theory. Here it must suffice to say that, in international law and politics, the idea has not as yet gone beyond the level of mere exhortation. [46]

The exhortations have assumed a highly specific character, however. In the 1960s, the UN Conference on Trade and Development, at the initiative of the developing countries, decided upon a target of net resource flows from the wealthy states to developing ones, of 1 per cent of gross national product per year, and, within that figure, a target of 0.7 per cent as the level of official aid flows (with the balance of the 1 per cent figure to come from private capital flows).[47] Several developed states (such as Belgium, The Netherlands and Sweden) accepted this standard. In 1990, however, only five donor countries met the 0.7 per cent official aid target: Norway, Denmark, Sweden, The Netherlands and France (the French figure, however, being inclusive of aid to its own overseas departments and territories). The least generous of the major developed states relative to the size of its economy was the United States, although it contributed the second-largest gross amount (after Japan).[48]

There have also been appeals to the naked self-interest of wealthy countries. It is in the interest of the developed states themselves (the argument runs) for Third World countries to be as prosperous as possible. They will then be better customers for the goods and services of the developed states themselves. This argument featured in the report of the Brandt Commission in 1980.[49] Whatever its merits, it is clear from its nature that it has nothing to do with the idea of rescue. The position regarding the legal duty on the part of affluent countries to provide economic assistance to poor ones may, then, be summed up with the utmost brevity. No such legal duty exists in the current state of international law.

4   Asylum for Unfortunate Persons

In this area, as in the others, international law has followed a trajectory from an older humanitarian tradition, in the natural law period, to a more positivist – and less generous – approach in which the stress is on the sovereignty of states, culminating in recent attempts to reinstate the older humanitarian ethos. The medieval natural lawyers and their early modern successors, such as Grotius, were clearly of the view that states had a duty to admit homeless persons into their territories for the purpose of passage or settlement. The example of the wandering Children of Israel was commonly invoked as a praiseworthy illustration.[50] This principle even extended to wartime. A neutral country was permitted, and indeed expected, to offer what were often called the 'offices of humanity' to both sides impartially. That included affording refuge to the victims of the war, but it also extended to permitting the armies of the two sides to transit its territory.[51]

At the same time, however, states possessed the right, as an inherent attribute of their sovereignty, to determine what persons (if any) to admit into their territories, and under what conditions. During the positivist era, this basic right of territorial sovereignty came to prevail over the older natural law duty to provide the 'offices of humanity' to persons in distress. The old natural law right of refuge, in other words, was in effect demoted to a mere 'imperfect right' of the kind outlined by Pufendorf and Vattel. The result is that modern international law goes no further in this area than to recognise that states have the *right* to grant asylum to persons in distress if they so choose. But they have no general *duty* to do so. The hard-edged right of territorial sovereignty prevails over the vaguer dictates of humanitarianism.

Although (as just observed) there is no *general* duty on the part of states to play host to persons in distress, there are several areas of life in which the law is concerned with various aspects of the question of asylum. We shall consider, first, and very briefly, the rescue of persons from hazards of the sea (and of outer space), an area in which states have assumed a duty to rescue by treaty; second, the question of asylum in neutral countries during wartime; and third, the modern law relating to refugees.

4.1   Rescuing Mariners and Space Travellers

In the maritime sphere, it was a very common practice in the eighteenth and nineteenth centuries for treaties of friendship to provide for persons shipwrecked in the territories of the contracting states. The typical provision was that nationals of either state who were shipwrecked in the territory of the other were guaranteed humane treatment and the general protection of the laws.[52] Modern international law has extended this principle to encompass the rescuing of persons in distress to the high seas. Article 12 of the Geneva Convention on the High Seas of 1958 requires each state party to impose on the masters of all ships flying its flag a duty to render assistance to persons in distress on the high seas.[53] (Note that, strictly speaking, the state is not required *itself* to undertake the rescue, merely to require that persons sailing under its flag do so.)

A similar provision exists regarding persons in distress in outer space. An international convention drafted in 1968 requires states parties to rescue and provide assistance to astronauts in distress who land in their territories. If the imperilled space travellers land on the high seas, then a duty to rescue and provide assistance arises on the part of any state party which happens to be in a position to take such steps.[54]

4.2   Asylum in Neutral Countries in Wartime

The law concerning asylum in neutral countries during wartime is fairly elaborate. We have observed above that the natural law writers exhorted neutral countries to afford the 'offices of humanity' to belligerents. In the course of time, this old natural law doctrine was subsumed into, and replaced by, the rather more precise rules of the law of neutrality. Under this newer body of law, which evolved from the seventeenth to the nineteenth centuries, neutral states, in the spirit of positivism, now had the right, but not the duty, to afford asylum to the victims of war. That is to say, they could choose to admit either civilian refugees or foreign armed forces into their territories, on certain conditions. Belligerent forces were not allowed to hold prisoners of war or maritime prizes (captured ships) in neutral territory, on the ground that such forcible holdings were warlike acts, which neutral sovereigns were not to allow. Consequently, prisoners of war and maritime prizes were commonly released when taken into neutral territory. In addition, the belligerent forces were not to use the neutral territory as a base of operations to conduct further hostilities. In other words, when entering neutral territory, the belligerent troops had to disengage from participation in the conflict.

In the nineteenth century, these conditions became increasingly detailed and strict. Three different categories of war-related asylum-seekers were recognised: able-bodied armed forces, prisoners of war (and, analogously, maritime prizes) and wounded and sick persons. Different rules were crafted concerning the treatment of each of these on neutral territory. We shall look briefly at each in turn. Belligerent troops being admitted to neutral territory were now required to be interned by neutral powers who chose to admit them to their territories. A notable example of this practice was the admission by Switzerland of a large French army in 1871, during the Franco-Prussian War, on the condition that the guests submitted to internment by their hosts.[55] This duty of internment was eventually inscribed into positive law, in the Hague Convention on the Rights and Duties of States in War on Land, of 1907 (as article 11).[56] The neutral host country is required, during the internment period, to supply the internees with food, clothing and 'relief required by humanity' (article 12). During the Second World War, Sweden and Switzerland adhered to this rule with respect to aircraft and aircrews from both sides which landed in their territories. The most recent occasion on which this law has been relevant was during the Gulf conflict of 1991, when a number of Iraqi air force pilots landed in Iran, which had declared itself neutral in the struggle. Iran, consistently with its duties as a neutral, did not allow these aircraft to fly military sorties from its territory. In fact, it went rather further and confiscated the aircraft, regarding them as an instalment of the reparations which Iran insisted that Iraq owed as a result of the war of 1980–88 between the two countries. (There appeared to be little concern over the fate of the Iraqi crews.)[57]

The law is more lenient regarding asylum for the second category of persons in the armed conflict context: prisoners of war. Prisoners who are held by belligerent troops admitted to a neutral country are to be set free by the host government. These liberated prisoners, along with any escaped prisoners of war who enter the neutral state are to be left 'at liberty', although at the same time the neutral host is allowed to restrict their residence to certain portions of the country if it wishes (article 13 of the Hague Convention on Neutrality in Land War).[58]

The Hague Convention on Land Warfare also deals with admission into neutral territory of a third class of unfortunates: sick and wounded persons from the armed forces of any of the combatants. These also *may* be admitted, at the choice of the neutral state. A neutral state allowing these persons in must ensure that the trains carrying the victims do not carry either military personnel or war material. The wounded and sick are not required to be interned, as able-bodied troops are; but it is required that they 'be guarded by the neutral Power so as to ensure their not taking part again in the military operations' (article 14).

It must be stressed that none of these provisions infringes the basic general right of neutral countries to exercise their *general* right to refuse admission to their territories at all, if they so choose. There is, accordingly, no question here of any duty to rescue the victims of war. In one area of the law of war, however, some question of a true legal duty to rescue has arisen: concerning the question as to whether neutral countries have the duty to protect foreign nationals who are prejudiced by a violation of the neutral rights of that state. Suppose, for example, that one belligerent engaged in military operations against his foe on neutral territory. Did the neutral sovereign have a duty to assert its sovereign rights and put a stop to the operations – and thereby to rescue the imperilled combatant? The United States made just such a claim in an arbitration against Portugal in 1851, regarding an incident that had occurred in the war of 1812. British forces had attacked Americans in a Portuguese port (Portugal being neutral) without any attempt at rescue on the part of the neutral host country. The Americans claimed that Portugal thereby violated international law. The decision in the case went in Portugal's favour, but on the ground that the Americans had not requested Portuguese assistance. There is some language in the award which indicates that, in principle, Portugal may have been under a duty to rescue the Americans if it had been duly notified of their peril.[59] If that is so, then this type of case is the nearest that international law comes to imposing a true duty to rescue on states. (It may be argued, though, that, strictly speaking, the duty would be an obligation on the neutral state's part to assert its own neutral rights, rather than a duty of rescue *per se*.)

4.3 Refugees

The law regarding peacetime asylum for civilian victims of persecution is similar to that governing wartime asylum, in that the basic foundation is the sovereign right of states to decide whether to admit such persons into their territory or not (and if so, under what conditions). This is a sovereign right which states have shown themselves most reluctant to give up. Where there has been innovation, it has not been on the question of admission of persons *per se*, but rather in the matter of how persons are to be treated during their stay – including the important question of whether they are protected from expulsion.[60]

In the twentieth century, the term 'refugee' has come to be a term of art in international law, as a result of the upheavals of the two world wars, and of the parade of lesser crises which have plagued the world. A refugee in the technical legal sense is a person who is animated by a well-founded fear of persecution by his home government, on such grounds as race, religion or political opinion. [61] This new kind of refugee first came to the world's attention in a forceful way in the aftermath of the First World War, when turmoil in the Middle East and Russia caused large numbers of civilians to flee from their homes. Unfortunately for these involuntary migrants, the principle of state sovereignty posed, at least in principle, an absolute bar to any question of a right of admission to foreign countries – or, by the same token, of any correlative duty on the part of a state to grant asylum. The only solution was to attempt to negotiate permission from various countries for these persons to enter and settle. To that end, the League of Nations entrusted a high commissioner, Friedrich Nansen (famous as a polar explorer) to undertake this task and to act as a sort of ombudsman to the refugees. This approach was tolerably successful.[62]

In the aftermath of the Second World War, the problem of homeless and destitute victims of war and oppression has become greater than ever.[63] But the state of the law remains as it has been: it is the sovereign prerogative of each state to decide for itself whether to allow victims of oppression to enter its territory or not. This state of affairs was clearly reflected in the provision of the Universal Declaration of Human Rights, of 1948, on the subject. Article 14(1) of the declaration states that all persons 'have the right to seek and enjoy in other countries asylum from persecution'.[64] But this is, as it says, merely a right to *seek* asylum, not a right to be granted it. The furthest that the international community has been willing to go in this area is to make provision for the humane treatment of refugees (as legally defined) *after* their admission to a host country. The principal instrument in this regard is the UN Convention on the Status of Refugees, drafted in 1951 (with an additional protocol drafted in 1966).[65] Supplementing the UN convention, and assisting in its implementation, are the activities of the UN High Commissioner for Refugees (UNHCR), whose function is to represent and protect refugees and to attempt to reach durable long-term solutions to refugee problems.[66] The general thrust of the 1951 UN convention is the requirement that states parties treat refugees either on a par with nationals or (in some instances) on a par with aliens of the most favoured category. One right contained in the convention is of particularly outstanding importance for a refugee: that of *non-refoulement*, which is the right not to be expelled or returned to the frontier of a territory where his life or freedom would be 'threatened' on grounds such as race, religion or political opinion (article 33). This right of *non-refoulement* is not an absolute guarantee against expulsion, because the refugee can be sent to a state where he will not be so threatened. Nor, importantly, is it a right to be admitted to the host country in the first place.[67]

The law relating to refugees may be said, then, to occupy a rather curious position in the moral order. States have a duty to treat refugees humanely, for example by not expelling them, *if* the refugees happen to be in their territory. But they have no duty to rescue them by allowing them to enter in the first place. An analogy might be made to the case of a person drowning at sea who encounters potential rescuers in a boat. The people in the boat would (on this analogy) have no duty to exert themselves to rescue the drowning person. But *if* he were somehow to clamber on board, then the people in the boat would be under a legal duty not to throw him overboard.[68] Attempts have been made to persuade states to accept a duty to admit refugees; but they have, so far, been unsuccessful. In 1967, the UN General Assembly adopted a Declaration on Territorial Asylum, which states that persons fleeing from persecution have a right of admission into states to whose frontiers they flee.[69] But this measure is merely a recommendation (as a resolution of the UN General Assembly) and is not legally binding. An attempt to draft a legally binding convention on territorial asylum in the 1970s proved an embarrassing failure.[70]

The only measure of success in this area has been achieved in a regional convention among member states of the Organisation of African Unity (OAU) on the subject of refugee problems in Africa, drafted in 1969. It does not go quite so far as to grant an explicit right of admission to the refugee, or a corresponding duty to admit on the part of the state, but it comes close by providing that no one 'shall be subjected ... to measures such as rejection at the frontier' if the effect of such rejection would be to 'compel' the person to return to a place where he would be threatened by persecution. [71] (This falls short of a duty to admit, because the state concerned might, say, arrange for the individual to go to some third country instead.) Unfortunately for asylum seekers, this convention has not been applied in practice to any significant extent.

Although states hold staunchly to their sovereign right to decide whom to admit to their territories, there is, in practice, a certain reservoir of sympathy for refugees – and even a willingness to grant them entry, as a matter of grace if not of right. States tend, however, to be exceedingly sparing in their generosity. They typically restrict their liberality to persons who qualify as refugees in the strict legal sense of the term; that is, to persons who have a well-founded fear of persecution by their home countries.[72] As a result, the question of qualification for refugee status, in the strict legal sense, becomes utterly crucial for the asylum seeker. It is important to note in this connection that many persons who are popularly thought of as 'refugees' do not qualify under this legal definition. For example, people who have merely taken flight from disorder out of, say, caution do not qualify as refugees under the definition in the 1951 UN convention. (Here again, though, the OAU convention of 1969 is more liberal than the UN one: it includes within its definition of 'refugee' persons who flee owing to 'external aggression, occupation, foreign domination or events seriously disturbing public order'.) Most notably, the UN convention definition excludes persons who flee from their home states on economic grounds, to improve their lot materially in a foreign country. The journalistic term for such a person is 'economic refugee', although this expression is, from the legal standpoint, an oxymoron. In all events, the law is clear on this point. The rules relating to refugees are *not* designed to promote general freedom of movement or migration.

This last question has presented itself forcefully in two cases: Vietnam and Haiti. Since 1979, some 675 000 'boat people' have fled from Vietnam by sea and been deposited on the coasts of various neighbouring countries – to the discomfiture of their involuntary hosts. These host countries have insisted that the vast majority of these boat people are not refugees in the legal sense; that is, that they are mere 'economic refugees', not victims of political persecution. In June 1989, the various states of refuge agreed a 'Comprehensive Plan of Action', the heart of which was a refusal of settlement rights to mere 'economic refugees'. The application of this policy by Hong Kong is instructive. While the crucial determination of refugee status is being made, the boat people are not allowed freedom of movement and residence in the colony. Instead, they are subjected to a form of administrative detention, a kind of legal limbo. If they are found to be genuine refugees, in the legal sense, they are allowed to remain in Hong Kong with the full protection of the 1951 UN convention. Otherwise, they are expected to return to their country of departure. Although Hong Kong and the other host countries are acting within their strict legal rights in adopting this policy, there has been some concern over whether the determinations of refugee status are being fairly made.

Various devices have been attempted to bring about the actual repatriation of the 'economic refugees' to their home states. The UN began a programme of cash payments as an inducement in 1989, which has been supplemented by a European Communities aid effort. These policies have had some considerable impact: since June 1989, some 36 000 Vietnamese have returned to their home country. But more drastic methods have been applied as well. In December 1989, Hong Kong forcibly repatriated 51 people to Vietnam. A further step came in October 1991, when Great Britain (on behalf of Hong Kong) concluded an arrangement with Vietnam for the immediate screening of new arrivals in Hong Kong, with prompt repatriation of those who were found not to qualify for refugee status. Vietnam, for its part, promised that it would not persecute persons for their attempted flight. The UNHCR was to provide monitoring in Vietnam to ensure that such persecution did not take place. This arrangement was followed in May 1992 by a more comprehensive one covering the pre-October 1991 arrivals. Under this new agreement, there is to be outright involuntary repatriation of all Vietnamese in Hong Kong who are merely 'economic refugees'. The UNHCR has made it clear that it opposes forcible repatriation (although it should be noted that 'involuntary' repatriation is not necessarily forcible).[73] These various efforts seem to have been effective. In 1992, nearly 17 000 Hong Kong boat people returned to Vietnam, while the influx of new asylum seekers into Hong Kong practically ceased.[74] A 'solution' to the boat people problem therefore appeared to be gradually evolving – a solution which carefully protects the sovereign rights of states and which sternly denies asylum to 'economic refugees'.

A problem similar to that encountered in Hong Kong faces the United States in the Western Hemisphere in the form of 'boat people' fleeing from Haiti to the shores of a land of would-be refuge and liberalism. Refuge and liberalism, however, have been found to be in very short supply. The American reaction has been, in many ways, more drastic than the British one in Hong Kong. The United States has taken stern measures to prevent the Haitians from landing in American territory at all. The basic policy is one of interdiction at sea by American vessels, followed by the immediate return of the would-be arrivals to Haiti. This policy is based on the thesis that the over-whelming majority of these persons (like the Vietnamese) are mere 'economic refugees'. To meet the concern over the fate of persons who are true refugees (that is, who have a well-founded fear of per-secution), the United States posts immigration officials on the inter-ception vessels who, in the course of the return voyage, interview the Haitians with a view to sifting the true refugees from the others. Those who are found, by this procedure, to be true refugees are then admitted to the United States; the others are unceremoniously re-turned to Haiti. Haitians who somehow slip through the interdiction-at-sea net and arrive in the United States face much the same fate as their counterparts in Hong Kong. They too are held in administrative detention pending case-by-case determinations of refugee status. Those held not to be refugees are also subject to involuntary repatriation, to which the UNHCR has expressed opposition. As in the case of Hong Kong, doubts have been expressed as to the fairness of the determinations of refugee status.[75]

One of the most obvious difficulties with the way in which coun-tries deal with asylum seekers is that the burden of hosting these unfortunate persons falls very unequally. Some writers insist that this question of 'burden sharing' really lies at the heart of the entire debate about duties to rescue.[76] This argument has particular force in the context of the international refugee crisis, in which the accidents of geography and the diversity of state policies combine to impose serious burdens on a small number of countries, while allowing oth-ers to sit back and enjoy their good fortune. There are many obvious examples of this phenomenon. In 1971–72, there was a huge flood of East Pakistanis into India as a result of the Bangladesh independence crisis. During the 1980s, the war in Afghanistan bequeathed to Paki-stan the world's largest horde of refugees. Warfare and oppression in the Horn of Africa resulted in the displacement of large numbers of persons in that region, beginning in the late 1970s. Thousands of Kurds fled from Iraq into Turkey in 1991 to escape repression. Soon afterwards, the chaotic collapse of Yugoslavia propelled large num-bers of people into the neighbouring states of Central Europe.

It is hardly surprising, therefore, that proposals for burden sharing in refugee crises have been advanced periodically. There have even been proposals for fixing legal liability on the state that generated the refugees – with the consequence that that state would be liable in damages to other countries that suffer as a result of the refugee influx.[77] To some extent, there has been voluntary burden sharing. In 1979, most notably, the UN arranged an 'Orderly Departure Programme' for the emigration of persons from Vietnam to various participating countries, to forestall the decidedly 'disorderly' emigration on small boats to neighbouring states. (In 1992, about 100 000 people left Vietnam under this scheme.)[78] In addition, Western countries have voluntarily resettled some of the Vietnamese boat people who took initial refuge in Southeast Asian states. For example, Western countries consented to accept some 547 000 Southeast Asians who had taken initial refuge in Thailand. But the Western generosity eventually faded. So, accordingly, did Thailand's own. In 1986, it refused to accept any more asylum seekers into its main refugee camp.[79] Nowhere was this lack of progress on burden-sharing more dramatically illustrated than at a conference in July 1992, called by the UNHCR to deal with refugees from Bosnia–Herzogovina. A proposal was advanced for a quota system to share out the numbers of refugees equitably among the countries of the world. But the plan was rejected. As a result, the refugees were largely left to their own devices for finding countries of refuge.[80]

One result of this refusal to share the burden of coping with asylum seekers (whether they are refugees in the strict sense or not) is that overburdened states will be driven to take unilateral measures to divert the flow of asylum seekers elsewhere. In the early 1980s, there were reports that Malaysia was pushing Southeast Asian boat people out to sea to avoid playing host to them. In the early 1990s, even Germany, one of the most liberal countries, began taking steps to tighten its asylum policy. In December 1992, agreement was reached by the main political parties to designate certain countries as non-repressive, so that claims of persecution relating to those states could be summarily rejected.[81]

In sum, the attitude of international law towards refugees is a very judicious blend of carefully measured humanitarianism, combined with a stony determination to uphold the basic sovereign right of states to accept or reject asylum seekers as they please. On the one hand, states have readily accepted, in the 1951 UN convention, the principle that, once admitted to their territories, refugees are entitled to humane treatment, essentially on a par with nationals. There is also a certain measure of genuine sympathy for the victims of persecution. At the same time, though, states have been, on the whole, grimly determined to withhold from refugees the most valuable right of all – the right to be admitted to the territory of a state that will provide them refuge from persecution. There appears to be, at present, no prospect of a change in the world's approach to this problem.

5   Humanitarian Intervention and Rescue of Nationals Abroad

Perhaps the single most obvious area of international law concerned with the question of rescue is that of humanitarian intervention, which is the taking of forcible action by one state to rescue persons in another state who are the victims of oppression. It is also one of the most controversial areas of the whole of international law. The reason is obvious enough. This subject, more than any other in international law, touches directly upon the delicate question of the right of states to treat their own nationals as they choose without interference from other states. It is also intimately concerned with issues about the lawful and unlawful use of force in international affairs. Here, more than anywhere, the demands of humanity and the traditional sovereign rights of states come into direct conflict.

We should note one important point at the outset of this discussion: our concern here is entirely with the question of a *right* of humanitarian intervention, rather than of a duty. The reason is that humanitarian intervention, by its nature, necessarily involves at least a prima facie violation of the sovereign rights of another state. For that reason, there is no doubt that, even assuming that it exists as a legal right, it must be exercised only with the greatest caution. When rescuers must necessarily be trespassers, the right of rescue will inevitably be carefully circumscribed.

Our story here is much the same, in outline, as in the categories considered above: an evolution from an early concern on the part of natural lawyers with the well-being of peoples, to a later emphasis, in the positivist era, on the rights of states, and in particular on the principle of non-intervention. The difference here is that even the medieval natural law writers trod very warily in this emotive field. The Jesuit writer, Francisco Suárez, for example, writing in the early seventeenth century, went no further than to hold that any Christian prince had a right to defend 'innocent people' who were seeking to 'accept the law of Christ' in the face of a wicked ruler who was attempting to coerce them into idolatry.[82] It is interesting that thinkers of a more secular outlook were willing to go much further along this line. A noted example was Gentili,[83] who explicitly asserted that 'kingdoms were not made for kings, but kings for their kingdoms'. This was, of course, a forthright rejection of any claim on the part of kings of an inherent right to rule as they pleased. Gentili stressed the existence of a general 'kinship of nature' amongst all peoples and the union of all peoples in a 'society formed by the whole world'. His views were not confined to the public law sphere. Rather, he was concerned to ensure that any lawful power of one person over another, such as parents over children or masters over slaves, should be exercised with moderation. Even wrongdoers, in Gentili's view, were entitled to protection against punishment 'with fury' and, if such excessive punishment was being inflicted, then any person could step in to protect the victim. The example that he gave was the assistance rendered by the English government to the Dutch insurgents against Spanish rule in the late sixteenth century. Even if the Dutch were in the wrong in rebelling, the excessive punishment inflicted by the Spaniards justified the assistance rendered by the English.

Grotius was clearer yet on the matter. He gave extended consideration to the question of undertaking war on behalf of others. This was largely a discussion of the law concerning alliances, but it included 'The question of whether a war for the defence of subjects of another power is rightful'.[84] Grotius answered this question in the affirmative. He maintained that, if a ruler 'should inflict upon his subjects such treatment as no one is warranted in inflicting', then foreign sovereigns were entitled to come to the rescue. The ultimate justification here, as with Gentili, was the general 'mutual tie of kinship among men, which of itself affords sufficient ground for rendering assistance'. Grotius, ever alert to private law analogies when they prove helpful, likened this principle to the case of a guardian acting for a pupil who was personally incapable of action, or to a counsel appearing without authority for a litigant who was absent. He reached the same conclusion, from a slightly different standpoint, in his discussion of the subject of punishment. Appealing here to the general principle 'that man should be helped by man', he concluded that it was lawful for anyone to exact vengeance from a wrongdoer. Applying this general principle to princes, he asserted that they 'have the right of demanding punishments not only on account of injuries committed against themselves or their subjects, but also on account of injuries which do not directly affect them but excessively violate the law of nature or of nations in regard to any persons whatever'.[85] At the same time, though, Grotius was conscious that his position was at variance with that of some previous writers on the subject. He candidly admitted that Vitoria, Vasquez and Molina held the opposite view. The reason was that they considered the matter as one of 'civil jurisdiction' (that is, of the rights of sovereigns over subjects), whereas he (Grotius) saw it from the more general perspective of the 'law of nature'.[86]

Advocates of the right of humanitarian intervention claim to be able to point to a number of historical examples of its exercise. The illustration that Grotius himself gave was of the Roman emperors warring against the Persians for their oppression of Christian subjects.[87] Gentili's example, as we have just seen, was the assistance by the English of the Dutch rebels against Spain. Various other incidents have been put forward as instances of this right of humanitarian intervention (as it came to be called). One was the British intervention in the Greek war of independence against the Ottomans in the 1820s, in which the action of the British fleet at Navarino helped to turn the tide in the Greeks' favour. In the 1860s, France intervened in a civil war in the Lebanon (then part of the Ottoman Empire) to prevent an attack and massacre of Maronite Christians by Druzes. It has been contended that the American war against Spain in 1898 was, at least in part, a rescuing of the Cuban insurgents from oppression by their colonial overlords.[88]

This supposed right of humanitarian intervention has been vigorously contested by a number of international lawyers.[89] These opponents of the doctrine are certainly no apologists for repressive governments. They readily accept that the UN possesses the right of humanitarian intervention – and, indeed, for the most part, they regret that the UN has not exercised this undoubted right more frequently than it has. What they contest is the existence of a *unilateral* right of intervention on the part of individual states, outside the framework of the UN. Humanitarian intervention, in their view, exists solely as a community right, exercisable by the UN through its powers under Chapter VII of the Charter. In support of their view, these writers point to the UN Charter's basic prohibition on the unilateral use of force, article 2(4), which forbids 'the threat or use of force against the territorial integrity or political independence of any state, or in any other manner inconsistent with the Purposes of the United Nations'. The Charter (as noted in Section 2 above) goes on to carve out two explicit exceptions to this general rule: self-defence (individual and collective) and forcible action under Security Council auspices. Since there is no mention of unilateral humanitarian intervention as an exception, it must be held to be forbidden. In other words, the UN Charter, on this view, places a higher value on the non-use of force than it does on the righting of wrongs through unilateral forcible action.

Putting this same line of argument in somewhat broader terms, it is argued that unilateral humanitarian intervention undermines the functioning of the UN Security Council. The UN machinery was set up precisely to deal with such crises. Since such machinery for dealing with gross abuses of human rights by states now exists, any right of unilateral, self-judging humanitarian intervention that might once have existed should now be seen as obsolete. In support of this last view is the fact that, on several occasions, the UN Security Council has actually mounted humanitarian interventions on behalf of the world community at large. The most notable example is Rhodesia, in which the real concern was more the oppressive character of the government within the country than fears of aggression against neighbouring states. From 1966 to 1979, the Security Council maintained comprehensive economic sanctions against Rhodesia in an attempt to force the 'illegal racist minority regime' out of power. (Success in that regard eventually came, but more as a result of guerrilla war than of the economic sanctions.)[90] Another case in which the UN Security Council has taken action on largely humanitarian grounds concerns South Africa. Since 1977, there has been a mandatory arms embargo in force against that country, largely as a response to its repressive racial policies.[91]

The UN took its most forceful action to date in the humanitarian sphere in 1992, in two separate crises. First was the ferocious civil conflict in Bosnia–Herzogovina, where publicity about shocking atrocities inflicted mainly (it appeared) by Serb irregular forces led to public pressure for intervention of some kind. In August 1992, the UN Security Council, having already invoked Chapter VII with respect to the Yugoslavian situation the previous year, authorised humanitarian action by member states at their own initiative for the protection of relief supplies – though 'in co-ordination' with UN peacekeeping forces present in the area.[92] Various European states responded by contributing troops. The other instance concerned Somalia, a country that had fallen into a state of near-anarchy, with widespread interference by various warlords in relief efforts intended to rescue large numbers of persons from starving. A small presence of Pakistani forces under UN auspices did little to improve matters. Accordingly, the Security Council, in December 1992, authorised the use of whatever force was necessary to ensure that the humanitarian aid was delivered without molestation. In this instance, the United States assumed the dominant role in the humanitarian effort.[93] In early 1993, it was far from clear how successful these forcible humanitarian efforts in Bosnia and Somalia would prove to be. The point for present purposes, however, is simply to emphasise that there is no legal barrier to humanitarian intervention under the auspices of the UN, and that such action has actually occurred in practice. To the opponents of the principle of unilateral intervention, these historical examples bolster the case against unilateral humanitarian intervention by illustrating the feasibility of multilateral action instead.

Another serious objection to unilateral humanitarian intervention – and the most obvious one - is that it is subject to the most serious abuse. What is to prevent a country from simply pursuing its own power politics goals under the guise of humanitarian motives? After all, nothing is easier than to put one's own selfish actions in the best light by claiming (possibly with the utmost sincerity) that they are in the interest of the world at large. It is indeed depressingly easy to point to examples in which interventions with a humanitarian element also, by coincidence, served the political ends of the intervening state. India's intervention in the Pakistan civil strife in 1971–72 is one example. Another is the Syrian intervention in Lebanon since 1976. The Tanzanian overthrow of the Amin government of Uganda in 1979 and the Vietnamese intervention in Cambodia that same year provide further illustrations, as do the American interventions in Grenada in 1983 and in Panama in 1989–90. Some would even go so far as to contend that concrete historical examples of true humanitarian interventions are virtually non-existent.[94]

This scepticism as to the existence of true humanitarian interventions is fortified by the fact that intervening states themselves have generally refrained from giving humanitarianism as a justification for their actions, even when they arguably might have done so. There are various reasons for this reluctance. States are fully aware of how serious a matter the use of force against another state is, and so they tend to take care to rely on the most firm (or at least firm-sounding) excuses. Reliance on so highly doubtful a ground as humanitarian intervention might be seen to weaken a legal case rather than to strengthen it, and also to lay the intervening state open to accusations of hypocrisy if (as is usually the case) it also has political interests at stake. Finally, there is the innate caution of governments: they hesitate to endorse a doctrine which might in the future be used against them and which is, in addition, dangerously open-ended in character. At all events, intervening states tend, in practice, to rely on conventional justifications such as self-defence or the defence of nationals when resorting to force.

Opponents of humanitarian intervention do, however, consider the possibility that a genuine humanitarian intervention might, in principle, occur, however rare it might be in practice. They would propose to deal with the matter by making a sharp distinction between morality and law. Such an intervention should be held, some have argued, to be unlawful strictly speaking – but, at the same time, to be praiseworthy from the moral standpoint, if it serves to relieve genuine suffering that would otherwise have been ignored. In such a rare case, the expectation would be that no action would be taken against the intervening state or states. They would be held to have committed a technical violation of the law, but one that was best overlooked because of the moral and humanitarian factors present. Ian Brownlie is the most prominent proponent of this 'double level' approach (as it has sometimes been labelled).[95] A variant of this line of reasoning has been advanced by Fernando Tesón. He takes the view that, while unilateral humanitarian intervention itself is lawful, it is nevertheless permissible in certain cases to recognise the legality of the situation created by such an intervention.[96]

The proponents of humanitarian intervention have countered these opposing arguments with gusto.[97] These champions of the doctrine concede the validity of many of the opposition's points but deny that they add up to a case for outright abolition, merely to the necessity for extreme caution and vigilance in its exercise (or purported exercise). The advocates of humanitarian intervention do not deny that the UN Charter, as well as general international law, contains a general prohibition against the use of force. But they contend that the prohibition is not absolute. In fact, the very provision of the Charter which contains the ban, article 2(4), also qualifies it. What is banned by that article is not, strictly speaking, the use of force *per se*, but rather 'the use of force against the territorial integrity or political independence of any state, or in any other manner inconsistent with the Purposes of the United Nations'. A humanitarian intervention, some argue, is not directed 'against the territorial integrity or political independence' of the state suffering the intervention. Its only purpose is the relief of suffering of the victim population. It is not a 'power play' by the intervening states. Furthermore, a humanitarian intervention certainly is not contrary to the purposes of the UN, since one of the UN's stated purposes (in article 1) is 'solving international problems of a humanitarian character', as well as promoting 'respect for human rights'. For these reasons, a humanitarian intervention falls outside the general prohibition of article 2(4) on the use of force.[98]

Champions of humanitarian intervention admit that, ideally, the community at large (the UN), rather than individual states, should undertake any humanitarian interventions that are necessary. Nor have they any doubt that the UN has the legal right to act in such cases if it so chooses. But the problem, they insist, is deciding what – if anything – is to be done in the all too numerous cases in which the UN fails to act. Certainly nothing is easier than to make a shamefully long list of such cases of UN inaction. In the case of terrible massacres of ethnic Chinese in Indonesia in the mid-1960s, for example, the UN did nothing. Appalling mistreatment of East Pakistanis by their ruling government in 1970–71, for example, led to no UN action. In Burundi in 1972, genocidal attacks by Tutsis against Hutus similarly provoked no UN response. The same was true of Uganda in the case of large-scale human rights abuses in the 1970s and 1980s by the Amin and Obote governments. The 'dirty war' in Argentina in the late 1970s attracted little interest at the UN. No effective action was taken against the murderous Khmer Rouge government of Cambodia in the same period. Nor did the 'Red terror' in Ethiopia in the late 1970s goad the Security Council into action.

Advocates of humanitarian intervention can point to the situation in Iraq in 1991 as a particularly dramatic illustration of the inadequacy of the UN as an enforcer of human rights norms. In the wake of the successful liberation of Kuwait by UN-approved forces, revolt broke out in Iraq amongst Shi'ite Muslims in the south of Iraq, and amongst Kurds in the northern mountains. The government reacted with characteristic ruthlessness, using massive military force against both groups. There was widespread coverage of these matters in the world press – and corresponding outrage at the obvious reluctance of either the UN or the victorious pro-Kuwait countries to take any action to stop the repression. The Shi'ite revolt, in particular, was taking place almost under the very guns of the victorious pro-Kuwait armies; yet they scrupulously refrained from any rescue action. The UN's response was clearly inadequate. The Security Council could have invoked its enforcement powers under Chapter VII by declaring these situations to constitute a threat to the peace. Instead, the UN went no further than to 'demand' that Iraq halt its repressive actions against its civilian population, while carefully refraining from invoking Chapter VII.[99] (The UN also entered into an agreement with Iraq, pursuant to which the UN would assist in the administering of humanitarian aid and provide some token security presence in a Kurdish safe haven; but this was an arrangement with the Iraqi government and therefore cannot be considered to be an *intervention* by the UN into Iraqi affairs.[100])

In the light of this timidity on the part of the UN, the Western powers proceeded to take unilateral action. Regarding the Kurdish revolt in the north, they made it clear to Iraq, in April 1991, that a clearly designated area of the country was to be treated as a 'safe haven' for Kurds and that, inside that designated area, Iraqi government forces were not to operate, on pain of military defensive action by the Western states. In effect, the Western powers insisted upon the establishment of an autonomous Kurdish area within Iraq (although the safe haven did not include, by a large margin, all of the territory of Iraq in which Kurds lived). In the south, the Western powers, in August 1992, imposed a 'no-fly zone' (a ban on Iraqi military flights in a designated area) to provide some protection for the Shi'ite population. In December 1992, they found occasion to enforce it by shooting down an Iraqi airplane in the zone. To the advocates of unilateral humanitarian intervention, the Iraq crisis graphically illustrates the shortcomings of reliance on the UN for effective human rights protection – and the consequent need for UN member states to step into the breach in emergency cases. The intervening states (it is argued) are, in effect, voluntarily filling the gap left by the UN and thereby exercising their duties as global good citizens. If the duly authorised global policeman is not available, or not able, to right serious wrongs, then, as a regrettable last resort, the individual states should be allowed to act.

Finally, the advocates of humanitarian intervention, while not denying the grave dangers that can arise from the abuse of the doctrine, deny that the dangers are so great as to lead to outright rejection of it. Grotius himself had considered the question in precisely these terms.[101]

The very real potential for abuse is merely a ground for extreme caution in the exercise of the right, and for casting a very sceptical eye indeed upon any claims to justify uses of force on humanitarian grounds. In the interest of providing appropriate safeguards for the exercise of this valuable, but dangerous, right, the proponents of the doctrine have advanced a number of criteria that must be satisfied before any intervention will be deemed to pass legal muster under this heading. The various proposals of this kind are of a broadly similar and commonsensical character. The human rights abuses in question must be exceptionally severe in character, so as to preclude any lighthearted exercise of this dangerous right. The intervention must be confined as narrowly as possible to the rescuing of the victims and avoid, to the greatest extent possible, interference with the sovereign rights of the state. The intervening state or states must give a full and prompt report of their actions to the UN, so that the world at large will be in a position to make an informed judgement as to the merits of the case.[102]

It would be difficult to find any other issue in the whole of international law about which the debate has been so robust, or, to date, so inconclusive, as over humanitarian intervention. [103] One reason for the difficulty in resolving the contest is that the basic philosophical and temperamental gulf between the two sides is so great. The proponents of the principle bring what is recognisably a just war perspective to bear on the question: force is to be permitted as a last option when the cause is a just one. Their stress is on the right of states to act on behalf of the general human interest for the promotion of human rights. This community interest, in their view, should have a higher priority than the traditional principles of non-intervention and the sovereign equality of states. The opponents of humanitarian intervention, in contrast, are somewhat more difficult to characterise. They are certainly not to be numbered, with Moore and Borchard, among the opponents of the very idea of collective security. On the contrary, they base much of their case on a concern that the authority and powers of the UN not be usurped by its more powerful member states. At the same time, however, they are firmly in the positivist tradition in their insistence on the principles of the sovereign equality of states and non-intervention. Perhaps the fairest way of summarising their position is to say that, in their view, the dangers posed to the rights of states are more real and immediate than the speculative benefits to oppressed peoples.

The two camps are sharply at odds in the views that they hold of the nature – or at least of the robustness – of international law. The opponents of humanitarian intervention are clearly sceptical as to the ability of the rules of international law to be finely enough tailored to fit precisely onto the rules of morality. It must therefore be accepted that sometimes the two will diverge. The supporters of the doctrine, in contrast, are confident that international law can be carefully crafted so as to conform to the rules of morality. The opponents of the principle are accordingly more conservative in the sense that they have more modest expectations about the ability of international law to deal with real-world problems in all their richness. The opponents are also conservative in the sense that they are more inclined to strict construction of legal texts, such as the UN Charter. The Charter makes no provision for (or even mention of) humanitarian intervention. Therefore, it is not allowed. The advocates of the principle, on the other hand, contend that the Charter must be interpreted in the light of the actual challenges which the world faces from time to time. In particular, the rule forbidding the unilateral use of force by states, praiseworthy as it might be in principle, must be applied with some flexibility during periods (such as the present one) when the collective security apparatus of the Security Council is so manifestly imperfect.

The World Court has, so far, dealt with the issue on only one notable occasion. This was in the *Nicaragua* v. *United States* case, in 1986, in which it pondered humanitarian intervention as a defence to an accusation of an unlawful use of force. The court held that the United States, by furnishing aid of various kinds to the Nicaraguan insurgents, violated the general prohibition against the use of force. It then went on to consider whether the American actions might have been justified as a humanitarian intervention for the promotion of human rights in Nicaragua. (The United States did not itself make this argument, as it declined to appear to argue its case at all.) The court had scant sympathy with such a defence in this case:

> While the United States might form its own appraisal of the situation as to respect for human rights in Nicaragua, the use of force could not be the appropriate method to monitor or ensure such respect. With regard to the steps actually taken, the protection of human rights, a strictly humanitarian objective, cannot be compatible with the mining of ports, the destruction of oil installations, or ... with the training, arming and equipping of the *contras*.[104]

This pronouncement, it may be noted, stops short of being a *general* rejection of the very idea of humanitarian intervention. But it does indicate that the World Court will scrutinise such claims closely.[105]

Similar to the problem of humanitarian intervention is that of the rescue by a state of its *own* nationals who are victims of either oppression or some other form of peril in a foreign state. The similarity lies, of course, in the fact that, in order to effect the rescue, the state of nationality must necessarily interfere with the normal sovereign rights of the territorial state. It is hardly surprising, then, that many of the arguments from the humanitarian intervention debate reappear here. For example, the opponents of forcible rescue of nationals point out that the UN Charter does not expressly allow it as an exception to the general ban on the use of force; consequently, it ought not to be permitted. Proponents respond that a rescue operation, like a humanitarian one, is not directed against 'the territorial integrity or political independence' of the host country and therefore falls outside the article 2(4) prohibition against force. The opponents contend that the task of rescue should be left to the UN. The advocates answer that the UN, in reality, seldom acts effectively.

There is, however, one important and obvious difference between the two situations: the presence of the nationality link necessarily gives the rescuing state a greater *self*-interest in the matter than it has in the case of humanitarian intervention. For this reason, the phenomenon of protection of nationals has not traditionally been seen in humanitarian terms, but rather in terms of the protection of the rights of the rescuing state. This approach originated with Vattel in the eighteenth century. He insisted that an injury inflicted by a state upon a foreign national automatically constituted an injury to the victim's home state.[106] The World Court later took that view to its logical conclusion by holding that, when a state makes a diplomatic claim on behalf of an injured national, it is, legally speaking, redressing an injury to itself.[107]

Some writers take this approach and justify the forcible rescue of nationals on the ground of self-defence. The value of this argument lies in the fact that self-defence (as observed in Section 2 above) is expressly provided for in the UN Charter as a permissible use of force. The problem is that it is questionable whether the concept of self-defence encompasses the rescuing of individual nationals. In everyday usage, the term is more commonly applied to the protection of the state as a whole, and particularly of its territory, from invasion. It may fairly be extended to encompass the protection of the sovereign machinery of the state outside the territory, such as a naval fleet that might come under attack on the high seas. But only with considerable stretching can the idea take in the protection of civilian nationals in the territory of another sovereign state. Legal scholars are divided on whether such a stretching is justified. The foremost proponent of an affirmative response to this question is the British writer, Derek Bowett, who is a noted proponent of the thesis that the right of self-defence extends to the protection of a state's vital interests generally – including the safety of its nationals abroad.[108] Not surprisingly, this view is endorsed by militarily powerful countries such as the United States. Other writers are doubtful about the self-defence argument and support the use of force to rescue nationals on a different basis: as a humanitarian measure. According to this argument, the rescue of nationals becomes merely a special case of humanitarian intervention,[109] which has already been discussed.

The arguments regarding the potential abuse of the doctrine of forcible rescue of nationals resemble those concerning humanitarian intervention. It may be noted, though, that the danger of abuse here is probably somewhat less than with humanitarian intervention. The rescue of nationals is less open-ended, since it can only take place when a nationality link is present. Nonetheless, the opponents of the practice insist that the risk of abuse is a serious one. They point to such incidents as the American interventions in the Dominican Republic in 1965, in Grenada in 1983 and in Panama in 1989–90, as well as to various French interventions in Africa, as illustrations.[110] It is therefore (on this view) in the overall interest of the international community to interpret the right of self-defence in the most sternly restrictive fashion, to insure against its future misuse as a cloak for aggression. That may be a harsh (and regrettable) result from the standpoint of the persons in peril, but the interest of the wider community in promoting the non-use of force should take precedence.[111]

It is interesting to note that some doubt has been expressed as to whether the consent of the country in which the rescue operation takes place will suffice to make the rescue lawful. This question came up in one of the most notable post-Second World War rescue missions, in the Congo in 1964. In that incident, insurgents were holding some hundreds of civilians hostage in Stanleyville. The Congo government requested the assistance of Belgium and the United States, which was duly provided. Paratroop forces from these two states succeeded in rescuing most of the hostages in a week-long operation. This incident sparked a long and bitter debate in the UN Security Council, in which a number of African countries abusively attacked the two intervening states, contending that the consent of the Congo government was insufficient to provide a legal justification. In the event, however, the resolution adopted did not condemn the two states but merely contained an anodyne general exhortation to countries to refrain from intervening in the domestic affairs of the Congo.[112]

The argument for the irrelevance of consent is based on the thesis that the international community as a whole has an interest in upholding the vital principle of non-intervention. Therefore it should not be possible for a single state – even the state most closely affected – to undermine it by waiving its rights. On the other side, the argument is that the purpose of the principle of non-intervention is to protect states from undesired interventions. Therefore, if a state genuinely wishes, for some reason, not to avail itself of the protection, there is no reason not to honour its wishes. The latter view appears the more persuasive one. But there has been, as yet, no judicial pronouncement on the question. More contentious, of course, is the case in which the rescue operation does not have the permission of the country in which it takes place. There have been a number of notable instances of this kind of rescue mission since the Second World War. One was the forcible rescue by American forces of the ship *Mayaguez*, which was captured by Cambodia in 1975. The single most spectacular one, however, was undoubtedly the forcible rescue by Israel in July 1976 of a planeload of passengers who had been hijacked and taken to Entebbe Airport in Uganda. A large number of Israeli nationals were on board – indeed, the hijackers carefully separated the Jewish passengers from the non-Jewish ones, releasing the latter. In a lightning commando raid, Israeli forces liberated the captives. In the process, three of the passengers and one Israeli commando were killed, along with seven hijackers and some 20 Ugandan soldiers. In addition, one airport terminal building was destroyed, together with 11 Mig fighters (representing a substantial portion of the Ugandan air force).

Fierce protest predictably ensued from African and other Third World countries. A telegram sent to the UN on behalf of the member states of the OAU condemned the Israeli action as a 'wanton act of aggression'.[113] The secretary-general of the UN, Kurt Waldheim, stated that the rescue mission was 'a serious violation of the sovereignty' of a member state of the UN[114] – without, however, committing himself on the crucial question as to whether it was a *justified* violation. American lawyers Myres S. McDougal and Michael Reisman contended that it was. They pointed out that Israel's action could not possibly have had an effect on 'the territorial integrity and political independence' of Uganda, and furthermore that the rescue action was 'entirely necessary and proportionate to the lawful purpose of the rescue'.[115] There was no judicial consideration of the legality of this rescue mission, but there was a debate, lasting some five days, in the UN Security Council on the incident. Great Britain and the United States introduced a draft resolution on the subject, which condemned aerial hijacking, deplored the loss of life which had stemmed from the hijacking (as opposed to the rescue operation) and reaffirmed 'the need to respect the sovereignty and territorial integrity of all States' in accordance with the UN Charter and international law.[116] In the course of the debates, the United States forthrightly defended the Israeli action, asserting that the right to rescue nationals abroad was clearly established and that it flowed from the right of self-defence.[117] A rival draft resolution by three African states took a predictably more strident line, condemning 'Israel's flagrant violation of Uganda's sovereignty and territorial integrity' and demanding compensation for Uganda from Israel.[118]

In the event, neither resolution was adopted. The African one was withdrawn without being put to a vote. The British–American draft failed to win the necessary nine votes for adoption. This vote, however, did vividly indicate the depth of the uncertainty of states on this question: of the 15 Security Council members, two abstained and no fewer than seven (including the Soviet Union and China) declined to participate in the voting at all.[119] Secretary-general Waldheim stated, rather vaguely, that the incident raised 'many issues of a humanitarian, moral, legal and political character for which, at the present time, no commonly agreed rules or solutions exist'.[120] Sweden adopted Brownlie's 'double level' position: on the one hand, it found itself 'unable to reconcile the Israeli action with the strict rules of the Charter', while at the same time it did not 'find it possible to join in a condemnation in this case'.[121]

The only occasion, so far, on which a court has commented on a rescue mission concerned the unsuccessful American attempt to rescue hostages held in its occupied embassy compound in Tehran in 1980. Shortly after the mission, the World Court handed down a decision in the suit which the United States had brought against Iran for the taking and holding of the hostages. Since Iran declined to appear and defend the action, it did not raise the question. But the court brought the matter up on its own initiative. It stated that it understood the preoccupation of the Americans with the matter and its frustration at Iran's intransigence. (Iran had been in breach of a court order to release the hostages for some four months before the rescue mission.) At the same time, though, the court noted its 'concern' over the rescue operation in the light of the fact that, at the very time that the mission was mounted, the court was preparing to adjudicate upon the claims that the United States itself had brought against Iran. The court was therefore moved to 'observe' that 'an operation undertaken in these circumstances, from whatever motive, is of a kind calculated to undermine respect for the judicial process in international relations. ...' It was also moved to 'recall' its order of December 1979, that neither state was to take action that might aggravate the tension between them. But the court then immediately pointed out that the question of the legality of the rescue operation was not before it.[122]

It is difficult to say what the legal significance of these remarks by the World Court actually is. The overall tone was clearly one of disapproval, but it should not be concluded that the court's statements amount to a definitive judicial rejection of the legality of forcible rescue of nationals in the general case. The main reason for caution is that a very special circumstance was present in this case: the fact that the matter was actively *sub judice* at the time of the rescue mission, and furthermore that the very party undertaking the mission was the one which brought the action. The basis of the court's disapproval, therefore, was the contention that the operation amounted to an undermining of the judicial process – a feature of this operation that could not be expected to be present in other such cases. The court therefore cannot be said to have condemned the idea of forcible rescue of nationals in principle. The question of the legality of the use of force to rescue nationals abroad is consequently, like humanitarian intervention, still an open one in international law, with stalwart (and passionate) champions on both sides.

Notes

1   The discussion of positivism in this chapter is concerned only with international law. For a more comprehensive discussion of legal positivism (which includes a portion on international law), see H.L.A. Hart, *The Concept of Law* (Oxford, 1961).

2   'Reply to Faustus the Manichaean', in 5 *The Works of Aurelius Augustine, Bishop of Hippo* (Edinburgh, 1872), 145, 463–8.

3   A. Augustine, *Concerning the City of God Against the Pagans* (trans., H. Bettenson, Harmondsworth, 1972), 862. For perceptive remarks on this aspect of Augustine's thought, see R.B. Miller, *Interpretations of Conflict: Ethics, Pacifism, and the Just-war Tradition* (Chicago, 1991), 18–23.

4   T. Aquinas, *Summa Theologiae: A Concise Translation* (ed. and trans. T. McDermott, London, 1989), 367–8.

5   On the medieval just war tradition generally, see A. Vanderpol, *La doctrine scolastique du droit de guerre* (Paris, 1925); F.H. Russell, *The Just War in the Middle Ages* (Cambridge, 1975).

6   On the role of neutrality in the medieval just war tradition, see F. Bottié, *Essai sur la genèse et l'évolution de la notion de neutralité* (Paris, 1937), 87–92.

7   N. Machiavelli, *The Prince* (trans. G. Bull, London, 1981), 121–3. On this development, see F. Bottié, op. cit., 133–8. Machiavelli's actual concern was with advancing the position of the ruler. With Hobbes came the emphasis on the state as a corporate entity with paramount interests of its own. Nevertheless, the modern science of statecraft may fairly be said to have originated with Machiavelli.

8   See C. Wolff, *The Law of Nations Treated According to a Scientific Method* (trans. J.H. Drake, Oxford, 1934), 107; E. de Vattel, *The Law of Nations; or, The Principles of Natural Law Applied to the Conduct and the Affairs of Nations and Sovereigns* (trans. C.G. Fenwick, Washington, 1916), 6.

9   H. Grotius, *On the Law of War and Peace* (trans. F.W. Kelsey, Oxford, 1925), 565–6. On Grotius's views on the just war question generally, see P. Haggenmacher, *Grotius et la doctrine de la guerre juste* (Paris, 1983).

10   A. Gentili, *The Three Books on the Law of War* (trans. J. C. Rolfe, Oxford, London, 1933), 31–3.

11   H. Grotius, *op. cit.*, 783–7.

12   For a classic positivist statement of the legal nature of war, see L. Oppenheim, *International Law: Disputes, War and Neutrality* (H. Lauterpacht ed., London, New York, Toronto, 7th ed., 1952), 202, which expressly rejects the older view of war as 'the legal remedy of self-help to obtain satisfaction for a wrong sustained', insisting instead that war is entered into by states for 'political reasons' and that international law simply recognises war as 'a fact' of international life.

13   This body of rules concerning neutrality was in part a matter of customary

law. For the most elaborate exposition of this law in its classical form, see R. Kleen, *Lois et usages de la neutralité d'après le droit international conventionnel et coûtumier des Etats civilisés* (2 vols, Paris, 1898–1900). Two of the multilateral conventions drafted by the Hague Peace Conference of 1907 concern neutrality: Convention V Respecting the Rights and Duties of Neutral Powers and Persons in Case of War on Land, Oct. 18, 1907, 205 Consolidated Treaty Ser. 299, reprinted in A. Roberts and R. Guelff (Eds), *Documents on the Laws of War* (Oxford, 2nd ed., 1989), 63–9; and Convention XIII Concerning the Rights and Duties of Neutral Powers in Naval War, Oct. 18, 1907, 205 Consolidated Treaty Ser. 395, reprinted in A. Roberts and R. Guelff, op. cit., 109–19. These two conventions are thought generally to be still in force.

14 See, for example, E. Winslow, 'Neutralization', 2 *American Journal of International Law*, 366 (1908); S.M. Robinson, 'Autonomous Neutralization', 11 *American Journal of International Law*, 607 (1912).

15 For a carefully balanced discussion of this question, see D. Stevenson, *The First World War and International Politics* (Oxford, 1988), 34–8.

16 2 J. Lorimer, *The Institutes of the Law of Nations: A Treatise of the Jural Relations of Separate Political Communities* (Edinburgh, 1884), 121–30.

17 1 R. Kleen, op. cit., *supra*, n. 13, at 155–8.

18 J. Westlake, *International Law: War* (Cambridge, 2d ed., 1913), 190–92.

19 Covenant of the League of Nations, June 28, 1919, 225 Consolidated Treaty Ser. 195, reprinted in I. Claude, *Swords into Ploughshares: The Problems and Progress of International Organization* (New York, 4th ed., 1971), 453–62.

20 See, for example, M.W. Graham, Jr., 'The Effect of the League of Nations Covenant on the Theory and Practice of Neutrality', 15 *California Law Review*, 357, 372–3 (1927); Q. Wright, 'Neutral Rights Following the Pact of Paris for the Renunciation of War', 24 *Proceedings of the American Society of International Law*, 79 (1930); N.D. Baker, 'The "New Spirit" and Its Critics', 12 *Foreign Affairs*, 1 (1933); H. Stimson, 'Neutrality and War Prevention', 29 *Proceedings of the American Society of International Law*, 121 (1935); J.T. Shotwell, *On the Rim of the Abyss* (New York, 1936).

21 Q. Wright, op. cit., *supra*, n. 20.

22 Quoted in R.A. Divine, *The Illusion of Neutrality: Franklin D. Roosevelt and the Struggle over the Arms Embargo* (Chicago, 1962), 19.

23 N.D. Baker, op. cit., *supra*, n. 20, at 16.

24 The leading exposition of this view was J.B. Moore, 'An Appeal to Reason', 11 *Foreign Affairs*, 547 (1933). See also L. Woolsey, 'The Fallacies of Neutrality', 30 *American Journal of International Law*, 256 (1936); E. Borchard, 'Neutrality and Unneutrality', 32 *American Journal of International Law*, 778 (1938); E. Borchard and W. P. Lage, *Neutrality for the United States* (New Haven, 1937); E. Borchard, 'Realism v. Evangelism', 28 *American Journal of International Law*, 108 (1934); E. Borchard, 'Sanctions v. Neutrality', 30 *American Journal of International Law*, 91 (1936); E. Borchard, 'The "Enforcement" of Peace by "Sanctions"', 27 *American Journal of International Law*, 518 (1933).

25 J.B. Moore, op. cit., *supra*, n. 24, at 579–80.

26 E. Borchard, 'Neutrality and Unneutrality', op. cit., *supra*, n. 24, at 778.

27 E. Borchard, 'The "Enforcement" of Peace by "Sanctions"', op. cit., *supra*, n. 24, at 523.

28 E. Borchard, 'Sanctions v. Neutrality', op. cit., *supra*, n. 24, at 94.

29 Resolutions and Recommendations Adopted by the Assembly during its Second Session (Sep. 5 to Oct. 5, 1921, in *League of Nations Official Journal*, Special Supp. No. 6, at 24 (1921); reproduced in J.F. Williams, 'Sanctions under the Covenant', 17 *British Year Book of International Law*, 130, 148–9 (1936).

30 E.C. Stowell, 'The Juridical Significance of World War II', 38 *American Journal of International Law*, 106, 107, 108 (1944).

31 North Atlantic Treaty, Apr. 4, 1949, 34 U.N. Treaty Ser. 243. On collective self-

defence generally, see D.W. Bowett, *Self-defence in International Law* (Manchester, 1958), 200–48.

32   Case Concerning Military and Paramilitary Activities in and Against Nicaragua v. *United States of America*), 1986 I.C.J. Rep. 14, 104–05 [hereinafter referred to as *Nicaragua v. US*].

33   Article 24(1) of the Charter provides that the Security Council, in matters relating to international peace and security, acts on behalf of the body of UN member states. Article 25 provides that the member states 'agree to accept and carry out the decisions of the Security Council'.

34   Security Council Res. 83 (June 27, 1950), and Security Council Res. 84 (July 7, 1950), 5 Security Council Off. Rec., Res. & Dec. 1950, U.N. Doc. S/INF/5/Rev. 1 (1950), 5.

35   Security Council Res. 660 (Aug. 2, 1990), in 29 *International Legal Materials*, 1325 (1990), and in E. Lauterpacht *et al.* (Eds), *The Kuwait Crisis: Basic Documents* (Cambridge, 1991), 88.

36   Security Council Res. 661 (Aug. 6, 1990), in 29 *International Legal Materials*, 1325 (1990), and in E. Lauterpacht *et al.* (Eds), op. cit., 88.

37   Security Council Res. 678 (Nov. 29, 1990), in 29 *International Legal Materials*, 1565 (1990), and in E. Lauterpacht *et al.* (Eds), op. cit., 98.

38   On this issue, see N. Rostow, 'The International Use of Force after the Cold War', 32 *Harvard Journal of International Law*, 411, 414–18 (1991).

39   For excellent discussions of medieval attitudes towards economics and trade, see R. H. Tawney, *Religion and the Rise of Capitalism: A Historical Study* (Harmondsworth, 1926), 27–67; also O. Langholm, 'Economic Freedom in Scholastic Thought', 14 *History of Political Economy*, 260, 273–83 (1982).

40   H. Grotius, op. cit., 186–90.

41   For the views of Grotius on the subject of necessity, and the legal consequences thereof, see H. Grotius, op. cit., 193–5.

42   S. Pufendorf, *On the Law of Nature and Nations* (trans. C.H. and W.A. Oldfather, Oxford and London, 1934), 304–6. The view that charity is an 'imperfect duty' is an enduring one, but contrast Pufendorf's use of 'imperfect duty' with that of Kant and others, who used it of a genuine duty which gives rise to no correlative right. The imperfect duty of charity is discussed in Chapter 1.

43   E. de Vattel, op. cit., 40–41.

44   *Nicaragua v. US*, (*supra*, n. 32, at 138).

45   For a brief, lucid explanation of unequal exchange theory, with references for further reading, see H.D. Evans, 'Trade, Production and Self-reliance', in D. Seers (Ed.), *Dependency Theory: A Critical Reassessment* (London, 1981), 119.

46   The restructuring of international economic relations generally is the goal of the demands of the Third World countries for the instituting of a 'new international economic order'. For a descriptive account of this programme, see L. Anell and B. Nygren, *The Developing Countries and the World Economic Order* (London, 1980). For a critical analysis, placing the programme in a broader historical perspective, see S.C. Neff, *Friends But No Allies: Economic Liberalism and the Law of Nations* (New York, 1990), 178–96.

47   UN Conference on Trade and Development, Res. 27 (II), in 1 *Proceedings of the UN Conference on Trade and Development, Second Session, New Delhi, 1 February – 29 March 1968*, U.N. Doc. TD/97, Vol. I (1968), 38. This call was endorsed by the Pearson Commission the following year: Commission on International Development (Pearson Commission), *Partners in Development* (London, 1969), 143–51.

48   19 *IMF Survey*, 232 (1990).

49   Independent Commission on International Development Issues (Brandt Commission), *North–South: A Programme for Survival* (London, 1980), 64–77.

50   H. Grotius, op. cit., 196–203.

51 Ibid., 783–7.

52 Innumerable examples could be given. See, for instance, the Treaty of Amity, Commerce and Navigation, Ecuador–France, June 6, 1843, 95 Consolidated Treaty Ser. 91.

53 Geneva Convention on the High Seas, Apr. 29, 1958, 450 U.N. Treaty Ser. 82, art. 12. See also the UN Convention on the Law of the Sea, Dec. 10, 1982, U.N. Doc. A/CONF. 61/122 and Corr. 1-11 (1982), art. 98. This 1982 convention was not in force as of the end of 1992.

54 Agreement on the Rescue of Astronauts, the Return of Astronauts and the Return of Objects Launched into Outer Space, Apr. 22, 1968, 672 U.N. Treaty Ser. 119.

55 See the Convention for the Entry and Reception of the French Army, France–Switzerland, Feb. 1, 1871, 142 Consolidated Treaty Ser. 475. On this incident, see A. W. Freeman, 'Non-belligerent's Right to Compensation for Internment of Foreign Military Personnel', 53 *American Journal of International Law*, 638, 640–45 (1959).

56 See note 13, *supra*.

57 P. Davidson, 'Iran Operating Planes Seized from Saddam', *Independent* (London), 3 August 1991, 9, col. 1.

58 See note 13, *supra*. Analogous rules govern the treatment of naval prizes (captured ships). Prizes are not to be brought into neutral waters, save in certain restricted circumstances. If they are brought in, then the neutral power is to release them (articles 21 and 22 of the Hague Convention of 1907 on Neutrality in Naval Warfare, *supra*, note 13). The Hague Convention allows neutral countries to permit prizes to be brought into their waters for sequestration pending adjudication by prize courts (article 23). This is a very controversial provision which a number of countries, including Great Britain and the United States, have refused to accept.

59 The General Armstrong (*United States* v. *Portugal*), Feb. 26, 1851, in J.B. Scott (Ed.), *Cases on International Law Principally Selected from Decisions of English and American Courts* (St Paul, Minn., 1922), 853–5.

60 The most notable legal provision in this regard is article 13 of the International Covenant on Civil and Political Rights, Dec. 16, 1966, 999 U.N. Treaty Ser. 171, reprinted in I. Brownlie, *Basic Documents on Human Rights* (Oxford, 3rd ed., 1992), 125–43. This article provides that (save in national security cases) an alien being expelled from a state must be allowed to submit reasons against his expulsion and to have the case reviewed by 'a competent authority'. As of November 1992, 114 states were parties to this covenant.

61 Convention on the Status of Refugees, July 28, 1951, 189 U.N. Treaty Ser. 137, art. 1; reprinted in I. Brownlie, op. cit., 64–81, and in G.S. Goodwin-Gill, *The Refugee in International Law* (Oxford, 1983), 247–69.

62 For a general history of international responses to refugee problems during the period between the two world wars, see J.H. Simpson, *The Refugee Problem: Report of a Survey* (London, New York, Toronto, 1939).

63 See generally J. Vernant, *The Refugee in the Post-war World* (London, 1953).

64 General Assembly Res. 217A (III), 3 U.N. General Assembly Off. Rec., Resolutions, U.N. Doc. A/810 (1948), 71; reprinted in I. Brownlie, op. cit., 21–7.

65 See note 61, *supra*. See also Protocol Relating to the Status of Refugees, Dec. 16, 1966, 606 U.N. Treaty Ser. 267, reprinted in G.S. Goodwin-Gill, op. cit., 270–73.

66 For the text of the Statute of UNHCR, see G.S. Goodwin-Gill, op. cit., 241–6. On the activities of the UNHCR, see L.W. Holborn, *Refugees – A Problem of Our Time. The Work of the UNHCR: 1951–1972* (Metuchen, NJ, 1975).

67 On the law relating to the status of refugees generally, see A. Grahl-Madsen, *The Status of Refugees in International Law*, 2 vols (Leyden, 1966–72); and G.S. Goodwin-Gill, op. cit.

68 Robert Nozick's position is identical. See Chapter 1, Section 3.

69   General Assembly Res. 2312 (XXII), 22 U.N. General Assembly Off. Rec., Supp. No. 16, U.N. Doc. A/6716 (1967), 81, reprinted in G.S. Goodwin-Gill, op. cit., 275–6.

70   For the abortive draft text of this would-be convention, see G.S. Goodwin-Gill, op. cit., 277–9. On this initiative, see P. Weis, 'The Draft United Nations Convention on Territorial Asylum', 50 *British Year Book of International Law,* 151 (1979). On the law of asylum generally, see A. Grahl-Madsen, *Territorial Asylum* (Uppsala, 1980).

71   Convention on Refugee Problems in Africa, Sep. 10, 1969, 1001 U.N. Treaty Ser. 45, reprinted in G.S. Goodwin-Gill, op. cit., 280–86.

72   For the position of the UNHCR on the determination of refugee status, see UNHCR, *Handbook on Procedures and Criteria for Determining Refugee Status under the 1951 Convention and the 1967 Protocol Relating to the Status of Refugees* (Geneva, 1979).

73   On the agreements of October 1991 and May 1992, see *The Economist,* 16 May 1992, 93, col. 1.

74   On the problem of asylum seekers in Hong Kong, see 'Vietnam's Prodigal Sons', *The Economist,* 13 February 1993, 62, col. 1. See also 'Boat People: Force If Necessary, Gently If Possible', *The Economist,* 1 November 1991, 70, col. 1. See also UK Foreign and Commonwealth Office, 'Background Brief: Vietnamese Migrants in Hong Kong' (London, 1991).

75   See 'Haitian Refugees: Huddled Masses', *The Economist,* 30 May 1992, 55, col. 3.

76   See the discussion of Robert Goodin's view in Chapter 1, Section 6. The argument of Chapter 1 is that the extent of the burden is a main obstacle in the philosophical justification of either a moral or a legal duty to rescue. That argument is given clear point in this discussion of the law relating to refugees.

77   See, for example, L. Lee, 'The Right to Compensation: Refugees and Countries of Asylum', 80 *American Journal of International Law,* 532 (1986).

78   'Vietnam's Prodigal Sons', *supra,* note 74.

79   'Indochina: No Refuge', *The Economist,* 21 February 1987, 53, col. 2.

80   For a table of statistics on the displacement of persons as a result of strife in former Yugoslavia, as of July 1992, see UNHCR, 'Emergency Report: Displacement in Former Yugoslavia' (1992), 6.

81   A. Lieven, 'Politicians Predict Asylum Bill Success', *The Times,* 8 December 1992, 11, col. 7.

82   F. Suárez, 'A Work on the Three Theological Virtues, Faith, Hope and Charity', in *Selections from Three Works of Francisco Suárez, S.J.* (trans. G.L. Williams, A. Brown and J. Waldron, Oxford, 1944), 826–7.

83   A. Gentili, *op. cit.,* 74–7. All of the quotations in this paragraph are from this source.

84   H. Grotius, *op. cit.,* 583–4.

85   Ibid., at 475–8.

86   Ibid., at 506.

87   Ibid., at 584.

88   For a survey of past incidents which can plausibly be argued to have been humanitarian interventions, see J.-P. Fonteyne, 'The Customary International Law Doctrine of Humanitarian Intervention: Its Current Validity under the U.N. Charter', 4 *California Western International Law Journal,* 203, 205–13. See also D.S. Bogen, 'The Law of Humanitarian Intervention: United States Policy in Cuba (1898) and in the Dominican Republic (1965)', 7 *Harvard Journal of International Law,* 296 (1965).

89   For opposition to the doctrine of humanitarian intervention, see T. Franck and N. Rodley, 'After Bangladesh: The Law of Humanitarian Intervention by Military Force', 67 *American Journal of International Law,* 275 (1973); I. Brownlie, 'Humanitarian Intervention', in J. N. Moore (Ed.), *Law and Civil War in the Modern World* (Baltimore, 1974), 217; N. Ronzitti, *The Rescue of Nationals Abroad through Military Coercion and Intervention on Grounds of Humanity* (Dordrecht, 1985); F.R. Tesón, *Humanitarian Inter-*

vention: An Inquiry into Law and Morality (Dobbs Ferry, NY, 1988); T. Farer, 'Human Rights in Law's Empire: The Jurisprudence War', 85 *American Journal of International Law*, 117 (1991).

90 On the Rhodesian crisis and the UN, see generally J. Nkala, *The United Nations, International Law, and the Rhodesian Independence Crisis* (Oxford, 1985).

91 Security Council Res. 418 (Nov. 4, 1977), 32 Security Council Off. Rec., Res. & Dec., U.N. Doc. S/INF/32/Rev. 1 (1977), 5.

92 Security Council Res. 770 (Aug. 13, 1992), in 31 *International Legal Materials*, 1468 (1992).

93 Security Council Res. 794 (Dec. 3, 1992). For a description of the contents, see U.N. Press Rel. DH/1282 (1992).

94 See T. Farer, op. cit., *supra*, n. 89, for the assertion (121) that 'there is not a single case in the entire postwar era where one state has intervened in another for the exclusive purpose of halting mass murder, much less any other gross violation of human rights'.

95 See I. Brownlie, 'Humanitarian Intervention', op. cit., *supra*, n. 89.

96 Tesón, op. cit., *supra*, n. 89.

97 In favour of the doctrine of humanitarian intervention are J.-P. Fonteyne, op. cit., *supra*, n. 88; R.B. Lillich, 'Humanitarian Intervention: A Reply to Ian Brownlie and a Plea for Constructive Alternatives', in J.N. Moore (Ed.), op. cit., *supra*, n. 89, at 229.

98 See J.-P. Fonteyne, op. cit., *supra*, n. 88, at 253–5; W.M. Reisman, 'Coercion and Self-determination: Construing Article 2(4)', 78 *American Journal of International Law*, 642 (1984).

99 Security Council Res. 688 (Apr. 5, 1991), in 30 *International Legal Materials*, 858 (1991).

100 For the text of this memorandum of understanding, of April 18, 1991, see ibid., at 860.

101 H. Grotius, op. cit., 584.

102 J.-P. Fonteyne, op. cit., *supra*, n. 88, at 229–32, 234–5, 258–68.

103 For a lively set of readings on humanitarian intervention (both for and against), together with valuable references for further reading, see R.B. Lillich, *International Human Rights: Problems of Law, Policy, and Practice* (Boston, Toronto, London, 2nd ed., 1991), 587–614.

104 *Nicaragua v. US, supra*, n. 32, at 134–5.

105 But see N. Rodley, 'Human Rights and Humanitarian Intervention: The Case Law of the World Court', 38 *International & Comparative Law Quarterly*, 321 (1989), for the view that the jurisprudence of the World Court rejects the legal validity of humanitarian intervention.

106 For Vattel's statement, see E. de Vattel, op. cit., *supra*, n. 8, at 136.

107 Mavrommatis Palestine Concession Case (Jurisdiction) (*Greece v. United Kingdom*), P.C.I.J. Ser. A, No. 2, at 12. For a more recent World Court pronouncement to this effect, see Barcelona Traction, Light and Power Co Case (*Belgium v. Spain*), 1970 I.C.J. Rep. 3, 44.

108 D.W. Bowett, op. cit., *supra*, n. 31, at 87–105.

109 See R.B. Lillich, 'Forcible Self-help by States to Protect Human Rights', 53 *Iowa L. Rev.*, 325 (1967).

110 In support of the legality of the Grenada intervention is J.N. Moore, *Law and the Grenada Mission* (Charlottesville, Va., 1984). Opposing the legality is W. Gilmore, *The Grenada Intervention: Analysis and Documentation* (Berlin, 1984). In favour of the intervention in Panama is A.D. Sofaer, 'The Legality of the United States Action in Panama', 29 *Columbia Journal of Transnational Law*, 281 (1991). Opposing the legality is L. Henkin, 'The Invasion of Panama under International Law: A Gross Violation', ibid., at 293. On various interventions by France in Africa, often justified by the

protection of nationals, see 'Mitterrand's Muddle: France in Africa', *The Economist*, 27 February 1993, 60, col. 1.

111   Ian Brownlie is the most noted advocate of this view. For his position on the forcible rescue of nationals abroad, see I. Brownlie, *International Law and the Use of Force by States* (Oxford, 1963), 298–301.

112   For an informative account of this incident, see H.L. Weisberg, 'The Congo Crisis 1964: A Case Study in Humanitarian Intervention', 12 *Virginia Journal of International Law*, 261 (1972). See also Security Council Res. 199 (Dec. 30, 1964), 19 U.N. Security Council Off. Rec., U.N. Doc. S/INF/19/Rev. 1 (1964), 18.

113   U.N. Doc. S/12126 (1976), in 31 U.N. Security Council Off. Rec., Supp. for July, Aug. and Sep. 1976, at 6.

114   U.N. Doc. S/PV.1939 (1976), at 2.

115   R.B. Lillich, op. cit., *supra*, n. 103, at 615–16.

116   U.N. Doc. S/12138 (1976), in 31 U.N. Security Council Off. Rec., *supra*, n. 113, at 15.

117   U.N. Doc. S/PV.1941 (1976), at 7–10.

118   U.N. Doc. S/12139 (1976), in 31 U.N. Security Council Off. Rec., *supra*, n. 113, at 15–16.

119   U.N. Doc. S/PV.1943 (1976), at 18.

120   U.N. Doc. S/PV.1939 (1976), at 2.

121   U.N. Doc. S/PV.1940 (1976), at 14.

122   Case Concerning United States Diplomatic and Consular Staff in Tehran (*United States of America* v. *Iran*), 1980 I.C.J. Rep. 3, 43–44. In support of the legality of the rescue mission, see O. Schachter, 'International Law in the Hostage Crisis: Implications for Future Cases', in P.H. Kreisberg (Ed.), *American Hostages in Iran: The Conduct of a Crisis* (New Haven and London), 325, 333–6.

Index